MAX WEBER'S SOCIOLOGY OF RELIGION

Max Weber's Sociology of Religion

Its Method and Content in the Light of the Concept of Rationality

M.M.W. LEMMEN

UTP-Katernen 10

GOOI&STICHT
uitgeverij gooi en sticht bv hilversum

UTP-Katernen 10

ISBN 90 304 0547 3
G en S 54 04 215
NUGI 639, 652/CIP

Original title: *De godsdienstsociologie van Max Weber. Haar methode en inhoud aan de hand van het rationaliteitsbegrip*
English edition:
©1990 Gooi en Sticht bv, Hilversum and Carolusstichting, Heerlen

Translated in English by: H.D. Morton

CONTENTS

FOREWORD

As the successor to Prof. Dr. M. M. W. Lemmen in sociology of religion and pastoral sociology at the University for Theology and Pastorate in Heerlen, I am grateful for the opportunity to present the English translation of Dr. Lemmen's doctoral dissertation, *Max Weber's Sociology of Religion: Its Method and Content in the Light of the Concept of Rationality.* Here, in an inimitable way, Lemmen sums up the characteristic features of Max Weber's work and elucidates its present importance for the practice of sociology today.

He does so on the basis of the concept of rationality, because this is the key concept in Weber's socology of religion whereby Weber analyzes and compares the most diverse cultures from a central vantage point. Yet Lemmen is also intent upon clarifying the concept of rationality as such, because it also plays an important and controversial role today, particularly in theory of science and in the comparative sociology of culture. This turns out to have been an excellent choice, as it conveys Lemmen to an objective and correct summary and incisive analysis of the results of Weber's sociological thought and research.

Thus Lemmen appears in this book as a Weber scholar of high rank, a rank to which he was able to grow under the masterly guidance of Prof. Dr. K. Dobbelaere of the University of Leuven, who sponsored the dissertation. The expertise that has been gathered into this book makes it unquestionably one of the 'classic works' of Dutch sociology which no sociologist may overlook.

On the occasion of the appearance of the English version of this book I therefore venture to hope it will enjoy a worldwide distribution and that through this volume as many people as possible will be able, in spite of Mathieu Lemmen's premature death, to make the acquaintance of the writer and to benefit from his work. This occasion brings to fruition a second wish too, namely, that the small circle of Mathieu Lemmen's immediate community, who remember him in the first place as a most amiable man, will be joined by an ever growing number of people who know him as an important sociologist and eminent scholar.

Finally, I want to thank all those who have made this publication possible and supported it. They are in the first place the dissertation's sponsor Prof. Dr. K. Dobbelaere, and Dr. L. D. Meijers, together with Herbert Donald Morton, Th.M., M.A., who made the English translation and index. After the writer's death Drs. P. L. J. Moonen resolutely saw through to a successful conclusion the initiative taken by Prof. Dr. Lemmen to realize the present project. I also thank the editors of UTP Publications, who were prepared to bring this book out in the scientific series of the University for Theology and Pastorate. Not in the last place I thank the *Carolusstichting,* who contributed financially to making publication possible.

Heerlen, The Netherlands   Prof. Dr. G. P. P. van Tillo
October 1989

INTRODUCTION

Anyone who takes a sociological interest in modern society and, in particular, in the altered place and function in it of religion, is confronted almost inevitably with the name of Max Weber (1864-1920). With Karl Marx (1818-1883) and Emile Durkheim (1858-1917) he is one of the classic figures of sociology of religion, the special discipline within sociology that considers the relation between religion and society as the object of its empirical scientific reflection.

From a scientific point of view, sociology of religion led a poverty-stricken existence throughout the early part of this century. It was restricted mainly to the sociography of churches and religions and it was the fruit mainly of pastoral concern. The problems it formulated were limited, and its theoretical insight was minimal. However, a clear change has come about in this situation, especially since the 1960's. Specifically, since the publications of Thomas Luckmann and Peter Berger there has been a breakthrough in the self-evident identification of church and religion, and both are now approached in the context of processes of societal development. The method and content of Weber's sociology of religion have acquired great relevance as a result of this development. His ideas continue to yield hypotheses for scientific research. The new, more theoretical literature being produced today on such fundamental problems of sociology of religion as the sociological view of religion, the manner in which questions in the field of sociology of religion must be formulated and investigated, the nature and method of sociology as science, and so forth, is inconceivable without Weber's universe of discourse. In other words, whenever the 'paradigm' of sociology or sociology of religion is at issue, many present-day writers engage in a dialogue with Weber. Their assessments of his work are divergent and often mutually contradictory. This plurality of attitudes arises not only as a result of the diverse sociological viewpoints of the writers concerned but also, very frequently, as a result of divergent interpretations of Weber's writings. Weber himself is partly to blame for this, for his scholarly German is complex and

11

difficult, and his style is often unpolished. Sometimes he commits his thoughts to writing in an ample and repetitious way; at other times his sentences are cryptic and forced. The line of his argument is often barely traceable. His enormous erudition tempts him again and again into countless excursions or forces him again and again to burden his generalizations with qualifications and nuances. On the other hand, the divergence of interpretations can also be explained (in part) from the fact that many sociologists evidently do not (or cannot) take the time to acquire more than a cursory acquaintance with Weber's original text.

With that, the purpose of this book is stated. I want to approach Weber's sociology of religion and present its characteristic features (and terminology) as objectively as possible in order to shed light, in an indirect yet responsible way, upon Weber's significance for the practice of sociology today. Thus I shall show, for example, the untenability of the prevalent view that Weber founded society unilaterally upon the human subjective sense of things at the expense of the impenetrable and hard factuality of objective structures. A 'dialectical' view of man and society underlies his factual analyses, as Peter Berger has explained with respect to theory and content, and as Zijderveld has shown in the area of theory and methodology. This dialectical view is so concretized in Weber that it can function as a model for differentiated empirical analyses.

My presentation of Weber assumes the concept of rationality, because it was a key concept for Weber himself, in his sociology of religion; with it he analyzed and compared the most diverse cultures from a central point of view. His main purpose in doing so was to communicate comprehensibly and to explain empirically the origin and typical nature of the modern Western rational and secularized pattern of life. Moreover, the concept of rationality continues to play an important and controversial role even today, especially in theory of science and in the comparative sociology of culture. Partly for this reason, clarifying this concept in Weber is one of my objectives.

It remains to explain briefly the scope and organization of this book.

The first chapter provides an inventory of all Weber's writings on the sociology of religion. I explain the purpose of each one, together with the role that the concept of rationality plays in it. From this survey alone it is clear that Weber's methodology, too, must be dealt with explicitly and that it will not suffice to present it merely to the extent it is more or less implicit in his concrete analyses. The concept of rationality (rationalism, rationalization) itself, which Weber repeatedly says has more than one meaning (he calls it *mehrdeutig*), is enough to require a closer examination of his conceptual apparatus and scientific frame of reference.

Thus the second chapter is devoted to this frame of reference, indispensable as it is for a correct interpretation of Weber's concrete analyses.

Following this introduction to what Weber calls 'rationalistic' sociology, the third chapter constitutes an introduction to the study of rationality as a socio-cultural reality. It describes rationality as structure (rationalism) in contrast to rationality as process (rationalization); the latter is the subject of the fourth chapter. The various forms of socio-cultural rationality treated in the first chapter, such as Occidental capitalistic rationalism, Protestant, Confucian, and Hindu rationalism, and so forth, are described here successively. It is beyond my purpose and competence to assess either the correctness of Weber's descriptions of these religions or the extent to which his analyses may by now have been superseded by more recent research. Because the matter entails ideal-typical descriptions, however, they will in any case be useful to the interested reader as a hypothetical orientation for further study. The scope of my presentation is linked both to the weight Weber attaches to these forms of rationalism and to a desire to afford the reader the degree of clarity he must have in order properly to assess the more systematic elements and also the elements relevant to the current sociology of religion.

The fourth chapter deals with rationality as it occurs empirically in our ever-dynamic reality, namely, as a process. Given the exposition presented in the third chapter, sufficient concrete material is on hand to commence the study of this process. I do so at a general theoretical and analytical level in the first place. Among other matters, I deal explicitly here with Weber's dialectical view of processes of change.

In the fifth and final chapter I return to the concrete historical forms of rationality that were described in the first and third chapters, now in order to compare them with one another and to explore their sociological origins, which were analyzed in a more abstract way in chapter 4. The focus of this final chapter is on modern Western rationality.

The following remarks remain to be made about the plan of this book.

Because the summary and the reflections it contains are based on one criterion of selection, an impression could be given of greater intrinsic unity or systematic coherence than can actually be found in Weber's writings themselves.

Consequently, this book is not to be taken as a sociological biography of Weber but as an objectively correct presentation of the results of his sociological thought and research. As a result, the notes serve a twofold function. In the first place, they refer to the location and context of Weber's statements [references to standard English translations and terms have been supplied by the translator and appear in brackets – HDM]. Beyond that, they deal with the controversial interpretations of Weber's critics, including, of course, those who share and those who do not share my views. My selection from the very extensive and still growing body of secondary literature on Weber aims at systematic completeness only with respect to books and articles devoted explicitly and exclusively to Weber's sociology of religion or concept of rationality. Otherwise, I make no claim to completeness.

For this English version, which has been translated from the original Dutch edition of 1977, I have significantly enlarged the bibliography to include relevant books and articles that have appeared in the meantime. The text itself has been amended just slightly, here and there, with a minor correction or clarification.

Heerlen, The Netherlands   Prof. Dr. M.M.W. Lemmen
September 1981

CHAPTER ONE

RATIONALITY AND MAX WEBER'S WRITINGS ON THE SOCIOLOGY OF RELIGION

Rationality occupies a central, or better said, *the* central place in Max Weber's sociology of religion. The problem Weber tried to bring closer to a solution with his sociology of religion was that of the typical nature of the culture and structure of Western society. This society was to him, from a macrosociological perspective, a form of 'rationalism.'

This rationalism found cultural expression in science and art especially. Sciences, such as astronomy, geometry, mechanics and physics, biology, chemistry, history, political thought, and jurisprudence were permeated in their systems and methods by rationalism. Various elements of this rationalism were to be encountered elsewhere in the world, certainly, but that in its totality typified Western culture alone. The same was true of the arts, such as architecture, music, and printing. In the structural area this rationalism found expression in scientific institutions such as universities, in the organization of systems of justice and administration and, of course, in capitalism.

This economic rationalism, specifically modern European-American capitalism, is central to Max Weber's sociology of religion. He was primarily interested in it as a cultural phenomenon, as a particular mentality, and not so much as a socio-economic structure. Yet he also links it directly to the social structure. After all, this mentality interested him precisely because it had an enormous influence on Western man's pattern of everyday life, that is, on human behavior of an abiding and inter-individual character. The connection between culture and structure ran mainly via the capitalistic work ethic conceived as a practical, operational motive inspiring a rational pattern of life. The question Weber poses is the following: Why did this rationalism in its totality arise in the Occident and only in the Occident? Why not in the Orient, where there were also societies with highly developed rational cultures? These societies too knew forms of capitalism; and, according to Weber, they can be called 'rationalistic' in other respects as well, even though they are irrational when viewed from the standpoint of a Westerner.

Thus Weber uses the term rationalism to signify extremely varied cases. He sees 'rationalization'-related phenomena in the most varied areas of life and in every sphere of culture. These forms, too, of rationalization of the conduct of life belong to the object of investigation of Weber's sociology of religion. However, Weber uses them mainly to explore Western rationalism, the unique character and origin of which they help to bring more clearly to light through cross-cultural comparisons. That they constitute the object of socio-religious inquiry is to be explained by the fact that the belief in magical and religious forces and the ethical ideas anchored in such belief were, according to Weber, universally among the most important factors influencing the pattern of everyday life in the past.

Weber explicitly formulated this purpose in a sixteen-page essay that served as a foreword to the publication of his collected writings on the sociology of religion, his 'Vorbemerkung' in the *Gesammelte Aufsätze zur Religionssoziologie*.[1] It is highly probable, moreover, that this is the last thing he wrote prior to his death 14 June 1920.[2] The *Gesammelte Aufsätze zur Religionssoziologie* consists of three volumes. First published in 1920-21, it has been reprinted many times.

In addition to the 'Vorbemerkung' to which I just alluded, the first volume contains the following themes, in the same order in which I present them here, which is also chronological order.

I. 'Die protestantische Ethik und der Geist des Kapitalismus'

Weber's essay on the Protestant ethic and the spirit of capitalism was first published in the *Archiv für Sozialwissenschaft und Sozialpolitik* in 1904-1905.[3] It was incorporated into the *Gesammelte Aufsätze* essentially unaltered, albeit with additions and citations in the text and footnotes meant to clear up misunderstandings that had arisen in the meantime.[4] F. Rochfahl, Werner Sombart, and Lujo Brentano in particular had offered critiques, and Weber had already responded to them in another context.[5] The study now contained 190 pages.

The theme Weber addresses in this opening essay is that of the close affinity between the capitalist spirit and Protestantism. He centers the capitalist spirit on the Protestant work ethic. By Protestantism he means its seventeenth-century Calvinist and sectarian orientations in Germany, the Netherlands, England, France, and North America. The Baptist movement of the sixteenth century opened and the Methodism of the eighteenth century closed the list. He sometimes designates these orientations, each of which he describes separately, by the general term 'Puritanism,' but more frequently and – given his subject – more pertinently he uses the term 'ascetic Protestantism'. The core of it, as he saw it, was the religiously motivated ascetic ethic, viewed not as a system of doctrine but as the mainspring of conduct.

Not only does Weber find a close affinity between the capitalist work ethic and the religious ascetic way of life; he also shows the causal connection between them. To use the present-day terminology, the ascetic attitude functions as the independent variable and the work ethic as the dependent variable. In Weber both the content of these variables and their conceptualizations are types of rationalism.

In imputing causal influence to Protestant asceticism vis-à-vis the capitalist work ethic, Weber consciously leaves aside important intervening variables. Namely, he does not explore the social structural forms of ascetic Protestantism and the processes issuing from them that have also influenced the ascetic attitude. This is by no means to say that Weber failed to perceive their importance for an adequate explanation. On the contrary, he calls explicit attention to them.[6] In the subsequent essay they are even subjected to explicit investigation. Likewise missing is a structural analysis of capitalist society – e.g., an analysis of the market, which is, after all, according to Weber, the prototype of rational social action.[7] All he desires to show here is that one of the constituent elements of the capitalist spirit originated in Christian asceticism. It is for methodological reasons alone that Weber restricts his inquiry to clearly defined religious factors, in order to determine whether and how these factors contributed to the origin, character, and expansion of rationalistic Western culture based on capitalism.[8]

It is irrelevant to the present survey to explore the extent to which Weber's parenthetical treatment of influential social, material, and political variables may have affected the results of the research of this essay; in other words, the validity of the way in which these results were obtained and the vulnerability of his thesis to falsification are not directly at issue here. Yet this problem, which has been the subject of a great deal of controversy, will arise indirectly.[9]

Although Marx is not mentioned in this essay, it is clear from both external factors and internal textual criticism that *Die protestantische Ethik* is also meant to be a refutation of vulgar marxist notions that would make religion just a reflection of technologically determined social production relations. In Weber's Germany this was a current and controversial subject of political and scientific importance that bore directly on the theme of his research. In the essay itself he repeatedly uses terms such as 'materialistic standpoint,' 'superstructure,' and so forth.[10] He dissociates himself explicitly 'from the idea that it is possible to deduce the Reformation, as a *historically necessary result,* from certain economic changes.'[11] The opposite, spiritualistic thesis that the spirit of capitalism is to be accounted for exclusively in terms of influences deriving from the Reformation – one he was often reproached for allegedly holding, as he himself noted – is a thesis he rejects as 'foolish and doctrinaire.'[12]

II. 'Die protestantische Sekten und der Geist des Kapitalismus'

This second, thirty-page essay from the first volume of *Gesammelte Aufsätze* was originally published in 1906 in *Christliche Welt* under the title 'Kirchen und Sekten in Nordamerika: Eine kirchen- und sozial-politische Skizze.'[13] It was an expanded and revised version of 'Kirchen' and 'Sekten,' two articles that had appeared in the Easter number of the *Frankfurter Zeitung* that same year.[14] The essay as it appeared in *Christliche Welt* is in two parts.

In the first part Weber examines how the structural features of American Protestantism served to advance economic rationalism. Its sect-like characteristics were eminently suited for breeding 'qualified members of an occupation,' and especially the reliable, creditworthy businessman. This structure functioned relatively independently of its religious content. This is evident from the fact that eventually countless 'secular clubs' of the most diverse sorts inherited this function of the religious communities.

The second part explains in an ideal-typical way the internal structures of the 'church' and the 'sect' and their consequences, both external (e.g., for the state) and internal (e.g., for the members of the 'church' or 'sect'). The church was the predominant type in Europe but the sect was the predominant type in America.

The first part of this essay of 1906 was revised, expanded, and incorporated under the above-mentioned title in the *Gesammelte Aufsätze*. Meanwhile, the church-sect polarity was adopted and worked out more fully by Weber's friend and colleague Ernst Troeltsch;[15] for this reason, Weber did not include this part of his original essay here – the more so since he had already had the opportunity to say a number of things about the subject in *Die protestantische Ethik*.[16]

III. 'Die Wirtschaftsethik der Weltreligionen: Vergleichende religionssoziologische Versuche'

Quantitatively the most extensive part of Weber's sociology of religion, this work takes up the rest of the first volume and, for that matter, the two following volumes as well. The first of these three volumes opens with an introduction of thirty-eight pages. It was originally published in 1916 in the *Archiv für Sozialwissenschaft und Sozialpolitik* under the title 'Einleitung in die Wirtschaftsethik der Weltreligionen.'[17] Weber expanded it some what for publication in the *Gesammelte Aufsätze*. He explains the purpose of the cross-cultural sociology of religion that is to follow. Namely, Weber wanted to explore the various forms of rationalization of the ethos or lifestyle in the five world religions that had multitudes of followers, namely, Confucianism, Hinduism, Buddhism, Christianity, and Islam. He makes no claim to offer a well-rounded picture of these world religions. He is interested primarily in the 'economic ethic' of each one. By the term 'economic ethic' Weber means the practical motives to economic action – in the broadest sense of that term – grounded in these religions themselves.[18] These practical motivations of the pattern of everyday life were of interest to him both as they contrasted to each other and to the extent that they differed from the economic rationalism of the West.

In this connection Weber reiterates that 'rationalism' may mean very different things.[19]

It is clear that Weber's objective in comparing the various religious ethics is to reinforce his Protestantism thesis. Namely, his research will principally reveal that the impulses to the typical Western rational ethos occurred in no other religion.

Although Judaism is not a world religion, Weber announces he will examine it because of its influence on Christianity and Islam and its influence, in part imagined and in part real, on the modern Western economic ethic. Here too Weber's intention is to shed more light on his Protestantism thesis.

Finally, in this introduction to 'Wirtschaftsethik,' Weber implicitly advances a third factor that reinforces the Protestantism thesis. Namely, his scientific objective is broadened here, in that in contrast to the first essay his research now pertains to more than the influence of religion on the pattern of economic life. Here, reversely, attention is also given to the influence of nonreligious factors in shaping the pattern of the religious attitude. Specifically, the meaning of social stratification and power relations for the nature and direction of religious rationalization is already broadly indicated in this introduction. This makes possible a more valid causal understanding of the capitalist ethos in its relation to typical Western religiosity.

Broadly speaking, one can say that Weber regards the various societies as complex wholes of variables within which one variable, namely, the religious attitude, always proves determinative for the possible rise of Western-type rationalism. The most diverse social situations turn out to have involved some factors that were favorable and some that were unfavorable to the development of modern Western capitalism. Finally, the religious factor is found to be decisive again and again.

A. 'Konfuzianismus und Taoismus'

Directly following Weber's introduction to the economic ethic of the world religions is his study of religiosity in China, that is, of Confucianism and Taoism.

It was originally published in 1916 in the *Archiv für Sozialwissenschaft und Sozialpolitik*, where it followed directly the 'Einleitung' mentioned above.[20] Weber expanded it extensively for inclusion in the *Gesammelte Aufsätze*. That Weber begins with Chinese religiosity and then proceeds to Indian and finally to Near Eastern religiosity is not a function of geography but pure coincidence. There are effective internal reasons for the East to West sequence.[21]

Chinese rationalism, as it will become clear, contrasts sharply with modern Western rationalism. Specifically, the former is a rationalism of adaptation to the world while Puritanism is a rationalism of world mastery. The Indian religiosity of world rejection is in this respect a type of rationalism that, logically speaking, occupies a position between Chinese rationalism and European rationalism. Lastly, Near Eastern Jewish rationalism is a form of rationalism present at the cradle of the European variety. This religiosity accordingly provides a historical basis of explanation for Western rationalism, which differs fundamentally from all Oriental forms of rational religiosity.

Confucianism and Taoism (together with Buddhism, which was imported) were the most important religious movements in which Chinese religiosity acquired form during a period of some two thousand years.[22]

The mandarins as a class of literate civil servants and functionaries are the key, from a sociological standpoint, to accounting for the orthodox Confucian orientation of life and (seen from their social situation) the heterodox, popular Taoist orientation. The former derived in part from the teachings of Confucius while the latter appealed – largely without justification – to the teachings of Laotse.

To a certain degree, but in vastly differing measures and in totally different ways, both were types of rationalism. Both, too, by virtue of their nature, were obstacles to the rise of capitalism in the modern sense.

The first volume of the *Gesammelte Aufsätze* closes with a thirty-seven page intermezzo, 'Zwischenbetrachtung.' This, too, had already been published earlier, in 1916, in the *Archiv für Sozialwissenschaft und Sozialpolitik.* It is linked to both the 'Einleitung' and 'Konfuzianismus und Taoismus,' together with which it forms a whole.[23] In both publications it bears the subtitle, 'Theorie der Stufen und Richtungen religiöser Weltablehunung.' This theory of levels and directions of religious abnegation of the world is a schematic construction intended to serve as an ideal-typical instrument of orientation for acquiring insight into the historical empirical forms of religious abnegation of the world.

The essay serves as a transition from Chinese to Indian religiosity. In India, in sharp contrast to China, one finds the earliest and most consistent forms of rational world renunciation ever seen on earth. Here Weber attempts to understand from within what the 'sense' or 'meaning' of world renunciation can be. What motives bring people to it? What spheres of values are rendered invalid by it (schools of world renunciation)? And what conflicts can arise from it?

Abnegation of the world tends to go progressively further, via the rationalization process, until it reaches the point at which the world seems totally devoid of value and meaning (levels of world renunciation).

B. 'Hinduismus und Buddhismus'

The second volume of the *Gesammelte Aufsätze* continues 'Die Wirtschaftsethik der Weltreligionen' with 'Hinduismus und Buddhismus.' This study of Hinduism and Buddhism appeared in 1916 and 1917 in the *Archiv für Sozialwissenschaft und Sozialpolitik.*[24] Incorporated practically without alteration,[25] it occupies all of this volume's 378 pages.

The name 'Hinduism' emerged only after the Islamic penetration of India. It indicated the indigenous national religiosity as against that of the conquerors and native converts to Islam.

Weber also employs the term 'Brahmanism.' It points to the fact that the Brahmans – a special sort of priests – formed the top of the Hinduistic hierarchical religious social caste system. They developed a pronounced rationalism that influenced even the conduct of the lowest castes. Within this system it was impossible for modern capitalism to arise.

Besides this orthodox rationalism, India developed two additional forms of rationalism, namely, Jainism and Ancient Buddhism. From the Hindu point of view, which was otherwise tolerant as far as dogma is concerned, these two currents were heterodox because they did not recognize the religious authority of the Brahmans. Both entailed a religiosity and class ethic of the the most prominent professional monks. The Jainist order regarded Mahavira as their founder, and Buddhism in this respect referred to Siddhartha, called Gautama, or Buddha (the Enlightened One), who was a generation younger than Mahavira.

The Jainist order was a sect with a core of professional monks, but it also included lay members. It bore a close resemblance, not only externally but also internally, to American sect religiosity.

Alongside many Puritan features, however, their religious rationalism also exhibited close affinity to Buddhist rationality. Jainism is by now (1911) just a small sect (0.4% of the population), although it was once, temporarily, a dominant confession in India. Weber took an interest in it because, among other reasons, the rationalism of this religiosity led to its becoming a specific and exclusive sect of traders.[26]

Ancient Buddhism, in contrast, was exclusively a religiosity of professional monks. They were cultivated, prominent, intellectually schooled, peripatetic, mendicant monks. There was no trace of a systematic influence or organization of laymen, as in Jainism. This followed from the unique character of their extremely consistently applied rationalism.

The three above-mentioned forms of rational religiosity are comparable in that all three were borne by intellectual strata. Neither orthodox Brahmanism nor the heterodox rationalisms fully satisfied the needs of the masses. They did not satisfy the needs for emotional religiosity and for help in times of external or internal distress. According to Weber, it was above all these emotional needs that were decisive everywhere for the 'psychological' character of the religiosity of the masses in contrast to the 'rational' character of every salvation doctrine of the intellectuals. Only two typical possibilities of salvation doctrine, according to Weber, meet these needs of popular religiosity. Like religiosity everywhere else in the world, Indian religiosity, too, took one or both of these paths, namely, that of magic, and that of revering or worshipping a (living or dead, and deified) savior.

After examining the three forms of religiosity of the Indian intellectuals, Weber devoted the final part of this second volume to describing the forms in which Indian religiosity adapted itself to these specific plebeian needs. This pertains both to Hinduism and Buddhism in India itself and to Buddhism as it spread through Ceylon, Burma, China, Korea, Japan, and Tibet.

C. 'Das Antike Judentum'

The third and final volume of the *Gesammelte Aufsätze* contains a study of Ancient Judaism, 'Das Antike Judentum.' It appeared between 1917 and 1919 in the *Archiv für Sozialwissenschaft und*

Sozialpolitik.[27]

As in the case of the study of Hinduism and Buddhism, this treatise was also incorporated into the collected works practically without alteration. The first 280 pages [of the German edition] deal with various aspects of the Israelite covenant society and Yahweh; then pages 280 to 400 examine 'the establishment of the Jewish Pariah People.'[28] Weber was unable to complete this study of Judaism because of his death. In the foreword to this volume his wife, Marianne Weber, states that he had wanted to add to it an analysis of the Psalms and of the book of Job. That, in turn, was to have been followed by an examination of Talmudic Judaism. The transition to it, namely, a study of Phariseeism, had already been prepared. It was incorporated into the third volume as an appendix.[29]

Studies of primitive Christianity and Islam that Weber had projected in his introduction to 'Wirtschaftsethik der Weltreligionen' and that were meant to round off his cross-cultural investigations were not finished. The preparatory work for them had been completed, however, according to Marianne Weber. Moreover, Weber had already discussed both religions briefly in his 'Religionssoziologie' in *Wirtschaft und Gesellschaft* [see the following section], namely, in connection with the relations between the cultural religions and the 'world.'

Although Judaism cannot be numbered among the world religions, Weber still deals with it because of its influence on Islam and, more especially, Christianity. Had it not taken over the Jewish religion, Christianity as an originally pneumatic sect with the cult of Christ the Lord would probably have disappeared, as did so many other mystery communities in the Hellenistic world.

The rise and development of the Jewish religion is of world-historical significance and is a turning point in the cultural development of the Middle East and the entire Occident. Yet that is not to say that Judaism achieved this of itself, for from a sociological perspective, later Judaism was the religion of a 'pariah people' that were separated by ritual boundaries from their social environment. In principle their ghetto existence was freely chosen, and it was related to, among other things, the historical self-knowledge of the Jewish people.

This historical awareness was the result of a typically Jewish rationalism that differed from all Oriental and from Protestant Occidental rationalisms alike. Its bearers were primarily the Levitic priesthood and the prophets.

24

IV. The Sociology of Religion in 'Wirtschaft und Gesellschaft'

Next to *Gesammelte Aufsätze,* Weber's work on economics and society, Wirtschaft und Gesellschaft, is especially important as a source for his sociology of religion.

Wirtschaft und Gesellschaft was planned as part of a grandly conceived multivolume work, an encyclopedic socio-economic handbook, *Grundriss der Sozialökonomik* [Outline of social economics]. It was to have been written by many authors under Weber's general editorship.[30] In addition to the part on economy and society, to which Weber was to have contributed something himself, there were plans for sections on economy and the science of economics; economy and nature; economy and technology, and so forth.

Weber got his *Wirtschaft und Gesellschaft* ready for the press himself, in part; but it was first published after his death, by Marianne Weber, in 1921-22. The fourth and fifth editions were prepared by Johannes Winckelmann, who published *Wirtschaft und Gesellschaft* as an independent sociological work by Max Weber. In doing so, he emancipated it from its ranking in the multivolume socio-economic work, *Grundriss der Sozialökonomik,* alluded to above, the traces of which had until then continued to appear on Weber's title page. Weber's *Wirtschaft und Gesellschaft* now stood by itself, a completed whole written by Weber alone. Winckelmann gave it the subtitle *Grundriss der verstehenden Soziologie.* On the basis of internal and external textual criticism supported by manuscripts discovered in the meantime and by Weber's other writings that had already been published, Winckelmann forged *Wirtschaft und Gesellschaft* into a systematic and coherent whole meant to present as purely as possible the actual course of Weber's thought. Winckelmann presents an extensive explanation and defense of his approach in the fifth, revised edition of 1972.[31]

Part One of *Wirtschaft und Gesellschaft* which Winckelmann, in keeping with Marianne Weber's terminology, calls 'Soziologische Kategorienlehre' (1-180),[32] embraces the more abstract and methodological questions. The historical empirical material found here serves to illustrate the exposition of theory. Weber wrote this part between 1918 and 1920.

Part Two bears the title Weber himself gave it, 'Die Wirtschaft und die gesellschaftlichen Ordnungen und Mächte' (181-868).[33] In contrast to Part One, this second part is more concrete and empirical. Yet here too is a study that is far from purely descriptive; it is systematic in conception. In Part One the historical material served only to illustrate conceptual and theoretical expositions. In Part Two, in contrast, the theoretical conceptual apparatus serves to facilitate 'an interpretive understanding' *(verstehen)* of the historical facts.

The fifth chapter [of the fifth German edition] of this second part is entitled 'Religionssoziologie.'[34] It was written between 1911 and 1913. The subtitle, 'Typen religiöser Vergemeinschaftung,' is more an indication of the connection between this passage and what has preceded it than it is a characterization of the content of Weber's sociology of religion. Namely, this passage can correctly be viewed as a relatively independent whole. The subtitle signifies that after the treatment of such forms of community as family, sib, business enterprise, tribe, folk, and the like, consideration will be given to constellations that (once they have assumed the form of general religions) work to penetrate all other possible sorts of communities.

That the form of religion in question must be viewed as a 'systematic' whole is asserted by Weber himself, in the passage in which he explains the limited objective of the *Gesammelte Aufsätze*.[35] Elsewhere he states that it was his intention to have his comparative studies in sociology of religion published concurrently with *Wirtschaft und Gesellschaft* so that they would interpret and complement the chapter on sociology of religion contained in it. Thus it is obvious that the systematic considerations are based on more detailed historical research. Yet the reverse is also true, according to Weber: some points in the comparative sociology of religion are to be interpreted in the light of the systematic sociology of religion.[36]

Here again the problem of rationality plays a great role. This is already obvious from the fact that in an essay of 136 pages[37] the word 'rationality' ('rationalism,' rationalization,' 'rational,' 'irrational') occurs some three hundred times. Yet in keeping with the line of thought, too, each of the twelve sections is directly concerned with the problem of rationality.[38]

To provide an overview of the problems addressed in this work, it will suffice at this point just to mention these twelve sections. The first section of 'Religionssoziologie: Typen religiöser Vergemeinschaftung' deals with the origins of religion [cf. E. Fischoff, trans. (Boston, 1963), chap. 1]. Then, successively, there are sections on gods, magicians, and priests [Fischoff, chap. 2]; the idea of God, religious ethic, and taboo [Fischoff, chap. 3]; the prophet [Fischoff, chap. 4]; the religious congregation *(Gemeinde);* canonical writings, preaching and pastoral care [these two sections are combined in Fischoff, chap. 5]; castes, classes, and religion [Fischoff, chaps. 6, 7, and 8]; the problem of theodicy; salvation and rebirth [these two sections are combined in Fischoff, chap. 9]; the different roads to salvation and their influence on the conduct of life [Fischoff, chaps. 10, 11, and 12]; religious ethics and the 'world' [Fischoff, chaps. 13 and 14]; the great religions and the 'world' [Fischoff, chaps. 15 and 16].[39]

Finally, mention needs to be made of another explicit source for Weber's sociology of religion, a thirty-nine page section of his 'Soziologie der Herrschaft,' or sociology of 'authority' [Gerth], 'imperative control' [Parsons], or 'domination' [Rheinstein], which constitutes the ninth chapter of *Wirtschaft und Gesellschaft*.[40] Namely, the sixth part of this sociology of domination,[41] 'Politische und hierokratische Herrschaft,' is devoted to 'political and hierocratic domination.' It deals with the mutual relationships and intertwinements of profane and religious authority, together with their effect on the pattern of conduct.

V. Other Writings on the Sociology of Religion

Without claiming to have made exhaustive mention of all the loci where Weber speaks incidentally of one theme or another from the sociology of religion, it is still necessary for the sake of completeness to take note of two less formal sources. Noteworthy in the first place are the proceedings of the first German *Soziologentag,* which convened in Frankfurt am Main, 10-22 October 1910.[42] In his 'Geschäftsbericht,'[43] where he speaks of the future tasks of the *Deutsche Gesellschaft für Soziologie,* Weber alludes in passing to the relation between 'worldview' in the broadest sense of the word and associational conduct, likewise in the broadest sense. Namely, he speaks of the mechanism that comes into play whenever sects set out to realize values.[44] In addition, he illustrated at this congress during the debate that followed Ernst Troeltsch's address how such religious associational types as church, sect, and mysticism, which Troeltsch had delineated, interpenetrate each other, empirically speaking.[45]

A second locus is provided by the lectures Weber delivered in the winter semester of 1919-20. They are entitled *Wirtschaftsge-*

schichte: Abriss der universalen Sozial- und Wirtschaftsgeschichte.
This posthumously published social economic history closes with
a fifteen page section on the rise of the spirit of capitalism, 'Die
Entfaltung der kapitalistischen Gesinnung.'[46] This section contains
Weber's sociology of religion in a nutshell.

CHAPTER TWO

THE METHOD OF MAX WEBER'S SOCIOLOGY (OF RELIGION)

Weber calls his sociology 'rationalistic,' and he regards it as a product of the Western process of rationalization. What he means by that he explains and justifies in his methodological essays.[1]

As the preceding chapter will have made clear, the concept of rationality (rationalism, rationalization) is a central instrument of analysis in Weber's sociology of religion. Yet Weber does not deal with it thematically. Becoming better acquainted with Weber's sociological method is thus a necessary first step towards understanding his writings on the sociology of religion – the more so since Weber's sociological framework of reference becomes clear in the process. Neglecting to assess that framework would mean risking answering today's questions directly from Weber even though he did not pose those questions in the same way himself. Not only would we misinterpret Weber in that case; we would likewise fail to do justice to material in Weber's work that could be of value for contemporary sociology.

In this chapter I shall restrict myself to explaining Weber's method without going on to ask whether he always applied it consistently in his sociological research. Because Weber's sociological method is, in turn, not easily understandable in isolation from both his more general scientific methodology and concrete means of empirical research, I shall also deal briefly with each of these.

This chapter accordingly has three sections: I deal first with Weber's more general scientific methodology, then with his sociological methodology, and finally with the techniques he used in conducting sociological research.

This does not mean I am about to present an extensive study of Weber's theory of science. That would be a theme in itself. Besides, even a cursory acquaintance with Weber's *Gesammelte Aufsätze zur Wissenschaftslehre* reveals that he did not write a systematic, coherent theory of science. The title *Wissenschaftslehre*, which might lead one to expect the contrary, was added uncritically by

29

Marianne Weber to a collection of separate essays, according to Winckelmann.[2]

I. Weber's Scientific Methodology

In this section I shall explain what Weber understands by science, how he regards the relation between science and values, and the consequences these conceptions have for the character of his sociology.

A. Weber's Conception of Empirical Science

The goal of an empirical science, in Weber's view, is to arrange intelligibly a given reality in such a way that science can claim to be reliable and valid as experiential truth. In other words, science desires truth conceived as the intelligible arrangement of empirical reality that would have to be recognized as correct 'even by a Chinese,' thus someone from a totally different cultural world, because when viewed from a particular standpoint it would be impossible not to infer it from the facts.

Hence science must bring to light intersubjectively verifiable and actual patterns. Science would attain the highest degree of an intelligible arrangement of reality if it attained absolute goal-oriented, purposeful, *instrumental rationality (Zweckrationalität);* that is, if from particular empirical facts it inferred other facts that would follow causally after the evidential model $2 \times 2 = 4$ or, in other words, showed that two or more empirical facts are related to each other in such a way that the one follows directly and unequivocally from the other as the exclusive means to a specified end. Such goal-oriented evidence is specifically suited to a 'generalizing causal approach,' that is, to 'nomological regularity' in empirical reality.[3] The 'laws' implied here yield knowledge characterized most notably by calculability.[4]

Of course, an empirical science (in contrast to purely deductive sciences such as logic) never attains that high a degree of rationality or intelligible arrangement of reality. Thus it is also true that goal-oriented, instrumental rationality functions only as an ideal, limiting case. Evidence is only one side of the science ideal. It still deals only with what is objectively possible. The scientist must go on to test his evidence without prejudice – that is, in an intersubjectively verifiable way. In other words, he must see if empirical reality actually works in keeping with his intelligible arrangement of it. If it does, Weber speaks of the rationality of objective correctness *(objektive Richtigkeitsrationalität)*. Logically speaking, this is entirely different to subjective instrumental rationality *(Zweckrationalität)*. That is because the rationality of objective correctness *(Richtigkeitsrationalität)* draws neither an intelligible nor a causal connection between facts; all it does is establish the pattern of their temporal association with each other.[5]

Absolute rationality of objective correctness *(Richtigkeitsrationalität)*, like absolute instrumental rationality *(Zweckrationalität)*, is a practically unattainable limiting case in empirical science. There can be a high measure of instrumental rationality (the intelligible arrangement of reality according to the goal-oriented scheme) without the rationality of objective correctness: in that case, actual reality does not correspond with the intellectual, or objectively conceivable reality. One can then speak of incorrect knowledge. The reverse could also be the case: a high degree of nomological regularity might be observed in the course of facts without the 'Why' of that regularity being at all intelligible.

For Weber the ideal of scientific knowledge clearly consists in having both forms of rationality coincide as closely as possible and in having each reach the highest degree attainable. Subjective clarity of insight *(Evidenz)*,[6] or the *conceivable* course of events *(Sinnadäquanz)*, and objective correctness, or the *actual* course of events *(Kausaladäquanz)*, then optimally coincide.

Hence rationality in science means methodically rendering empirical reality intelligible, so that it can be calculated. 'Calculability' must be understood here in the broad sense and not reduced to mathematical calculability. Weber employs this concept synonymously with predictability. The optimum in scientific intelligibility, namely, goal-oriented rationality, is likewise the optimum in calculability, since here the 'Why' of empirical regularity is immediately evident. In anticipation of what is to follow, we can at this point characterize science as a form of 'technical' rationality.

In establishing what science is, Weber has in mind principally the empirical sciences of human action such as history, economics, and other social sciences.[7] It is from this vantage point that he also alludes to natural sciences such as physics, biology, chemistry, etc. What has been said above holds in the full sense only for the cultural and human sciences. Both kinds of science proceed on the basis of the principle of causality. Logically speaking, both entail precisely the same 'causal imputation": the demonstration of 'adequate grounds' upon which to establish rules. However, this nomological knowledge acquires a different meaning in each case. Our need for causal explanation demands as much rationality – that is, intelligibility and calculability – as possible. Well now, nomological knowledge in the cultural sciences has more intelligibility and in that sense less irrationality than nomological knowledge in the natural sciences has. Namely, in the first case we can 'understand' *(verstehen)* reality; that is, we can empathically and subjectively comprehend and 'interpret' *(deuten)* it.[8] In other words, in the cultural sciences we can adduce a concrete motivation or complex of motivations that more or less straightforwardly accounts for human social actions in causal terms. Weber speaks of 'adequate' causality[9] in contrast to contingent causality – neither of which corresponds to 'necessary causality.' Deviations from nomological knowledge, the knowledge of empirical regularity, are possible in concrete instances in the cultural sciences, concerned as they are with human conduct, without any inherent impairment to their nomological validity.

Causality in the natural sciences is not intelligible. It can only be observed from the outside. Here causality, together with the nomological knowledge it yields, means no more than that empirical reality matches certain rules of experience. The 'why' of the matter remains obscure: the pertinent reality is in this sense obscure. There is only *Richtigkeitsrationalität:* objectively verifiable nomological regularity, with problematical causal meaning. Weber distinguishes between interpretive understanding *(deutend verstehen),* the kind of understanding by means of which insight into the 'Why' of human action is gained from the inside, and another kind of (noninterpretive) cognizance, *begreifen,* which serves only to establish nomological regularity. In the natural sciences one is restricted to external, noninterpretive cognizance in the sense of *begreifen.* Whether explicitly or implicitly, the ultimate goal of the natural sciences is conceived to be to arrange empirical reality in a system of general laws, via hypothesis formation and verification.[10] If a hypothesis proves inadequate in just one instance, the presumed natural law is invalidated. Accordingly, today's inductive work is 'preparatory work' on account of the imperfect current state of science. People remain ever hopeful of arriving at a perfect scientific system of laws from which every concrete system can be deduced. The concrete instances would in that case be subsumable to general rules. In the cultural sciences the opposite is the case: nomological knowledge is not an end in itself but merely a means to accounting for concrete meaningful coherent patterns. The reality in which the cultural sciences are interested involves human actions that are concrete and unrepeatable *(Einmaligkeit)* and always qualitatively unique *(Einzigartigkeit)*. Nomological knowledge is possible in the human sciences none the less, because the researcher is able, in the process of interpretively understanding *(deutend verstehend),* to abstract the causes from these concrete aspects. Even the natural sciences abstract from the individual, but then for other reasons. Namely, they are primarily interested in the general aspects of phenomena.

The cultural sciences cannot be captured in a finite system of laws. They have a historical character because the eternally onward-flowing tide of culture bears new problems with it. This accounts for the tentative character of all cultural-scientific concept formation and for the necessity of constantly devising new concepts and laws. Cultural-scientific work consists of constantly acquiring new knowledge of the infinite historical store. The old intellectual heritage is accordingly permanently subject to dispute in the light of newly acquired knowledge. Thus concepts and laws must be constantly revised. Progress in the field of the social sciences is essentially a question of changes in the practical problems of culture and, more specifically, in the form of a critique of the existing conceptual apparatus. This does not mean that the proper task of the social sciences must be the perpetual pursuit of new conceptual constructions. Their goal, after all, is to be serviceable to the knowledge of real, coherent patterns. It is not a question of gathering as much material as possible, nor is it one of the subtlety of ever new thoughts. The social researcher must be devoted exclusively neither to facts *(Stoffhuber)* nor to meanings *(Sinnhuber).* The one approach would make him insensitive to new perspectives as a result of his constantly assembling more material through statistics, polls, etc., while the other would ruin his taste for facts by leading him constantly to spin new-fangled webs of thought.

Once a science has established itself and adopted its methodological principles, it tends to regard itself as a goal and to be unconcerned about the presuppositions of the acquired knowledge. And this can be a good thing, according to Weber. Yet the great problems of culture go beyond that. Hence even a science must be prepared to alter its established standpoint and its conceptual apparatus in order to get a grasp on the stream of events. What is typical of science (as distinct from art, for example), is that its lot, indeed, its very goal is to be overtaken by developments.[11] This ever-changing character pertains not only to the object of the social sciences but also, most importantly, to the framework of reference in terms of which these sciences look at social reality. That framework too can change.

Anyone who regards science as a quest for definitive synoptic nomological knowledge of reality in terms of which concrete events would be logically deducible applications is standing, whether knowingly or not, on the old scholastic epistemology.[12] According to this doctrine, concepts would be imaginable representations of 'objective' realities. However, according to Weber, anyone who accepts the basic ideas of modern epistemology, which is traceable to Kant, knows that concepts are rather the rational means of arranging empirical givens. Now, in principle, this can be done in an infinite number of ways. Weber rejects as 'inherent nonsense' the notion that the goal of the cultural sciences could ever be to grasp reality definitively in one or another closed conceptual apparatus.[13] Often a science's framework of reference is determined by what was experienced as problematical in a particular period or by the strictly personal choices of some scientist. To Weber it is accordingly not the material object a science studies that determines its character but the specific viewpoint in terms of which it arranges reality, i.e., its methodology.[14]

This Copernican revolution in epistemology is the second reason (shared, for that matter, with all sciences) why the social sciences have a historical character. Not only the social reality itself but also the vantage point in terms of which the scientist can examine it is subject to perpetual change. It is for this reason that Weber advocates concepts formulated as sharply and unambiguously as possible. Clearly formulated concepts make the specific orientation of an investigation plain and clear not only to the researcher himself but also to others. Moreover, they make it possible to see whether the conceptual apparatus to be employed is suitable to the intended goal or whether it might better be exchanged for another one. At this point, however, we have arrived at the matter of investigative techniques, which I intend to examine in the third section of this chapter.[15]

Clearly Weber regards a social science as problem-oriented and historical in character. That brings us to the question of how he views the relation between science and values.

34

B. The Relation Between Science and Values

Weber argues most emphatically for 'value-free' science.[16] He means by that that the scientific researcher should distinguish between establishing empirical facts and making value judgments about such facts, whether in terms of an ethical or some other standpoint. The freedom of science from values is based on the assumption that the fields of science and of values are entirely heterogeneous. Science can neither prove nor refute values. Science is not 'the 'way to true being', the 'way to true art', the 'way to true nature', the 'way to true God', the 'way to true happiness."[17] It is meaningless in the sense that it provides no answer to questions like 'What must we do?' and 'How must we live?' This is in contrast to theology, which proceeds on the basis of the *a priori* that the world has a meaning. This *a priori* is at the foundation of every religious rationalization, as we shall see. Thus Weber rejects the scientific optimism that has dominated many fields since the Enlightenment. The two questions, namely, that of how a concrete situation will develop with a certain degree of probability and of whether man should contribute to the development, on the one hand, and secondly, of the opinion people will form on any given issue, on the other hand, are fully heterogeneous and fundamentally different questions.

Science and values may in that case be heterogeneous; yet they are inseparable. In the first place, they are inseparable because people already implicitly recognize that science itself is a value by practicing it. Of course, even this value is not subject to scientific demonstration. Like all other values it arises from what, from the scientific viewpoint, is an irrational decision of the scientist. One who adopts science as a value does not yet thereby render a judgment of the fact that there can be no other valuable conceptions of science than our Western ones, which are the fruits of the Western process of rationalization. By virtue of its own intrinsic nature, this process requires freedom from values in the sense I have just described. Like every other value, the value of science too presupposes certain *a priori*s, the so-called logical principles of science, such as the validity of the principle of causality and the principle of non-contradiction. Beyond that, it of course also demands intellectual honesty and the courage to entertain inconvenient facts. The latter is especially true in the human sciences. Value-free science imposes upon its practitioner the duty (read: value) of keeping a cool head in order to be able, when necessary, 'to swim against the current of prevalent cultural ideals.'

In the second place, science and values are inseparable because every cultural science is 'value-related' *(Wertbezogenheit, Erkenntnisinteresse);* that is, what a science adopts as the problem of its research and the way it handles it are determined by subjective valuations, whether people are aware of it or not.[18] Thus Weber is sensible of the rise of Western rationality as a problem of values.[19] He finds it worth the effort of being deeply involved with the problem.

Sometimes a value judgment (or series of value judgments) is at the basis of a scientific theory, though no one seems alert to the fact, and it is incorporated into the theory as seemingly self-evident. For example, liberal economics regards the principle of free trade, the market principle, and a radical laissez faire public policy as self-evident values. Yet as a result it sometimes not only fails optimally to achieve its own explicit objectives; it can at the same time jeopardize other (e.g., ethical or religious) human values. The only legitimate judgment a scientific theory can make is whether in the case of the goal x the measure y is the only suitable means for x, or whether besides y we have y^1 and y^2 as well. In the latter case it can also judge whether certain differences in effect exist between y, y^1 and y^2, and whether it is therefore to be anticipated that the attainment of the goal x will be accompanied by the side-effects z, z^1 and z^2. Such judgments are merely inverted laws of causality. Thus the only legitimate 'value judgments' in science concern the degree of rationality of the proposed actions. This is valid without qualification for all scientific rationality. However, that is to say nothing as yet about the value of the ends to be achieved or about other values that may also be at stake in the pursuit of a specific objective.[20]

This example can serve at the same time to clarify the extent to which, in Weber's view, the value-relatedness of science can influence scientific praxis in a legitimate way. Depending upon the nature of the problem, different concepts and combinations of concepts have to be employed to reach the appointed goal (which belongs to the sphere of values). Thus values do, indeed, have a definite impact on the way science is conducted, although science and values are fundamentally different from each other. Technically speaking, value rationality *(Wertrationalität)* penetrates instrumental rationality *(Zweckrationalität)* – in this case, science – intrinsically. This happens, however, without impairment or adulteration of the typical character and specific nature of either of the two forms of rationality. Were the contrary the case, scientific value would be damaged. Of course, it is exclusively the province of value rationality to legitimate the value of science and the value of what science studies. Science cannot legitimate itself. Often, however, the two types of rationality either are not distinguished or are unconsciously mixed. In this connection Weber argues in favor of scrapping from the vocabulary of the social sciences such terms as 'adaptation' and 'progress' or 'evolution' that are borrowed from biology.[21] After all, these words can be used for both explaining and valuing certain facts. Such dual functions and meanings often are inadequately distinguished from each other. For example, people may regard modern economic development as 'natural,' and they may regard development and adaptation to it as something 'good.' Liberal economics thereby confuses science and values. The Marxist conception of history does the same: society develops according to a certain scheme, and adaptation to it advances human values. The state, thanks to its modern rational administrative techniques, has acquired tremendous power and prestige, leading some to regard it as the ultimate value.

Every social order that people might want to value needs to be scientifically examined in order to determine what type of people it offers the best chances. Without such an examination there is no factual basis for valuing a certain development.

Now, the implication of all this is that from a methodological standpoint value-relatedness can entail neither a positive nor a negative assessment of the rationalization process. This is a global process of development that originated in the Occident and that is now spreading over the entire world, but it is at the same time a development upon which people can pass highly divergent judgments.

A third connection between science and values that deserves brief mention is the fact that values themselves can be the object of scientific inquiry. When values become the object of scientific investigation, they lose their normative character. They are viewed as objects, as 'being' rather than as 'obtaining.' In that case they are simply rules of conduct that occur empirically, in certain circles of people, with lesser or greater frequency. The question concerns their empirical 'being,' not their (normative) 'correct meaning.' If a scientist lacks the capacity to understand empathically *(einfühlend zu verstehen)* actions which, from his standpoint, are incorrect, then he will also lack the capacity to explain them scientifically *(deutend verstehen* or *verstehend erklären* or *erklarend deuten)*. Hence the capacity to 'understand' *(verstehen)* is necessary, although 'one need not be Caesar in order to understand Caesar.' Obviously a scientist may make appraisals or value judgments, as long as he is mindful of the distinction between values and method. Yet it is especially important that he avoid making premature judgments when studying ideals that are alien to him, since damage to science would be the result: the scientist who prematurely disqualifies alien ideals as decadent will never reach the point of understanding them. It goes without saying that the scientist studies values only to the extent that they fall within the problem under investigation and have causal relevance to its solution. Meanwhile, important and valuable side-effects might result from the scientist's research: justice might be done to others, or the research might prove to have practical pedagogical significance.

The fourth connection between science and values Weber calls 'values-interpretation.' At the foundation of every scientific investigation there lies a value (hence the value-relatedness of science). It is an empirical fact, Weber states, that in our age an enormous diversity of values exists and that when they are thought through consistently, values are often mutually contradictory, like 'God and the devil.' In the conduct of their everyday lives, people are often unaware of the fact that their actual behavior is determined by a complex pattern of contradictory values; nor are they aware of how that is so. Yet in carrying on scientific research it is vitally important to the scientist to know what values he holds himself and what values govern the behavior of others. The fact that people disagree, the reasons why they disagree, and the points in dispute between them are questions for science. After all, truth is at stake here – truth that can provide clarification of the values in terms of which the scientist himself or the actors under study actually act. Even if absolute agreement about certain values should exist in a community, there would be a task for science: namely, the veritable self-evidence of the matter would be a specific problem for science. For that 'self-evidence' would be the very thing least likely to be 'thought,' since 'deep-rooted in man's conceptual universe.'[22] The interpretation and discussion of values are essential to the scientist above all because it is usually not clear what values are involved in any given case.

Such interpretation is partly rational and partly empirical in character. Rationally it can consist of logical analysis or the exposure of the inconsistencies that arise when a particular thesis is extended. What can be established empirically is the means required to realize a certain value, the secondary or side-effects involved, and the possible practical consequences for other values that could be affected.

Such interpretation of values is something entirely different from a philosophical treatment of values; hence such interpretation also does not lead of itself to the adoption of a certain position. It is possible, to be sure, that one would arrive at a different choice of values than had previously been thought possible. Science in that case would be drawn into a new set of questions charged with values, or in other words, new areas of interest for knowledge, which would of course then have to be dealt with in terms of the scientific method. It is not the scientific method but the values-orientation of the scientist that changes in such circumstances.

Finally, just a few words about science and the application of science. The value component of a research project does not exist as an empirical fact for the scientist; it is to be found rather in the goal of the research at issue. As my preceding remarks implied, a discussion of that goal will reveal that it has been selected from various values. Moreover, as I have shown, science contributes to the disclosure of the value (or values) people have selected. According to Weber, anyone who lives his life consciously is confronted by a chain of decisions whereby one chooses the meaning of his life and actions. In this sense a person chooses his own destiny. Human dignity consists, according to Weber, precisely in man's consciously choosing values. Science, however, can assist in making choices. Every ethic, for example, requires substantive content. Thus the choice for 'justice' says nothing about the concrete measures to be taken. What science can do, once agreement concerning ends has been reached, is to stand causal attribution on its head, so to speak, or, in other words, to translate the necessary consequences of facts into means and ends. The empirical law 'From x follows y' means, when translated for scientific application, 'The measure x leads to the result y'. Scientific rationality is translated into technical actions (in the broader and the narrower senses of the word *technique,* depending on whether reference is being made to application of the cultural sciences or of the natural sciences). In this sense a value-free political science is possible. Science can offer exceptionally valuable help in dealing with complex socio-economic problems the implications of which can only be vaguely sensed. That is also true of areas lying more in the personal sphere. Sociology of religion, for example, does not of itself make the religiously 'musical' person, that is, the one who has chosen religion as a value, either more or less religious, although either outcome would be a possible side-effect. In this sense one could, via science, become either more or less religious. Accordingly, Weber considers science, too, to be a means to introspection and personal choice.

C. Empirical-Nomological, 'Verstehende', and Socio-Critical Sociology

If we follow Vaskovics's[23] typological distinction between three methodological conceptions in present-day sociology, namely, the empirical-nomological, the interpretive *(verstehende)* and the socio-critical, then Weber's interpretive method is closer to the socio-critical than it is to the empirical-nomological method – at least if one may be permitted to abstract from the philosophical theory of society, which comprises an actual moment of socio-critical sociology. For in Weber nomological knowledge is not a goal in itself that would be required to grow, through cumulative theory formation, into a general, definitive, intrinsically consistent whole. Weber emphatically rejects every tendency towards an identification of the social sciences with the natural sciences. In Weber nomological knowledge is just a means to understanding concrete reality in its value-related coherency of meaning, and scientific theory has a decidedly open and provisional character. Furthermore, Weber shares the preference of the socio-critical conception which views society as a whole, as in his 'Wirtschaftsethik,' for example. Moreover, in Weber the scientist is positioned not only against but likewise decidedly within the historical process, as a co-player,[24] something critical sociology also strongly emphasizes. (Again, I am abstracting here from the philosophical or scientific consequences drawn in this regard by the critical school.) The purely value-free scientist is able, via his value-related situation, to arrive at a critique of a given state of affairs because scientific praxis provides the opportunity for posing new problems more appropriate to the times or relevant to the society. The interpretation and discussion of values fulfill a function similar to that of scientific praxis.

A conspicuous difference between Weber and the socio-critical school, certainly, is that Weber does not regard the choice of values as arising directly from scientific praxis itself, and therefore also does not take a very optimistic view of the possibility of arriving at some future, general consensus about values. On the contrary, Weber finds in our present-day society a 'polytheism' of many mutually different and contradictory valuations. It is only via conscious application that his (always technical) science will ever be able to be directed towards man's emancipation. The possibility of an 'emancipatory' sociology, as the critical sociology calls itself, would undoubtedly have been labelled an unrealistic utopia by Weber, given the values 'polytheism' in present-day society, among other factors.

Insofar as the application of science is concerned, Weber often informally uses the so-called decisionist model adopted by B. C. van Houten, following Jürgen Habermas.[25] According to this model, science can only indicate alternative means of achieving given ends. What these ends themselves should be is decided by the politician, for example, since they are based on an irrational choice that cannot be scientifically grounded. Insofar as the application of science is concerned, Weber is thus close to the empirical-nomological conception in sociology, which likewise distinguishes sharply between science and its application. In this respect Weber deviates fundamentally from the principled normative critical sociology.

However, to leave the matter at that would be to do Weber's views on the theory of science an injustice. Methodologically, he is relatively close to the so-called 'pragmatic model' developed by Habermas.[26] This model is based on a dialectical relation between values and scientific knowledge. In that case a strict distinction between science and politics, for example, creates room for critical interaction. Scientists translate practical questions into scientific problems, and practical needs are more sharply delineated scientifically through testing the technical possibilities. Inversely, the direction of scientific praxis is largely determined by the practical questions of the politicians. Now, this all bears a strong resemblance to Weber's problem-oriented sociology and to the emphasis he lays on the interpretation of values as a condition for empirical inquiry. From the above, it is clear that for Weber the value-free character of sociology is strictly a methodological question.

As we have seen, rationality in science means rendering reality methodically intelligible so that it becomes calculable in the broader sense. Rationality in science lies in the sphere of technical, goal-oriented rationality *(Zweckrationalität)*. It is distinct but never isolated from values-oriented rationality *(Wertrationalität)*, which we have yet to examine. The latter even penetrates the former intrinsically. Scientific method is, after all, always determined by the problem posed, and the problem always involves one value or another. The nature of the problem contributes to determining the course to be followed, since it leads to a particular conceptual apparatus. Sociology is accordingly 'subjective,' on Weber's view, in virtue of its implicit belief in the value of scientific knowledge in the Western sense and also in virtue of the sphere of interest in terms of which it interrogates reality. It is 'objective' in virtue both of its demand for intersubjective verifiability and of its need to be inferred absolutely from the facts.[27]

II. Weber's Sociological Methodology[28]

The observations made in the preceding section about the cultural and social sciences in general are valid for sociology as well. I have already discussed the problem-oriented and historical character of Weber's sociology, together with its critical function, because these follow directly from his general conception of science. That discussion applies without restriction to Weber's conception of sociology, in spite of the fact that in his essay of 1904 he still rejected the notion of a science of society as such. The reason he did so, after all, was his conviction that the concept 'social' was too general and vague to serve as a specific vantage point for arranging particular contents of meaning; in other words, society was too amorphous to be the object of a separate science comparable to history or economics. Thus his skepticism touched only the desirability of a new, separate social science, not its general methodology.[29] After 1909, however, Weber called himself a sociologist and regarded even his earlier works as belonging to sociology, including his *Protestantische Ethik* of 1905, which he of course included in his *Gesammelte Aufsätze zur Religionssoziologie*. The inducement to call himself a sociologist was his role in founding the German Sociological Association *(Deutsche Gesellschaft für Soziologie)*. His objective was an organization for value-free, pure scientific research, which he could not realize within the existing *Verein für Sozialpolitik*.[30] From that time onward Weber developed the specific perspective whereby sociology became for him a distinct cultural or social science.[31]

In the last phase of this development he defined sociology as 'a science concerning itself with the interpretive understanding of social action and thereby with a causal explanation of its course and consequences.'[32] This (nominal) definition suffices to show that the general methodology I described above is also valid for the methodology of sociology.[33]

Weber calls his sociology 'individualistic.'[34] I shall begin with this trait. In connection with it I shall also have a look at how Weber views social structures. Then, secondly, in order the more precisely to delineate sociological understanding *(verstehen)* and the corresponding concept of meaning, I shall go on to examine the relation between sociology and psychology. At the same time. I shall undertake to say what Weber understands by rationality.

Because Weber's sociology is 'historical sociology,' I shall in the third place indicate briefly the connection between history and sociology. This needs to be done both in order to make possible a better understanding of the nature of Weber's sociology and in order to facilitate, at a later stage, the better placement from a sociological standpoint of the rationalization process, which is also a historical category.

Finally, I want to deal in this section with the relation in Weber between general sociology and sociology of religion.

A. 'Individualistic' Sociology

The individualistic character of interpretive *(verstehend)* sociology follows from its material object: social action *(handelen)*. By social action Weber means covert or overt human action,[35] including 'both failure to act and passive acquiescence,'[36] to which the actor attaches a subjective meaning *(subjektiv gemeinte Sinn)* that takes account of the equally meaningful action of another actor or actors.[37] Social action is determined by this intentionality and can therefore be explained, in some measure at least, in terms of it. This typically human, meaningful action bearing upon others is the specific object of sociology. Meaningful behavior by a plurality of persons would not, of course, be 'social action' in the absence of an orientation towards others. For example, the behavior of a number of people on the street who simultaneously put up their umbrellas in reaction to a sudden shower is not 'social action.'[38] Typically nonhuman, meaningless facts or nomological regularities studied by physics, chemistry, biology, geography, and so forth, fall outside the purview of sociology. Material culture, however (for example, a machine), falls within its field of inquiry, as a product of meaningful human action. This is not to say that facts devoid of meaning would be unimportant for interpretive sociology; it is to say rather that they would assume an entirely different place from a methodological standpoint: namely, they are the conditions, occasions, obstacles, challenges, etc., for meaningful human social behavior. Thus the interpretive sociologist must take them into account as his problem requires. When considered in isolation from these situational factors, meaningful social behavior cannot be understood in its course and operation. Weber desires to avoid every form of monocausalism. Now, since the days of W. I. Thomas it would be feasible to call the 'definition of the situation' the object of Weber's sociology.[39] The sociologist studies situations as they exist from the standpoint of the actors defining them.

Weber warned as early as 1904 of the danger of using concepts borrowed from the ordinary parlance of politics, such as 'the interests of the agricultural economy.' Not only do the subjective notions of it vary from one farmer to another and not only are there conflicts of interest between different kinds of farmers (dairy, grain, etc.), but nonfarmers too define 'the interests of the agricultural economy.' These definitions are often correlative to a particular social situation: for example, the situation of the ruling classes, who are interested in maintaining the status quo, or the situation of the underprivileged, who desire change. There is talk here of a hopelessly tangled ball of values and interrelated interest, all of which contribute in some way or another to setting these definitions. This is especially true of the concepts that indicate a social collectivity[40] *(Kollektivbegriffe),* such as the 'state' or 'the interests of the state.' Such concepts of collective entities are simply a cover for an extremely tangled web of valuations to which definition makers link the state time after time.[41]

From these examples, what Weber meant by 'individualism' and 'subjective meaning' is clear. In an interpretive sociology the individual is at once the lower boundary and the upper boundary of social action: after all, physiological or chemical processes in terms of which the individual might be further analyzed are not 'meaningful.' Social collectivities are not subjects, that they should define situations. For other sciences it could be useful to regard such formations as subjects. Law entertains 'juridical persons' – corporations, for example – as bearers of rights and duties. For an empirical social science, however, such social collectivities can mean only the 'likelihood' that individuals will behave in such a way that a corporation, a state, or a family will arise. In the absence of that likelihood, the pertinent corporation, state, or family would vanish. 'Subjective meaning' can be purely individual, i.e., the meaning 'attached' or 'intended'[42] in a concrete case by a specific actor; usually, however, subjective meaning is the 'average or approximate' meaning that social action acquires in a particular cultural context. In other words, the so-called 'objective' meaning will have sociological relevance.[43] As I see it, one can best regard this objective meaning as a general culture that is internalized, via the socialization process, in individual subjective 'intentions.' An illustration is afforded by 'consensual action' *(Einverständnishandeln)*, a sociological category that indicates that one orients his action to the anticipated behavior of others, while an empirically valid likelihood exists that the others will also actually behave as expected, regardless of their personal intentions. As examples of 'consensual action' Weber mentions 'a language group' and 'a market.'[44] *A market structure is an objective meaning* or 'purposive' *(sinnhafte)* orientation; that is not to say, however, that that objective meaning is identical to the sum of subjective intentions. Here actions are oriented to culturally determined expectations that countless known and unknown others will accept money, now and in the future. This *objective meaning* does not exist as the result of subjectively agreed intentions or goals, although the action transpires as if there were such an agreement. On the contrary, the differences in subjective goals are rather the condition for the *objective meaning* that traffic in money acquires in social life – that is, for the meaning of a market structure.[45]

Thus if sociology seeks the causal explanation of meaningful actions – which is to say, if it seeks explanation in terms of 'motives' – then by 'motive' it does not mean so much the strictly individual motive of the actor; it means more especially the meaningful ground of such an *objective meaning.*[46]

Thus sociology is 'individualistic' because only individuals attach or intend meaning and because they are the sole source of social action. There is a suggestion, however, of 'methodical individualism.' Weber acknowledges in the first place the tremendous power that social structures can have over individual behavior. As we shall see, Weber speaks elsewhere with some frequency of 'the strait jacket of serfdom' *(das Gehäuse der Hörigkeit)* in which man is confined in modern bureaucratic society. In his methodological writings too, however, Weber stresses this phenomenon. One can neither understand social behavior nor causally account for it without taking into consideration the fact that social structures like the state, family, etc., are realities in the everyday conceptual world of individuals and that individuals orient their actual behavior towards these realities. This is especially the case when these conceptualizations pertain to institutions that are viewed as normative and towards which one must therefore perforce attune his behavior. Yet Weber rejects an 'organic' method à la Albert Schäffle or the 'universalistic' method of Othmar Spann.[47] Such 'functional' approa-

45

ches that proceed in terms of the whole and that view the individual as just a part ("cell' or 'functionary") of that whole have important illustrative or heuristic value for interpretive sociology, but they are only 'preliminary preparation' for the real work of sociology. Weber grants that we must know what kind of action is 'functionally necessary for 'survival" or, more importantly, 'for the maintenance of a cultural type"; the reason we must know that, however, is only so that we will be able subsequently to raise the real sociological question concerning the motives that are determinative for the actions of the differentiated functionaries or members of a particular community. One must know what a king, official, entrepreneur, pander, or magician does before one can go on interpretively to analyze and classify the meaning of such deeds. The superior value of inner interpretive *(deutende)* as against outer observational *(beobachtende)* explanation is purchased, it is true, at the cost of a more fragmentary and hypothetical character to our knowledge – notwithstanding which sociology must do what it alone can do, given its specific character: investigate the 'How' and 'Why' of meaningful social behavior. The 'Why' can only be discovered by examining the intentions of individuals. Methodical individualism is indispensable to the pursuit of understanding beyond the level of functional classifications in the sense of the nomological regularities associated with natural law.[48]

One may not conclude from all this, however, that for 'verstehende' sociology the analysis of social collectivities *(Kollektivgebilde)* would be nothing more than preparatory work best relegated to other sciences such as law. In that case sociology would not address institutional structures at all; it would address only the social action of individuals within these structures.[49] Weber's individualism is strictly methodical in character and intended only to obviate every reification of structures. The structures as such fall directly within his purview, which should not be surprising in someone who wants to understand social action precisely in its *structured coherency* of meaning. The fact that individuals are the only source of meaning is not meant to imply that they are likewise the only units of analysis. On the contrary, a clear and central unit of analysis in Weber is the 'social relationship,' the *inter*individual social action. Now, this social action may be a structure or an element of a structure: a certain more or less stable form of social action. Structure is in that case an objective unit of meaning that abstracts not only from the subjective action of individuals whose actions produce and maintain this structure but also from the concrete individual himself. We have already seen an example of this in the case of consensual action *(Einverständnishandeln),* a specimen of which was a market structure. Weber also recognizes organizational structures. If we take the church and the sect, respectively, as examples, they are religio-sociological particularizations of the general sociological concepts of 'institution' or 'compulsory association' *(Anstalt)* and 'voluntary association' *(Verein, Zweckverein).* One speaks of 'voluntary association' or of 'compulsory association' the moment and to the extent that a social 'organization' *(Verband)* has rational rules.[50] In the case of a 'voluntary association' these statutory rules apply to members only by virtue of their voluntarily joining; in the case of an 'institution' or 'compulsory association,' these rules are imposed from on high without more ado for everyone having certain characteristics (birth, residence in a certain place, etc.). Thus the state is a political 'institution' and the church is a hierocratic 'institution.' One is a member by birth, and certain norms are internalized through socialization, or in Weber's parlance, the individual is "born into' and 'drawn into' this connection.'[51]

What is of interest to us in this matter is that on Weber's view too individual action can be typically structured in character. In the case of a 'voluntary association' (a sect, for example), this is so to the extent that members follow the pertinent rational rules. In the case of an 'institution' Weber makes a distinction in this regard between the action of the administrative staff in upholding the pertinent rules and the action of members in permitting themselves to be governed by these rules. Furthermore, beyond action pertaining to the 'institution' as such, one can distinguish action regulated by the 'institution' (such as action oriented towards implementing civil law in a state). This latter is not, however, typical 'institutional action' *(Anstaltshandeln)* and hence is not action belonging typically to this structural unit. Perfectly in keeping with the problem-oriented character of his sociology, Weber remarks that it is purely a question of expediency whether one views a structure as a structural unit or as a substructure.

I believe what has now been said will suffice to show that an individualistic method (the necessary consequence of the interpretive character of Weber's sociology) does not reduce social reality to an individualistic reality. The method does avoid the reification of structures. Yet the objectivity of structures is not impaired. Structures are realities whose coercive powers are proportional to the empirical predictability of situationally determined behavior.[52]

B. The Relation Between Sociology and Psychology

The relation between sociology and psychology presents the opportunity to have a closer look at the concepts of 'meaning' and 'understanding.' We have seen that sociology seeks to understand social action interpretively *(deutend verstehen)*. According to Weber, 'understanding' *(verstehen)* can have many senses, but in sociology it always signifies subjectively apprehending the 'meaning' of human action. 'Interpretation' *(Deuten)* too can be used in various senses, but in sociology it is a scientific category that accounts for human action 'causally' in terms of the 'motives' of the actor.[53] In social reality meaningful activities are seldom entirely consciously motivated. A variety of semi-conscious or just vaguely sensed motives may underlie them. Even for the actor himself, the real motive may be concealed, 'repressed,' or denied entry. It is a part of the sociologist's task to discover the real motivational nexus even here. Yet in such an instance the matter is one of the interpretation of meaning as a limiting case.[54] If the social action at issue were entirely devoid of all conscious intentionality and thus not meaningful, it would fall as such outside the specific terrain of interpretive sociology. Then it might still belong to the field of psychology.

Weber notes that 'psychology' may mean quite different things to different people. I believe one can distinguish three senses of the term in Weber himself.

One can take psychology to mean the study of totally noninterpretable nomological regularities through the use of a natural-scientific method (differences in reaction speed to certain stimuli, memory function, fatigue phenomena, etc.). In that case psychology lies outside the terrain of sociology. Obviously such regularities can be pertinent to sociological causal explanation if they occasion or are the condition for the direction in which meaningful social action occurs. Methodologically speaking, there is in that case no difference from other sciences that study noninterpretable processes, as do physiology and geography, for example.

Weber also knows an interpretive psychology that comprehends the goal-orientation of human passions (e.g., the sexual drive). Yet methodologically speaking, it too assumes no place apart because it too pertains to nonmeaningful phenomena. This interpretive psychology can be as pertinent to sociology as the psychology of nomological regularities, but then by way of analogy (for example, the phenomena of being born and of dying). After all, the 'meaning' of action is entirely different from the psychological nomological regularities that codetermine it. For example, the struggle for profits is not a psychological category. In different persons it can even be determined by quite different 'psychic' patterns. Even if a direct connection could be established scientifically between the capacity for rational orientation and the cephalic index, for example, this would entail no consequences for sociological method. Psychological nomological regularities are data to be taken into account by the interpretive sociologist only insofar as they codetermine human intentionality. Generally speaking, there is a closer connection between sociology and psychology than there is between sociology and all other sciences.[55]

In a third sense of the term 'psychology,' it is self-evident to Weber that 'psychological' motives directly determine concrete social action.[56] 'Psychological' action contrasts here to rational instrumental action *(subjektiv Zweckrationalität)*. While the latter contains a maximum of scientifically certain meaning, it seldom occurs in its pure form in social reality. It is closely approximated at a stock exchange, for example. There the sociologist can speak of nomological knowledge in the strictest sense of the word. Usually, however, social behavior transpires 'psychologically' and can be interpreted and explained only in psychological terms, which is to say that the course of social behavior and the causal explanation of it have 'irrational' components. This 'only psychologically' interpretable and explicable behavior embraces a fluid transitional zone between conscious teleologically oriented action and totally 'noninterpretable' psychological behaviors. It is irrational from the vantage point of goal-oriented instrumental rationality – perhaps in the objective sense: e.g., when the action is based on mistakes, whether they be errors of thought or of calculation; or perhaps in the subjective sense: whenever the action is based on interpretable nonteleologically oriented motives such as ecstasy, mystical experience, or religious surrender.

Weber does not go into the possibility of distinguishing between sociology and an interpretive psychology. Most likely he perceived no distinction here. The absence of the term 'structure' or its equivalent in his definition of sociology points in this direction. To my mind his terminology is then also often psychologically colored – for example, where he describes sociological explanation as 'explanation in terms of motives.'[57]

Thus in Weber's view what I have called 'psychological' in the

49

third sense of the term – that is, irrational instrumental social behavior – belongs to the direct object of study of sociology. By 'subjective meaning' *(subjektiv gemeinte Sinn)* Weber understands not only conscious goals but all meaningful human behavior. In keeping with that, he distinguishes between rational and irrational understanding *(verstehen)*, both of which may be either 'direct observational understanding' *(aktuelles verstehen)* or 'explanatory understanding' *(erklärendes verstehen)*.[58]

As examples of *direct observational rational* understanding Weber mentions the understanding of propositions such as the meaning of the formula 2 x 2 = 4 or of actions such as aiming a gun to fire. One can speak of *direct observational irrational* understanding in the case of meaningful affects such as a fit of rage readable on someone's face.

An example of *explanatory rational* understanding would be the case of the oral or written expression of 2 x 2 = 4 in the context of a commercial calculation or scientific proof. Here *direct observational rational* understanding appears within a coherent pattern of meaning. That is likewise the case when one aims a gun on command in order to execute a criminal or fight an enemy *(rationales Motivationsverstehen)*.

Yet *explanatory irrational* understanding also belongs directly to sociology. For example, someone could aim a gun to take revenge *(irrationales motivationsmässig verstehen)*. Whenever there is an interpretable coherent pattern of meaning, to which directly observable interpretable behavior in the subjective sense belongs, one can speak of a sociological explanation. Thus there is a sociological explanation of anger towards others in cases where the anger is known to be based on wounded pride, jealousy, or an insult.[59]

It needs to be noted that the rational or irrational character of the interpreting and explaining pertains not to those activities but to the nature of the social behavior under study. Conceivably this behavior would have to be explained by both a rational instrumental *(zweckrational)* and an irrational instrumental *(zweckirrational)* motive.

'Meaningful' action is specifically human and involves a more or less cerebral or intellectual clarity. Hence 'meaning' always has something to do with rationality and vice versa. Weber distinguishes two directions in which human intentionality can take its course *rationally*.[60]

In the first place, rational action can be oriented to values *(Wertrationalität)*. Here one speaks of 'a conscious belief in the value for its own sake of some ethical, aesthetic, religious, or other form of behavior, independently of its prospects of success.'[61] Someone is acting in a 'value-rational' way if by virtue of his convictions he does what seems to him to be required by duty, honor, beauty, religious vocation, or the interests of a 'cause' of any sort whatsoever.[62] Such action is always action in compliance with 'commands' or 'demands' an actor accepts as binding upon him. To the degree that human action is consciously and consistently oriented to such considerations – which is usually only in some small measure – Weber speaks of value-rationality. The degree of rationality increases in proportion to the degree to which an actor self-consciously formulates the final values governing his behavior and consistently orients his behavior to conform to these values. Values are thus more than an emotional state. They can be the object of a hypothesis, and they can be assessed. Therefore values are accessible to interpretation *(verstehen)* in the sociological sense, and they can be accounted for in terms of motives.

The second direction in which rational action can be motivated is that of teleological or goal-oriented rationality *(Zweckrationalität)*. Here there is the suggestion of action in relation to goals, means, and secondary effects. People consciously weigh means against ends, or investigate what secondary effects must accompany proposed goals and what alternatives are possible.

With this twofold distinction Weber is not aiming at exhaustive, mutually exclusive categories of rational action. On the contrary, social action seldom moves in just the one direction or the other. Real social action often approaches the one or the other form of rationality in greater or lesser measure; and even more often, the two forms of rationality are present in mixture. The choice between competing goals and effects may happen to be 'determined in a value-rational manner,' in which case 'action is instrumentally rational only in respect to the choice of means.'[63] At other times an actor may treat competing ends simply as 'given subjective wants' scaled according to the urgency of the felt need for their satisfaction. This would be instrumental rationality without value-related orientation. However, *absolute* instrumental rationality – 'the orientation of action wholly to the rational achievement of ends without relation to fundamental values' – would in Weber's opinion (like pure value rationality) be a hypothetical limiting case hardly to be found in social reality.[64]

Thus value-rational orientation can relate to instrumental rationality in the most varied ways. Viewed in terms of instrumentally rational orientation, value rationality is, however, always irrational; and that is all the more so when an actor comes to regard a value as absolute in its own right, with the consequence that he reflects ever less upon the possible consequences of his value-oriented action. Then he may act out of pure duty, or pure sectarianism, for example, and not concern himself with consequences. In this sense he acts irrationally: he does not weigh the consequences of his actions. Then there is no instrumental rationality *(Zweckrationalität);* there is just value rationality *(Wertrationalität).*[65]

Weber distinguishes two more types of social action, namely, in the first place traditional action, which by virtue of internalization via the socialization process *(durch eingelebte Gewohnheit)* occurs naturally, as a matter of course. Such traditional action is at the boundary of sociology's area of concern. If it is in fact no more than a simple reaction to habitual stimuli, then it constitutes habitual behavior that falls outside the forms of meaningful action that are *directly* of interest to the sociologist. In that case it can in principle still belong *indirectly* to the sociologist's field of research – often in some important measure – in the same way that all other meaning-vacuous, nomological knowledge or every purely mass-conditioned, purely imitative and reactive behavior can. If, however, it is 'sublimated' – that is, if it becomes self-conscious in some degree – then it may be classified as a form of value-rational action, or of instrumentally rational action, or of both.

The last type of social action that Weber distinguishes is affectual action that is determined by directly observable affects, or in other words, emotional action that is based on an emotional state. What is true of traditional action is true of affectual action as well: only to the extent that emotional life implies meaningful action bearing upon others can it belong to the specific terrain of sociology. Affects as such are not meaningful, but they may be the occasion for or the consequence of meaningful action. Thus Weber regards the impassioned and emotional performance of the prophets as being of undoubted sociological interest because it was meaning-oriented, and because it is explicable, in part at least, in terms of intentionality [mission].[66]

The four types of social action (value-rational, instrumentally rational, traditional, and affectual or emotional) will seldom occur independently of each other in reality. Besides regarding them as four distinct types of action, it is therefore also acceptable to view them as four elements that normally constitute any social action.

This conclusion follows from the nature of Weber's ideal types (which I shall discuss shortly); furthermore, Weber makes an emphatic point of the matter himself.[67]

C. History and Sociology

I have characterized Weber's sociology as historical sociology because it is based on the assumption that insight into social reality is, inherently, provisional in character and in principle never definitively apprehensible in a scientific system. This is not to say, however, that sociology and history were identical for Weber, notwithstanding that historians and sociologists have each regarded his work as belonging to their own fields respectively and that Weber began to call himself a sociologist only in 1909.

In considering the question of the relation between sociology and history in Weber, the most appropriate approach will be to go beyond strictly methodological matters to have a look at the nature of sociology of religion as such. At the same time, we shall be able to comment on the nature of Weber's sociology of religion.

In his last essay Weber himself stated explicitly what the difference between sociology and history is.[68] Sociology addresses social action that occurs with a certain regularity; it works with typological concepts and seeks general rules. History aspires to elucidate discrete patterns (individual events) and personalities. The concept formation and nomological work of the sociologist are aimed in part at aiding in the imputation of historical causes to phenomena of cultural importance.[69] As a generalizing science, however, sociology must, in its very nature, have recourse to abstraction; its concepts thereby become relatively empty with respect to concrete historical reality: conceptual 'intension' is gained at the expense of conceptual 'extension.'

If we adopt this distinction between sociology and history, then we must call *Die protestantische Ethik* – Weber's central essay in sociology of religion which the other essays in *Gesammelte Aufsätze* are meant to support – in the first instance a historical essay. Here Weber undertakes to explain the 'spirit of capitalism' in terms of 'ascetic Protestantism.' Both are typically Western, which is to say they are individual phenomena restricted with respect to both place and time. There is a genetic-causal relation between them: ascetic Protestantism appeared first in a particular place and time and gave rise to an equally place- and time-bound, later capitalistic culture. Hence Weber also calls the spirit of capitalism 'an historical individual,' by which he means a unique 'complex of elements associated in historical reality.' Certainly we abstract or isolate this complex of elements from the inexhaustible wealth of concrete reality, but we do so in keeping with *historical* methodology in order 'to grasp historical reality – in concrete genetic sets of relations which are inevitably of a specifically unique and *individual* character.'[70]

Yet we can justifiably maintain that this historical essay is equally sociological in character. By incorporating it into the *Gesammelte Aufsätze zur Religionssoziologie* Weber gave this time- and space-bound essay, which showed concretely the actual historical influence of the ascetic religious motivation on the rise of the capitalistic work ethic, a more *general* and *analytical* character.

In interpreting Weber it is in my opinion correct to think that this initial investigation, in which he demonstrates the causal significance of the religious factor in a genetic-historical way, acquires the function of a hypothesis: the religious motivation becomes the independent variable subject to further testing through comparative research. The differentiating influence of religion on society is thereby rendered accessible to examination in a generalizing, analytical way, independent of the concrete, spatial-temporal (historical) context.

I want to go further, however, to assert that *Die protestantische Ethik* has a sociological as well as a historical character even apart from the place it later assumed in Weber's collected works on the sociology of religion. For this inquiry of 1905 was intended to refute the popular Marxist proposition which regarded religion as being no more than a reflection of material economic factors devoid of causal influence on patterns of behavior. Weber wanted to show how ideas function in history. This essay thereby acquired a purport that went beyond showing an actual genetic-causal relation. Weber wanted to examine not only the fact but also the *nature* of the relation.[71] His research showed that the religious factor could be a valid explanatory factor for social behavior. In a footnote that on his own testimony he never revised, Weber argues that only empirical research can determine whether this factor actually did function elsewhere as well. He does not wish to work like a 'dilettante' who takes the results achieved and proceeds to reason further in a logical deductive way or who reduces everything to a single formula. Weber is reacting here against one-sided *a priori* 'materialistic' or 'spiritualistic' views of culture or history.[72]

Thus it remains a fact – partly because of this remark made in a footnote – that even this pre-1909 essay has a generalizing, sociological character as well as a historical character.[73]

Weber's other writings on the sociology of religion are less clearly concomittantly historical in character, even though they often contain explicitly historical views and can be called historical in tenor. Thus Weber commences the foreword to his collected writings on the sociology of religion by posing a historical problem:

> A product of modern European civilization, studying any problem of universal history, is bound to ask himself to what combination of circumstances the fact should be attributed that in Western civilization, and in Western civilization only, cultural phenomena have appeared which (as we like to think) lie in a line of development having *universal* significance and value.[74]

To Weber the problem is at bottom historical: it is to account for a unique Western phenomenon and its failure to appear elsewhere. The scope of the problem, which touches the entire world of culture, does not detract from the fact that it is at bottom historical in nature.

Yet this problem is solved in a sociological way: the *'universal* significance and value' of Western rationalism must be explained not only in their historical, temporal-spatial context but also, and more desirably, in a typological, generalizing sense. This is clear from Weber's explicit objective: his research is intended to be a contribution to the 'typology and sociology of rationalism' itself.[75]

The monographs on Confucianism and Taoism in China, Hinduism in the Indian caste system, Buddhism in India and the rest of Asia and, finally, ancient Judaism must also be characterized as nonhistorical, according to Weber. They are 'typological' studies that consciously select from the various historical religious ethics that which is of importance to the economic ethos and the shaping of the practical everyday pattern of behavior. In other words, Weber investigates what the religious factor actually means as a possible causal element. This is a typically sociological problem. That is not to say, however, according to Weber, that the results can be faulted from a historical standpoint.

Eminently typological among Weber's writings are the 'introduction'[76] and, especially, the 'intermezzo'[77] in 'Die Wirtschaftsethik der Weltreligionen'; and, of course, the 'systematic' sociology of religion in *Wirtschaft und Gesellschaft*.[78]

55

D. The Relation Between General Sociology and the Sociology of Religion

As the preceding discussion shows, Weber's sociology of religion is an integral part of his general sociology, and especially of his chosen problem: accounting for the rise and character of Western capitalist society. In his main sociological study, *Wirtschaft und Gesellschaft,* it is a part of the whole – a relatively independent part, to be sure – just as his sociology of law and his sociology of politics are. Hence Weber's sociology of religion poses no new problems of methodology. Since what is distinctive about it pertains to its substantive side, namely, the cultural phenomenon of religion, we now need to look briefly at Weber's sociological view of religion as a cultural phenomenon. Needless to say, the question is a subject of lively controversy in sociology today.[79]

In the first place, we can say that Weber makes a clear distinction between a theological or believing and a sociological approach to religion:

> What to a theologian is valuable in his religion cannot play a very large part in this study. We are concerned with what, from a religious point of view, are often quite superficial aspects of religious life, but which, and precisely because they were superficial and unrefined, have often influenced outward behavior most profoundly.[80]

Yet we may not misunderstand this 'superficial and unrefined' aspect. Weber aspires to be an 'interpretive' *(verstehend)* sociologist and therefore attempts to put himself in the believer's shoes to the extent necessary to understand him from the inside. Because Weber as a sociologist is mainly interested in religion in order to understand its influence on the practical pattern of everyday life in society,[81] he must know the religious motivation. To this end he turns to the literature of theology. It is not the speculative dogmatic or the moral theological treatises that are pertinent to his objective but the writings which give evidence of having originated in the practice of the pastoral care of souls.[82] Weber often defends this approach in footnotes devoted to the selected literature underpinning his case. Thus Weber assumes the believer's vantage point solely in order to ascertain what religion actually means to the believer. Even within the framework of a 'single' religion Weber differentiates its meaning and motivational force in keeping with someone's social position. In particular, social stratification plays an important role in Weber. The most extensive section of his systematic sociology of religion, entitled 'Stände, Klassen und Religion,'[83] is devoted explicitly to it. Given their various socio-economic and cultural situations, farmers, nobles and warriors, petit-bourgeois merchants and artisans, leading intellectuals, plebeian intellectuals, etc., display various religious affinities in keeping with the requirements of their specific class ties.[84]

Not only does Weber not define what religion is; he declines to do so as a matter of principle. He commences his systematic sociology of religion by asserting:

> To define 'religion,' to say what it *is*, is not possible at the start of a presentation such as this. Definition can be attempted, if at all, only at the conclusion of the study. The essence of religion is not even our concern, as we make it our task to study the conditions and effects of a particular type of social behavior.
>
> The external courses of religious behavior are so diverse that an understanding of this behavior can only be achieved from the viewpoint of the subjective experiences, ideas, and purposes of the individuals concerned – in short, from the viewpoint of the religious behavior's 'meaning' *(Sinn).*[85]

Accordingly, we can say that, in his sociological view of religion, Weber in principle consistently upholds his value-free, interpretive method.[86]

III. The Techniques of Sociology

Sociological techniques as the more concrete instruments of method in empirical research are what lead Weber to call sociology 'rationalistic.' They are likewise indispensable for understanding the scope of his sociological generalizations.

Weber considers two techniques in his thematic writings on methods and methodology, namely, 'ideal types' and statistics.

What he has to say about statistics is very general in nature and of little pertinence here. Statistics are not even really a specifically sociological technique as far as Weber is concerned. Statistics can relate in precisely the same way to nonmeaningful and to meaningful events. One can speak of 'sociological' statistics only in the latter case, as with respect to such categories as crime statistics, vocational statistics, etc. Such statistics represent interpretable types of action or, in other words, 'sociological rules.' Statistics often pertain to matters that rightfully belong to both categories at the same time, e.g., crop statistics.[87]

Statistics as such are a form of what in the context of general methodology I have already called the rationality of objective correctness *(Richtigkeitsrationalität)*, which ascertains only the actual occurrence of nomological regularities. Because sociology seeks genetic, or causal, insight that must be intersubjectively verifiable and valid, it must constantly invoke, besides intelligibility, the help of 'external' experience as a test. Now, statistics lie in this external sphere and can, given certain favorable circumstances – namely, countable, unambiguous, collective phenomena – ascertain whether (and if so, with what frequency) sociologically intelligible action actually occurs in empirical reality. In that case statistics offer a (relatively) optimal proof of the objectivity of a sociological statement.[88] For this reason statistics are important. Naturally, says Weber, the sociologist too uses 'average types' that reflect 'typical' cases in a statistical way. Average types are possible only where the matter involves differences of 'degree' in qualitatively 'comparable' meaningful actions.[89]

Yet the specifically sociological types are 'ideal types.' It is these Weber has in mind when he speaks of types and describes his method as 'rationalistic.' The so-called 'ideal type' *(Idealtypus:* a term Weber prefers to all others) serves to make nomothetical knowledge of the sort desired by the social sciences possible. For this reason it belongs to the problem-oriented and historical character of these sciences. 'Ideal types' are not the sort of categories that represent characteristics common to as many phenomena as possible, as in the natural sciences. These reduce reality to general laws to which the concrete instance can be subsumed. The social and cultural sciences, in contrast, strive to understand empirical reality to the extent it is value-related and hence meaningful. Their specific sphere of interest, for that reason exactly, is not in whatever it is a phenomenon may have in common with as many other phenomena as possible. In other words, the matter is not one of concepts having the greatest possible scope or extension but one of concepts having the greatest possible content or intension. What is essential to the natural sciences, however, is that which is general; so concepts in the natural sciences are intensionally circumscribed. What is essential in the cultural sciences is that which is rich in meaning; so the scope of concepts in the cultural sciences is not as general and broad; concepts in the cultural sciences are, relatively speaking, extensionally circumscribed. Discovering and explaining the meaning or significance of empirical phenomena can be accomplished in countless ways, consistent with the problems germane to a given period and the interests of the researcher. These are the factors that determine what is essential and what is peripheral, sociologically speaking.

Natural science and sociology both seek knowledge that can be generalized. In contrast to the strictly quantifiable laws of the natural sciences, however, social nomological regularities are always qualitative in character. The chance of attaining a valid causal explanation of concrete, interpretable events is enhanced by the expansion and certainty of general knowledge. General knowledge is not an end in itself; rather, it serves to explain ever-changing cultural problems – problems, moreover, which can be approached in terms of various spheres of interest.

Now, an ideal type belongs in this framework. It is a means of establishing a causal relation between meaningful phenomena. The ideal type is used, whether consciously or not, in every science that seeks to characterize cultural phenomena. The ideal type differs specifically from concepts, which embrace only what is common to many phenomena, because the ideal type is meaningful and because it establishes a connection between phenomena. In other words, it contains a judgment about a coherent pattern of meaning, about the conditions in which such a pattern arises, or about the consequences which follow from it in the nature of the case. Concepts of kinds yield only categories, but the ideal type yields the value moment, the cultural core that furnishes categorical concepts with their inner coherence. The moment the term 'typical' is used, there is something more involved than the mere classification of phenomena. When someone working with sociological statistics speaks of a 'typical' magnitude, there is something more involved than an average. Consequently, the difference between the average type and the ideal type is fluid. The better a specifically cultural complex of meaning is represented, the more one can speak of an ideal type:

> An ideal type is formed by the one-sided *accentuation* of one or more points of view and by the synthesis of a great many diffuse, discrete, more or less present and occasionally absent *concrete individual* phenomena, which are arranged according to those one-sidedly emphasized viewpoints into a unified *analytical* construct *(Gedankenbild)*.[90]

Thus such an ideal type will never be found to exist anywhere in concrete reality: as such, it is a utopia. Yet such an ideal type is designed by the historical or sociological researcher's inventiveness, which is oriented to empirical reality and nourished by it. Such an ideal type is meant to illuminate the problem at issue in an adequately motivated and 'objectively possible' way. From a logical standpoint an ideal type is just an evident rational possibility free of contradiction, but from a material standpoint it is an evident objectively possible hypothetical law. Whether or not (and if so, to what extent) this objectively possible form of adequate causation is also valid in empirical reality can only be determined by testing the ideal picture against the empirical reality. Then it can be determined to what extent reality actually approaches this ideal picture and to what extent it deviates from it or contrasts with it. With the results of such testing in mind, the researcher must revise or perfect his ideal type and then test it once again against reality in order to arrive finally at a responsible presentation of an actual historical phenomenon or sociological law – a presentation that will never, however, reflect empirical reality in its concreteness. Thus such an ideal type fulfills its function even when its incorrectness is demonstrated empirically. In that case it functions as a hypothesis that is not empirically corroborated.

Often one ideal type will be pitted antithetically against another of the same sort in order to discover more certainly the causes of particular cultural phenomena. The artisan society may be pitted antithetically against the capitalist society, for example, or the church against the sect. In empirical reality such polar opposites occur only as mixed forms of the two. And naturally so, since such ideal types are constructed limiting cases analogous to physical reactions calculated on the assumption of an absolute vacuum. We have already seen that the four types of (social) action can also be viewed as components of one and the same social behavior. Scientifically speaking, according to Weber, it is necessary to construct an ideal type as unambiguously as possible from a logical standpoint in order to attain the indispensable clarity and intersubjectivity.[91] Moreover, to do that is also necessary in order to facilitate criticism of the formation of concepts, without which the advancement of science would be impossible. This applies both to deepening a given problem that is approachable from various sides and to remaining flexible in the face of new problems as they arise, as they inevitably do. The 'one-sided selection' or abstraction from empirical reality whereby the ideal type is constructed is intended precisely to achieve the desired freedom from ambiguity.[92]

Given the need for unequivocalness of meaning and the greatest possible certainty *(Evidenz)*,[93] sociologists prefer to construct ideal types of social action that go on in a strictly goal-oriented, instrumentally rational way – types 'von einem rein konstruieren rein zweckrationalen Verlauf.' We have already seen in connection with general scientific methodology that science attains the highest degree of certainty in the case of absolute instrumental rationality *(Zweckrationalität)*. Instrumental rationality likewise proved to be the most satisfactory for a generalizing causal approach. Weber expressly states that the construction of instrumentally rational ideal types does not result from a rationalistic prejudice on the part of sociology. The construction of such types does not imply that instrumentally rational action will actually predominate. In fact, the reverse is true: most action is 'psychologically' motivated. The construction of instrumentally rational types is just a matter of methodical adequacy; it has no direct bearing on actual social action, which will have irrational as well as rational elements. Such subjectively constructed ideal types indicate only how a social action would go on if it were purely goal-oriented. Now, given such an ideal type it is possible, through comparison with empirical reality, to gain insight into the degree to which an action was in fact instrumentally rational and into the magnitude of any discrepancy between the actual course of events and ideal-typical instrumental rationality. Where such a discrepancy exists, it can be asked what irrational (i.e., nonteleological) factors affected the action. For example, there may have been 'miscalculations'; problems may have been altered by the intrusion of other purposes or considerations or deliberate misinformation;[94] or people may have acted in value-rational, traditional, or affectual ways. All these possibilities may deserve consideration as (causal) elements of social action. Whether they have actually been elements in a given instance can be learned through the use of rational ideal types. Thus it is possible, for example, with the help of economic theory (which is constructed, of course, of ideal types and which makes statements about how economic action would go on if people were to act in a strictly rational way) to investigate the extent to which an action was in fact rationally economical and, likewise, the extent to which power politics or other extra-economic factors such as traditional restraints, feelings, mistakes, etc., were involved. Irrational feelings during a panic on the stock exchange are easily identified with the help of economic theory.

It will by now be clear that the 'rationalistic method' no more implies the actual predominance of instrumentally rational behavior than the 'individualistic method' denies the existence of social structures.[95] Rationally constructed ideal types are in themselves nothing more – but then, of course, at the same time nothing less – than definite causal hypotheses. Weber even acknowledges the research value of ideal types having an 'irrational' content. These may turn out to be value-oriented and to belong to the fields of ethics, aesthetics, or religion; or they may be more affectual or emotional in character. Moreover, the two types will often accompany each other, as in the case of mystical, prophetic, and pneumatic phenomena. It is even possible to design ideal types of pure facticity – for example, that of objective correctness *(Richtigkeitstypus),* which is used in statistics. Such ideal types of meaning-vacuous events are also called 'rational' by Weber, but then in the word's narrower, empirical-technical sense, which indicates nothing more than shedding light on probability factors.

From a logical standpoint there is no difference between these ideal types in so far as they are always obtained through the isolating process of abstraction and in so far as they always strive for unequivocalness of meaning. Naturally, an ideal type is more specifically sociological in character in proportion to the degree in which it is not just 'causally adequate' and productive of *correct knowledge* but more especially 'meaning adequate,' that is, accessible to *understanding (verstehen).* The latter status obtains in the case of ideal types whose content is 'rational' in the broader sense of the term: value rationality or instrumental rationality.

Yet it should be realized, Weber asserts, that ideal types are utopian constructions not only in the objective 'external' sense but also in the subjective 'internal' sense: the 'intended meaning' of empirical social action is something of which the actor himself is usually only vaguely aware.[96] In actuality, fully conscious meaningful action is just a limiting case. Thus it can be said that 'social action' in the sense in which it is defined as the object of sociology is an 'ideal type' in Weber's sense.[97]

CHAPTER THREE

RATIONALISM AS A SOCIO-CULTURAL STRUCTURE

The preceding chapter was about scientific rationalism as it pertains to sociology. The study presented in that chapter provided a way of discovering what Weber means by socio-cultural rationality – the rationality that can be confirmed empirically in everyday human behavior. This rationality was the central focus of Weber's sociology of religion.

The best way to proceed will now be to devote a chapter to rationality as a set, more or less static condition of a society or subsociety. In this regard Weber employs the term 'rationalism.'[1] Subsequently, I shall go on to devote a chapter to rationality as a process: 'rationalization.

I have named the subject of the first of these pivotal chapters socio-cultural 'structure.' By 'structure' I mean definitions of reality that are fixed temporally with respect to various mutually related positions. The question in this context is not one of structure versus culture but one rather of an analytical distinction between structure and structuring (de-structuring, re-structuring) as the diachronic process of (re-)defining reality.

To contrast the various forms of rationalism was an explicit objective of Weber's sociology of religion. Yet for the moment I am concerned only to provide an initial, relatively cursory introduction to the problem of rationality. Matters of comparison and contrast can be taken up only later, after an examination has also been made of rationality as a process. Although Weber himself did not deal separately with the structure and the process of rationality, they are distinguishable in his thought.[2]

In the five sections of this chapter, I describe – in an ideal-typical way, to be sure[3] – the 'rationalistic' structures that Weber himself treated explicitly and that I alluded to in chapter one. These are, in order, modern capitalistic rationalism and, further, the rationalisms of ascetic Protestantism; of Chinese Confucianism and Taoism; of Indian Brahmanism, Jainism, and ancient Buddhism; and of Judaism. My approach is basically the following. First, I look at what affects the social situations of the respective structures – I look at the 'bearers' of the respective rationalisms, to use Weber's terminology. Then I examine more closely the concrete systems of norms – the teleological behavioral rationality – of these structures, in order to illuminate, finally, their central value-orientations. Because of the unique character of Jewish rationalism, I in that case examine the central value first and only thereafter the social and the teleological rationality.

I. Modern Capitalistic Rationalism

Modern capitalistic rationalism is a substructure of global, rationalistic Western society. The distinctive feature of this society is that the social situations which control its everyday life are held by specialists who have been scientifically trained for them. Modern rational and systematic scientific practice has transformed man into a 'specialist.' Weber speaks of *Fachmenschentum*. Naturally, specialization and the division of labor are old and familiar phenomena in a wide variety of cultures.

> But no country and no age has ever experienced, in the sense of the modern Occident, the absolute and complete dependence of its whole existence, of the political, technical, and economic conditions of its life, on a specially trained *organization* of officials. The most important functions of the everyday life of society have come to be in the hands of technically, commercially, and above all legally trained government officials.[4]

Now, modern capitalistic rationalism cannot be understood apart from its interdependence on the global, rationalistic society of which it is a substructure. The free enterprise method of production would be unable to calculate the results of enterprise rationally in the absence of a rational legal and administrative structure – in the absence, that is to say, of an administrative organization that operates reliably and predictably according to formal rules. On the other hand, however, it would be a mistake to regard the typical character of modern capitalism as nothing more than an element of a general Western rationalization process. For according to Weber the rationalization of the various departments of life has not been a parallel development, temporally or spatially. Thus economic and juridical rationalization cannot be inferred from each other. Both can be advanced or obstructed by extremely divergent factors. Here, however, we have already encroached upon an area that belongs to rationality as a process and that is to be reserved for explicit treatment in the following chapter.

In his sketch of capitalism, Weber is concerned above all to discover the pattern of motivation in terms of which modern man actually lives in his ordinary, daily comings and goings. He repeatedly insists that by 'modern' man he does not mean only those involved directly in the economic process. He speaks of the man with a 'calling' who ascetically restricts himself to 'specialized' work at the expense of 'Faustian universality.' The 'spirit of capitalism' is therefore also the spirit of modern culture in general.[5] Now, the modern pattern of motivation is especially conspicuous in the actual system of economic norms. In his sociology of religion Weber is not interested in these norms as such so much as he is interested in the central meaning-giving system of which they are the concretization; Weber is interested in 'the core of culture,' the dominant value or, in his own terminology, the 'spirit' of capitalism: *der 'Geist' der Kapitalismus.*[6] Even the socio-economic structure as analytically distinct from culture is only of secondary importance to him. Nevertheless, we shall have to describe briefly this system of norms and this socio-economic structure because the spirit of capitalism is evident in them.

By capitalism as socio-economic structure Weber understands: the free enterprise method of production, which is oriented to a market. The private entrepreneur, whose origins are traceable to the long-established free urban burgher class hires (formally) 'free' wage laborers. The objective of the enterprise is to make a profit, expressed in terms of money. This is accomplished in a rational way through purposeful calculation of market risks. An indispensable means to the achievement of this objective is the constant comparison of the costs of capital and labor with their yields – that is, bookkeeping calculations before, during, and after the production process. The most characteristic elements of modern capitalism, besides rational entrepreneurial bookkeeping and the accompanying legally guaranteed separation of personal resources and corporate capital, are the market and (formally) free labor. It is the market that distinguishes modern capitalism from all the other forms of capitalism that have appeared throughout history in all civilized countries and that still appear today, even in the West. These other forms of capitalistic enterprise were also marked by a – frequently unbounded – quest for profits and by rational calculation aimed at acquiring profits. Weber has in mind all kinds of 'adventurer' capitalism that by calculated violence can incidentally rob others of their possessions; he is thinking, too, of chronic systematic exploitation of subjects through such means as fiscal regulations. In addition to such mainly politically oriented forms of capitalism there are also everywhere more peace- and economy-oriented forms of commercial and speculative capitalist enterprise. Modern capitalism is distinguished from all these forms, however, by the fact that its quest for profits is oriented to the risks of trade in the market. Thus it is based on (formally) pacific speculations structurally anchored in society.

Free wage labor stands in contrast to the slaves, serfs, servants, or otherwise traditionally bound workers of the pre-capitalist period. It is this (formally) free labor that makes possible an exact economic calculation and that gives rise to the uniquely Western rational organization of labor.[7]

As I have said, Weber is less concerned with this rational socio-economic structure than he is with the central system of meaning-giving, or intentionality *(zingevingssysteem)*, that underlies it, namely, the mentality of capitalist man, the factor which motivates his behavior from within. In order to identify this mentality, Weber first presents by way of illustration a series of norms that typify the actual normative pattern of life of modern man. In doing so, he cites two of Benjamin Franklin's writings, *Necessary Hints to Those That Would Be Rich* (1736) and *Advice to a Young Tradesman* (1748). Here Franklin advises the young businessman to remember that *'time* is money'; that *'credit* is money'; that 'money is of the prolific, generating nature'; that he that 'murders a crown, destroys all that it might have produced...'![8] – 'even scores of pounds.' Franklin advocates punctual repayment of borrowed money. He also commends industry, frugality, and justice because they raise one's creditworthiness. In short, Franklin recommends a careful life of exact calculations unmarred by wasted time or money, to the end that one may become as rich as possible.[9]

However, neither in Franklin nor in the present-day capitalist entrepreneur and worker are these seemingly purely utilitarian norms of conduct expressions of a fundamentally purely egocentric code of conduct. Something more is involved here than 'simply a means of making one's way in the world,' or 'business astuteness,' or morally indifferent commercialism. What is involved here is a 'peculiar ethic,' an 'ethos.'[10] Violating these maxims and norms would not only be foolish; it would be a form of unscrupulous, conscienceless behavior.[11]

In terms of the distinction I noted earlier between various kinds of rationality, it can be said that what we have here are not only goal-oriented (*Zweckrationalität*) but also value-oriented (*Wertrationalität*) considerations. The combination is typical of modern capitalism, distinguishing it from all earlier forms of capitalism. In traditional forms of capitalism there was ruthless and even highly formally rationalized greed or acquisitiveness. In modern capitalism, however, the matter is one of an ethic:

> In fact, the *summum bonum* of this ethic, the earning of more and more money, combined with the strict avoidance of all spontaneous enjoyment of life, is above all completely devoid of any eudaemonistic, not to say hedonistic, admixture. It is thought of so purely as an end in itself, that from the point of view of the happiness of, or utility to, the single individual, it appears entirely transcendental and absolutely irrational.[12]

When we go on to describe more precisely what the substance of this 'transcendental' or even 'irrational' value-orientation might be, we find that it is 'proficiency in a calling.'[13] This proficiency in a calling is today, for the ideal-typical entrepreneur and modern man in general, as it was for Franklin, 'the Alpha and Omega' of morality. This 'social ethic' of duty in a calling is the typical feature of capitalistic culture, and even 'the fundamental basis of it.' That is not to say that particular individuals such as entrepreneurs or workers must consciously adopt it. The survival of present-day capitalism is no longer dependent on anything like that. This 'social ethic' is basic as a result of the fact that it possesses objective, self-evident social validity. There is an established capitalistic cultural order in which the individual can simply experience the obligation of his calling as the imperative to earn money through labor and through the efficient use of capital. If one were to ask such individuals about the 'meaning of their restless activity' in the perennial pursuit of ever more wealth, then they might answer – if indeed they were able to reply at all – that it was 'to provide for my children and grandchildren.' More often, however, and more correctly, they would reply that they simply could not live without the business, the 'continuous work' of which had become 'a necessary part of their lives.' This indicates, of course, that the calling had become an end in itself, that 'a man exists for the sake of his business, instead of the reverse.'[14]

Weber mentions that the ascetic quest for ever greater productivity is obviously also based on the ideal of making rational provision for the material goods required by humanity. While one may have no desire to enjoy his money himself, he may be quite pleased and proud of having provided employment for many people, of having contributed to the 'economic progress of his home town,' etc.[15] Naturally, this success too, which belongs specifically to the 'spirit of capitalism,' is rationally calculated and expressed in numbers.

To the 'natural'[16] man, by which Weber means the person who has not been reared in a capitalistic environment, this value-orientation of the capitalistic society is irrational and even reprehensible. To him it is obvious that man works to live and not vice versa. Opposed to capitalism is the attitude Weber calls 'traditionalism.'[17] We shall explore this traditionalism a bit further to gain better insight into the nature of capitalism.

The difference between the two, economically speaking, does not lie in the socio-economic structure of the enterprises or in the fact that here, too, far-reaching economic rationalism can be developed in the sense of exact and technically accurate calculation. Many pre-capitalist enterprises surpassed the first typically modern enterprises in both respects. The fundamental value-orientation of the traditional economy differed from that of modern capitalism, however, as night from day. Everywhere and in all times, the prevalent ethical teachings and, more pertinently, the practical action they inspired, regarded life as obviously more important than work. This is clear from the fact that an increase in wages did not contribute inevitably to an increase in productivity, but had instead precisely the opposite effect. People experienced no inner need to work more than was necessary to satisfy the needs tradition imposed upon them. Even the entrepreneurs worked only to meet their current needs. The distinction made by Werner Sombart between an economy based on satisfaction of needs (*Bedarfdeckungswirtschaft*) and an economy based on acquisition (*Erwerbswirtschaft*) reflects the difference between the traditionalistic and the capitalistic entrepreneur very well, provided that 'needs' is taken to mean requirements that are determined by tradition. Because Sombart fails to make this distinction, many enterprises that he typifies as belonging to the economy of acquisition and which bear a resemblance to modern capitalistic enterprise in their external form in fact fall outside the category of typically modern acquisitive economy. Namely, they lack the attitude or value-orientation that Weber 'provisionally' calls the 'spirit' of (modern) capitalism.'[18] Traditionally, people work to live, and even to enjoy the fruits of their labor. The quest for profits for their own sake is treated as reprehensible. In the Western Middle Ages, for example, the merchant was proverbially unable to please God; *Deo placere vix potest* was even a part of the canon law, and an 'ethical attitude like that of Benjamin Franklin would have been simply unthinkable.'[19] Economic practices à la Franklin were usually viewed as ethically unwarranted or dangerous, or at best as something 'morally indifferent.' Such practices were never ethically vindicated nor did they ever derive their inspiration from typically ethical norms.

II. Ascetic Protestant Rationalism

Weber's approach to Protestant rationalism[20] is comparable to his approach to capitalistic rationalism. His objective in this case is to ascertain the values by which the Protestant believer actually allows himself to be led in his everyday life. Weber deals mainly with the ascetic Protestantism of the second half of the seventeenth century; in this period ascetic Protestantism was still an effective motivating force in everyday life. I shall again deal first with the concrete normative pattern of conduct in order thereafter to establish the central pattern of intentionality in terms of which this system of norms becomes intelligible.

In so far as society is concerned, the matter is mainly one of the religious conduct of the merchant and artisan bourgeois middle class. In order to determine the actually obtaining system of religious norms, Weber relies largely but not exclusively on the *Christian Directory* of Richard Baxter (1615-1691), an extensive compendium of English Puritan moral theology that reflected the actual practice of the pastoral care of souls. Baxter condemns wealth as dangerous and the pursuit of wealth as senseless. The reason why wealth and the immoderate pursuit of profits are morally suspect is to be found in the fact that they distract people from the pursuit of a righteous life focussed on the dominating importance of the Kingdom of God and the life to come. The activity of the Christian in the world should be solely to the greater glory of God. The Christian must fulfill God's calling. This is accomplished by working systematically and methodically in this world. It is not labor in itself but methodically rational labor that God requires of man on earth. 'Waste of time is thus the first and in principle the deadliest of sins.'[21] It is for this reason and for this reason alone that wealth and the pursuit of it are morally objectionable. They lead to idleness and to the enjoyment of possessions. The span of human life is finite and short and therefore precious. 'Loss of time through sociability, idle talk, luxury, even more sleep than is necessary... is worthy of absolute moral condemnation.'[22] Every hour lost is lost to labor for the glory of God. Contemplation, too, is without value if it is at the expense of one's calling. 'Besides, Sunday is provided for that...'[23]

Baxter's passionate plea for continual physical or mental work is based on a twofold argument.

In the first place, work is a proven ascetic antidote to every temptation, such as an 'unclean life': sexual intercourse must be to the glory of God and is therefore permitted only for the propagation of the human race.[24] Religious doubts and a sense of moral unworthiness can also be overcome through the motto, 'Work hard in your calling.'[25]

Furthermore, rational ascetic labor in a calling is a divinely ordained end in itself. 'St. Paul's 'He who will not work shall not eat' holds unconditionally for everyone'[26] – even for those who are wealthy enough to live without working. This contrasts sharply with the medieval conception. Thomas Aquinas, for example, holds that this saying of Paul's applies only to the human race, not to every individual; moreover, he also holds that contemplation, as spiritual work in the service of the Kingdom of God, 'takes precedence over the commandment in its literal sense.'[27]

What God's providential purpose is in the moral obligation to work, together with how the division of labor should be organized, is known to the Puritan in practice through labor's fruits. Everything that leads to a quantitative or qualitative improvement in production must be regarded as God's finger[28] indicating the proper course of action. A certain calling is preferable to irregular work; a change of work is pleasing to God if it leads to more important work for the common good or – and in practical terms this is the more important point – if it is privately more profitable.

Wealth and the pursuit of wealth in the pursuit of duty in a calling are thus not only morally permissible but also even obligatory. Everyone must make the most of his talents. Wishing to be poor is comparable to wishing to be ill, and it is damaging to the glory of God. One who can work and still begs sins not only through slothfulness but also against brotherly love. According to Weber, the 'emphasis on the ascetic importance of a fixed calling provided an ethical justification of the modern specialized division of labor' (*Fachmenschentum*); likewise, the 'providential interpretation of profit-making' justified the activities of the modern businessman.[29]

Clearly the ethos of rational bourgeois business and the rational organization of labor was the basis of Puritanism as well as of capitalism, however much the central intentional value orientation of the two differed. Let us look at this matter more closely now, with Weber.

'Ascetic Protestantism,' or 'puritanism,' is a collective name for various movements within Protestantism. Accordingly, the dogmatic background of the way of life rationalized in the Puritan sense is not the same everywhere.

In its most pervasive, most effectual, and most consistent form (*in Reinkultur*), this dogmatic background is to be found in Calvinism as it actually acquired form in the seventeenth century outside Germany, especially (for a while) in Holland and England. The subject under study here is not Calvin's personal theological views[30] or even the official dogmatics found in the theological literature[31]. Rather, it is the – ideal typical – religious ideas of the average person of that period. The middle classes in those days reflected on the abstract contents of faith to an extent that 'we' (Weber means himself and his contemporaries) can now scarcely imagine. This is understandable from 'the connection of these dogmas with practical religious interests' – namely, the attainment of eternal salvation[32]. In that age this concern was paramount, surpassing every other, temporal matter in importance.

In Calvinist dogmatics the doctrine of grace is the centerpiece. According to this doctrine man has, through original sin, totally lost the capacity to do anything religiously good. God has from all eternity, according to His unsearchable, immutable and arbitrary decree, predestinated some people to everlasting life and others to eternal damnation. Nothing in the creature has moved God to this foreordination, either as conditions or as causes. God's only motive for extending or withholding grace is His self-revelation: the revelation of His almighty, sovereign power, majestic glory, and unsearchable justice. Only by virtue of God's grace are some effectually called and determined 'to that which is good.'[33] By virtue of God's withholding grace, the 'natural' man remains totally wicked

71

and sinful and is unable to convert himself.

In an age in which eternal salvation was the most important thing in life, the individual, confronted by the decree of predestination, experienced an 'unprecedented inner loneliness.'[34] No one and nothing in the world could help him: no priest, no sacrament, no Church, indeed, even no God. Salvation was set from all eternity. Everything in creation was absolutely worthless. With the elimination of the Church as a sacramental force, the world was deprived of 'magic' altogether. 'The genuine Puritan even rejected all signs of religious ceremony at the grave in order that no superstition, no trust in the effects of magical and sacramental forces on salvation, should creep in.'[35] Friendship and, indeed, any confidence whatsoever in one's fellowman was equally suspect, for it involved placing one's confidence in the 'flesh' and in the creature. All that mattered was God's greater honor and glory. All else was idolatry, the worship of the creature. Brotherly love hereby acquired a typically objective and impersonal character.[36]

The elected Christian could fulfill God's commandments only by bringing God's created cosmos further towards completion and thus also transforming it to serve the 'utility' of the human race. Only by the purposeful, useful organization and arrangement of this cosmos according to God's will is His glory promoted and every form of idolatry avoided. This is taught in a direct way by divine revelation in the Bible, and it can also be inferred indirectly from the creation order. One's 'vocation' became one's only Christian 'calling.' Naturally, the most conscientiously practiced calling had no effect whatsoever on one's salvation. Nevertheless, in the Calvinist view – and this is of the utmost importance for understanding why this conception of calling could become so deeply rooted amongst the people – the way in which the calling was put into practice was the basis of knowledge about election. It was a 'sign' of God's grace. The conscientious practice of one's calling assured the individual that God was at work in him. It provided him with the assurance of salvation, the *certitudo salutis*.[37]

In this way Calvinism became in practice a form of the salvation by 'works' that it found so horrifying in Catholicism: works in Calvinism 'are the technical means, not of purchasing salvation, but of getting rid of the fear of damnation'; hence 'in this sense they are occasionally referred to as directly necessary for salvation or the *possessio salutis* is made conditional on them.'[38] Still, there is an enormous difference between the Catholic and the Calvinist. The Catholic could confess his shortcomings and sins, and they were forgiven him. Although the Catholic ethic too required a new lifestyle in principle, it did not lead to a systematics of good works because the Church as the vouchsafer of grace reconciled fallen man to God again and again. The *average Catholic layman* lived ethically 'from hand to mouth,'[39] as it were. His life consisted of the balance of merit of individual good works. The *inspired Catholic* who wanted to devote his entire life to God's service did more than was strictly required. He not only kept the commandments (*praecepta*) but followed the evangelical calling (*consilia evangelica*):[40] he lived in poverty, obedience, and chastity, withdrew from the world, and entered a cloister. There he led a systematic, methodical, purposefully rationalized existence aimed at overcoming the 'natural' man and escaping irrational passions and attachment to the world. He subjected his life to continual self-control and self-reflection in order to become a Kingdom 'worker,' thereby to attain his salvation.

The systematic 'works' salvation of the Calvinist greatly resembled that of the monk but differed from it in principle in two ways. In the first place, the distinction between the monk and the layman fell away: only work in a calling had significance for salvation. Extra good works going beyond the requirements of the normal Christian life had no significance for salvation. The Calvinist faced the alternative of election or damnation; there was no middle way. The Calvinist's labor in a calling had to lead to permanent self-reflection and the systematic control of his life as a whole because there was no other means available to him to gain assurance of his election. The quiet disappearance of confession as a means of regaining favor with God is symptomatic for the nature of Calvinist religiosity. Besides, it gave this religiosity new impulses. No church or priest could provide any assistance, so the Calvinist had to take the pulse of his religious life himself.[41] This led to a re-definition of the meaning of his life. His life as a whole must stand in the service of God. This led him to motivate *all* his conduct from a single, central point of view:

> The Puritan, like every rational type of asceticism, tried to enable a man to maintain and act upon his constant motives, especially those which it taught him itself, against the emotions. In this formal psychological sense of the term it tried to make him into a personality.[42]

In short, the Calvinist motto was actually 'God helps those who help themselves.'[43] The nature of the work, namely, its rationalized, systematic character, was the guarantee of God's help. In Calvinism, in so far as the rationalization of life was concerned, there was accordingly no formal difference between believing Christians. Every believer was a 'monk.'

This resulted in a second difference from the systematic 'works' salvation of the Catholic monk. The specific task of the monk was to surpass the ascetic morality of every Catholic by withdrawing from the world. Calvinism, however, placed a religious premium on inner-worldly asceticism, the rational methodical fulfillment of a calling:

> Christian asceticism, at first fleeing from the world into solitude, had already ruled the world which it had renounced from the monastery and through the Church. But it had, on the whole, left the naturally spontaneous character of daily life in the world untouched. Now it strode into the market-place of life, slammed the door of the monastery behind it, and undertook to penetrate just that daily routine of life with its methodicalness, to fashion it into a life in the world, but neither of nor for this world.[44]

In addition to Calvinist dogmatics as the central, meaning-giving religious foundation for the concrete rational system of norms, Weber also deals with Pietism, Methodism, and the sects of the Baptist movement as related phenomena. From the Calvinist standpoint, these nonCalvinist forms of ascetic Protestantism are to be regarded as vitiations of the inner consistency of the doctrine of predestination.

Pietism (England, the Netherlands, Germany) accented the *praxis pietatis,* the actual fruits of faith, but sometimes weakened Calvinist consistency by also cultivating the emotional dimension of religion as being equally a sign of God's election. Pietism hereby detracted from the motivation to actively rationalize conduct in the world.

Methodism (Anglo-American) even went so far as to cultivate the emotional side of religion methodically in order to attain assurance of salvation, the *certitudo salutis.* This could be carried so far that the doctrine of predestination was abandoned altogether so that only a purely emotional experience of rebirth, or 'regeneration,' remained relevant to the assurance of salvation. Because this emotional experience was of short duration, as a rule, and because it sometimes only occurred once in a lifetime, it did not lead to an emotional enjoyment of communion with God, to a permanent 'mystical union' (*unio mystica*). Thus this 'regeneration' fulfilled precisely the same function as the doctrine of predestination: it gave religious support to an active ascetic rationalization of conduct in the world, aimed especially at vocational work.

The central religious meaning of the sects generated by the Baptist movement in the sixteenth and seventeenth centuries differs completely from that of the Calvinists. Here we have to do with Mennonites, and especially Quakers. Weber regards them as 'a second independent source'[45] for the rise of the rationalization of the way of life in the world. These groups took root especially amongst the petty bourgeoisie.

Here the concept of the church assumes central importance. It is essential that the church be exclusively a believer's church, comprised solely of those who are born again and know it. This is symbolized externally by adult believer's baptism: only adults who had 'personally gained their own faith' were to be baptized.[46] Saving faith is granted to individuals solely through the operation of the Spirit of God and solely in an individual revelation. The individual has to let this divine voice come to him and permanently lead him by waiting patiently and methodically for it and by avoiding this world as something bad in itself. The inner witness of the Spirit, together with personal conscience, is the guarantee of God's working in man, as well as the source of inner sanctification.

The church is thus not

a sort of trust foundation for supernatural ends, an institution, necessarily including both the just and the unjust, whether for increasing the glory of God (Calvinistic) or as a medium for bringing the means of salvation to man (Catholic and Lutheran).[47]

Here, too, by the rejection of sacraments magic is radically eliminated from the world. The church is in no sense a means to God's justification. Externally, the church assumes the form of 'the believer's church,' a church organized exclusively on the basis of voluntary membership and limited to saved persons. The visible church does not on that account have to embrace all believers. It is on the basis of this voluntary character of the religious community that Weber speaks here of 'sects' in the sociological sense of the word;they were self-designated members of the invisible 'true church.' This church had no official theology, and the Quakers even dispensed with baptism and Holy Communion. Even good works or cloister-like asceticism had no importance for salvation. Yet it was precisely this radical elimination of magic from the world, this rejection of 'works' salvation and in particular of the merit of all public or political functions, which led, via the methodical and sober consultation of conscience that accompanied all activities, to a religiously motivated conception of calling. A conscientious, systematic lifestyle and pursuit of calling were legitimated as the *conditio sine qua non* of a Godly life.

III. The Rationalism of Chinese Confucianism and Taoism

A. *Confucian Rationalism*

The bearers of Confucian rationalism were the mandarins: a class of literate officials in the Chinese polity.[48] This polity can be characterized as an ecclesiastical-political entity in which the emperor was at once the high priestly 'son of heaven' and the supreme bearer of profane authority. The mandarins were advisors to the emperor and princes and they occupied official positions. They enjoyed enormous prestige in Chinese society. This prestige was based not on wealth or birth but exclusively on education and development. At the same time, they shared in the religious consecration of the theocratic state polity. They were at once secular lay officials and initiates in the ritual. Secular and religious authority formed an unbreakable unity.

In China there was no other *kind* of schooling than that of the mandarins. Thus the only differences in education were a matter of the level. While there were in fact various forms of official patronage, qualification by examination was the only legal route to acquiring a position in the state administration. For the successful who were unable to obtain a state function there were other important functions open in society, as in guilds and clubs. Such persons were also 'confessors' and advisors in important matters of their native sib.

In general, there were three levels of examinations, the Chinese names of which can be roughly translated as the bachelor's, master's, and doctor's degrees. However, there were many interim, preparatory and requalifying examinations, so that their actual number was much greater. There were ten kinds of examinations for the first degree alone. Thus the stereotype question put to a stranger of unknown social rank was that of how many examinations he had passed. In spite of the strength of the ancestor cult in China, it was not the number of ancestors that determined prestige but rather the reverse. The privilege of having an ancestral temple (instead of the mere table of ancestors allowed the illiterate) and the number of ancestors commemorated in such a temple depended on someone's official rank. 'Even the rank of a city god in the Pantheon depended on the rank of the city's mandarin.'[49]

We can characterize the class culture of the mandarins as typically Chinese. Regions not administered by mandarins were in Chinese eyes heterodox and barbarian. A knowledge of the nature of the mandarin's education is a first step towards discovering the central value of Confucian rationalism.

In general Weber distinguishes three types of education, using the educational objective as the criterion. Because these objectives flow into each other and overlap, one can represent them as a continuum.[50] At the one pole is the formation of the charismatic (magician, hero, saint). Here the matter is one of 'awakening' and testing personal capacities. Charisma cannot be 'taught"; it exists as a natural aptitude: help is needed only for a kind of 'regeneration' or 'conversion.' At the other pole is the formation of the 'expert.' Here the objective is to 'teach' or 'train' for practical employability in a rational structure (modern business, office or army). Between these two extremes is an entire scale of educational objectives aimed at the cultivation of a particular secular or religious stratum, that is, at the education of pupils for a lifestyle suitable to their class.

Now, mandarin education clearly belongs to this pedagogy of cultivation, which aims at forming the pupil into a bearer of culture. It assumes that the young Chinese has already become acquainted at home with the ceremonial expression of feelings of piety and respect towards parents, those in authority, and one's elders.

Higher education is typified by two characteristics in particular. The first in importance is that it is mainly literary and aimed at inculcating ways of thought suitable to a cultured person. This literary education is to be understood in the most literal sense of the term. The Chinese 'literati' (the literate class) were schooled especially in calligraphy more than in oratory and argumentation. The painting of the characters, the mastery of a beautiful writing style, thorough knowledge of the classical writings – all this suited the Chinese 'gentleman.' Counting, physics, mathematics, logic or speculative philosophy were practically absent from the program.

This brings us to the second characteristic of mandarin education. It was a secular political education, partly ritual-ceremonial and partly traditional-ethical in character. At the center, next to 'beauty,' stood 'benevolence' in the sense of social-ethical reliability and loyalty. In the eyes of the people, a mandarin who had completed his studies was by no means just a candidate official qualified by knowledge; no, he was a certified bearer of magical qualities. In this respect he was comparable to a Catholic candidate official who has completed his studies and been consecrated to the priesthood. This comparison holds in another respect as well. The end of a mandarin's studies did not mean the end of his tutelage. He remained subject to control throughout his life. His record of good or poor conduct was published periodically. The retention of his post, together with promotion and demotion, depended on his grades. There was no such thing for a Chinese official as tenure in a permanent position. He constantly had to prove himself through a 'harmonious,' uninterrupted, smoothly running operation. The imperial high priest, or a school, or a college of censors stood above him to reward or punish, censure or commend.

This school system, whose character dominated the mandarin's entire life, provides us with the key to a better understanding of the central values of Confucian rationalism.[51]

The mandarins had to prove themselves unremittingly through study of the classical texts, whose canonical validity was accepted as a matter of course. This study was the only means to ethical perfection.

Formally, the highest ethical good was defined as 'propriety,' that which was appropriate for a cultivated man. In substance, this meant that the ethically perfect person had to be continually alert to keep to the 'correct middle' and control all emotions. Nothing in the world was radically evil. Friendship, wealth, sexual satisfaction, etc., were self-evidently of value and were only to be condemned, were only irrational, when they threw the 'cultivated man' off balance. Therefore too every form of 'professional expertise,' the self-conscious cultivation of just one facet of the personality, was ethically objectionable. The cultivated man who became a professional specialist degraded himself to the level of an instrument, in order to earn money, for example, and thereby broke his inner harmony and his all-around perfection, which was a goal in itself. The possession of means, especially in the form of an important state function, was therefore also a prerequisite to being able to lead a 'virtuous' life. One can say that this ethic idealized and legitimated the position of the official who lived from prebends. Only an official post could put a man in a position to develop his personality harmoniously. This is all the clearer from the fact that 'propriety' meant, more precisely, what society held it to mean. All rules of class convention and stylish living found their limit in a sober social utilitarianism that was intended to uphold and advance the established social order. Hereby alone could one be a personality in the Confucian sense of the term. 'The 'reason' of Confucianism was a rationalism of order. Chen Ki Tong says, 'Rather be a dog and live in peace than be a man and live in anarchy'.'[52]

It is thus also not astonishing that the only really absolute duty was piety. The unrestricted, reverent allegiance of children to their parents constituted the model for all their social hierarchical relationships. The established social order was unconditionally canonized by this fundamental social obligation. Confucianism was in essence an exclusively inner-worldly ethic of adaptation to the social order. The official language knew no distinct word for 'religion.' There were only 'teachings' and 'rites'; there was no distinction as to whether these were more religious or more social-conventional in character. The rites were inevitably simple, sober, and inner-worldly in orientation. They were observed for the sake of having longevity, children, or wealth, and in lesser measure for the beatitude of ancestors, but never for the sake of living on in the hereafter. In China death was considered an absolute evil.

Through these teachings and rites the mandarins adapted themselves harmoniously to the established social order and thereby concomittantly to the cosmic harmony: 'Tao,' a basic concept shared by all Chinese thinkers, indicated the eternal order and course of the cosmos. The social order was a part of that. This harmony was not viewed as an absolutely perfect ordinance. There were good and evil spirits. The social order too was not viewed as perfect. However – the point is essential – this order was dependent upon the level of development of the people and especially on the ethically correct conduct of the emperor and state officials. Even natural catastrophes were attributable to ethical misconduct on the part of the emperor or mandarins, who therefore always had to prove themselves through strict fulfillment of their duties.

Magic had no direct saving significance in this purely inner-worldly utilitarian ethic of the lay intellectual. One who lived in the 'classical' manner need not fear the spirits. Only unethical conduct by those in high places afforded the evil spirits power. Although magic had no direct saving significance, its reality was taken for granted socially. Fear of evil spirits contributed to determining the Confucianist's lifestyle. Indeed, magic was the final, irrational source of legitimation of the theocratic-bureaucratic social system. The emperor or officials who failed to do their duty forfeited their magical-charismatic character and with it their divine legitimation (whatever the construction placed upon 'divinity'). They thereby became the cause of every conceivable disaster. Thus every catastrophe could be an indication of unethical conduct on the part of those in power. While the official class as such retained the basis of its charismatic legitimation, a particular official or emperor could be deposed for failure to act in keeping with the traditional 'sacral' doctrine. Even the people could appeal to it. Oppression or natural adversity were identified with severe shortcomings of the rulers.

Thus magic was a Magna Charta, so to speak: the ultimate irrational source of legitimation of a closed, purely inner-worldly traditionalism that found its internal anchorage in the duty of piety, upon which it consistently based its ethic of adaptation. Moreover, magic was a particularly effective source of legitimation: every deviation from the orthodox teaching could be attended by evil or even by the fall of the dynasty. So while magic functioned internally to sanction the rational performance of obligations by individual bearers of authority, it also and especially functioned externally, in the hands of the people, as an effective weapon against every form of official abuse of power. At the same time, it legitimated the power of the officials as a class so strongly that a separate, independent hierarchy was officially impossible. Socially, this meant the legitimation of an absolute traditionalism.

Weber mentions in addition to magic a second irrational basis of Confucian rationalism.[53] Even this optimistic, enlightened rationalism of officialdom could not avoid 'the perennial problem of theodicy': lack of education or charismatic inadequacy of the regime were (still) insufficient to account for the actual division of happiness and the unpredictability of fate. Consequently, a kind of 'predestination belief' developed that suited the class character of the Chinese mandarin. It consisted in having an awareness of an irrational destiny. Unlike the common man who devoted himself in ignorance, anxiety, or resignation to the pursuit of happiness or well-being, the 'superior' man, being fully aware of an irrational destiny, was prepared to accept worthily what could not be changed. Inner preparedness made him equal to the inevitable, and that was the proof of his aristocratic attitude. Thus here too the educated man relied not on birth but on achievement. Here too he exhibited no concern for the transcendental. He knew how to die proudly. What concerned him about the period following his death was the honor of his name.

Although this value-orientation fostered the Confucian pattern of life, it still bore a strained relation to the Confucian system as a whole, because this belief in the irrationality of fate – at least that of the particular individual – pierced Confucianism's totally rational, inner-worldly-oriented theodicy. Because of this tension, this belief was rejected as ethically dangerous by many Confucians. For that matter, Confucian practical rationalism regarded every metaphysical speculation as perilous, as a possible source of innovations.

B. The Rationalism of Chinese Taoism

Confucianism and Taoism[54] together form the Chinese world picture. By itself, Confucian rationalism was inadequate to satisfy the religious needs of the people. The people had from time immemorial been acquainted with a more familiar celestial deity, personal spirits, countless functional gods of thunder, wind, and the like, apotheosized heroes, enchanted natural objects and artifacts, all of them of immediate practical significance for the everyday life of the common man. Although Confucian rationalism found its ultimate support in this very same magical world picture, it had emptied the magic of its saving significance for the sake of the practice of virtue. He who lived a life of classical virtue need fear no evil spirits. The spirits were hereby increasingly deprived of their personal characters, and the cult was exchanged for bureaucratic ritual devoid of all emotional elements. The cult, equated with pure social convention, thereby came to lack any direct connection to the needs of the people. Such high-handed repudiation of the saving significance of the world of the gods and, even more importantly, of personal, individual assurance of salvation in this life was possible only within a circle of cavalier intellectual laymen.

Now, Taoist rationalism met the needs of the people. Consciously and systematically cultivating magic, it turned the entire world into an immense enchanted garden and then set out to influence its spirits directly in a magical sacramental way. While the Confucians despised sorcery, they had to tolerate it in principle or risk having the foundations of their own system undermined. The bearers of this Taoist rationalism were both intellectuals fleeing from the world and, more especially, a plebeian priesthood, a more or less organized class of professional magicians who carried on an inner-worldly and lucrative practice, on which they were economically dependent.

Now, in China this final category rationalized ancient empirical knowledge and technological know-how in the direction of a magical world picture. They developed a magic-'rational' science that functioned as a superstructure to block completely the progress of empirical knowledge and technique. Thus the original astronomy and chronometry that had served to guide the activities of the agricultural seasons were converted into astrology and chronomancy: an esoteric doctrine of soothsaying meant to determine whether the spirits found the time favorable for certain activities. Meteorology likewise became meteoromancy, and medicine and pharmacology became knowledge of 'spirits of illness,' whereby the remedy was determined as well. Very important was the development of geomancy: the shapes of mountains, high places, plains, rocks, trees, rivers, and so forth were decisive for the actions of good or evil spirits. Geomancy dictated whether a particular spot was suitable for constructing a house, street, canal, or mine. The spirits of the tombs made burial sites especially pestilential. It was of enormous importance for merchants to consult a god of wealth, etc.

As a result of the influence of intellectuals, this magical rationalism grew into a 'Universist' (de Groot) philosophy and cosmogony. Through speculations with the sacred number five (five planets, five elements, five human organs, etc.) the macrocosm (the universe) and the microcosm (man) were linked together and the entire world was transformed into an 'enchanted garden.' The world became an indivisible whole of irrational magic: wild, unmotivated *dei ex machina,* capable of anything, inhabited the world. Only countercharms could help. Hence Taoism knew nothing of an 'ethos.' Magic, not one's conduct, determined one's lot. This was in contradiction to Confucianism, in which magic was powerless in the face of a virtuous life.

The Taoist priesthood traced its teaching and cult to Laotse, an older contemporary of Confucius. While this was largely unjustified, Laotse's teaching did provide a modicum of occasion for it.

The two systems were not diametrically opposed. Laotse belonged to the same social stratum as Confucius and naturally esteemed the government, as indeed every Chinese did. Man's salvation depended upon the conduct of the rulers. In Laotse, the ruler's charisma consisted especially in his mystical union with the eternal order and course of the cosmos, Tao. Here the patriarchal tutelage of Confucianism gives way to a laissez-faire attitude of noninterventionism. To a Confucian, education and rules of conduct were important means to adapting to the divine harmony, but to a Taoist they were just an external surrogate if not an outright impediment.

It is understandable that the priests of magic whose practices Confucianism considered worthless should have felt drawn to an a-literate or anti-literate Taoism, which offered mystical, apathic ecstasy as early as the days of the literate Laotse. The cultivation of ecstasy pointed naturally towards sacramental magic (which meant as little, for that matter, to the blessed mystic as it did to the Confucian). Such magic could satisfy the emotions and salvation requirements of the masses in such matters as health, wealth, happiness, and immortality.

IV. The Rationalism of Indian Hinduism, Jainism, and Ancient Buddhism

A. *Hindu or Brahman Rationalism*

The bearers of Hindu rationalism were the Brahmans, a typical priestly class distinct from the bearers of profane authority. Their social position and their rationalism cannot be understood without insight into the Hindu social system, the 'caste system.'[55] Because this system determined the normative pattern of life of every Hindu, it offers a suitable means for apprehending the 'spirit' of the Hindu pattern, Brahman rationalism.

The caste system was essentially a system of social ranking; as such, it could cross all political and territorial boundaries. The Brahmans constituted the highest rank. Their prestige was based partly on priestly magical power, partly on personal cultivation and education. Their central position derived more especially, however, from the fact that the social rank of other castes was measured in terms of their greater or lesser proximity to the Brahmans. Even where certain castes did not recognize the Brahmans as priests or as authorities in the fields of education, ritual, and so forth, their social rank was still measured in terms of their relation to the Brahmans, at least in the final instance. Namely, the caste system as such was tied closely to the professional activities of the various castes.

It is irrelevant to this survey to examine these specific activities.

Moreover, the criteria underlying the caste distinctions were sufficiently irrational and the result of random historical factors that even a broad look at the professional activities of the four principal groups would carry us too far afield. We shall have to be satisfied with the indication that the Brahmans belong to priestly castes, the Kshatriyas to political and warrior castes, and the Vaishyas to artisan and mercantile castes, while the Shudras are manual workers and serfs.

It is relevant to our insight into the normative pattern of life of the Hindu that professional activities were among the factors determining who belonged to a particular caste. Weber therefore compares them to the Western guilds[56] on the one hand and to classes as typical associations of social rank on the other hand.

In the first place, the castes differed from the guilds in that membership of the former was determined in principle by birth, while in the West the practice of a particular profession and, with it, membership of a particular guild depended in principle upon free choice.

A more important difference was that the castes, given their exclusive orientation to social rank, existed in permanent enmity to each other. They were radically alienated from each other. Physical contact or even nearness without touching between members of different castes made someone ritually unclean. Fraternization between the castes was impossible in principle because commensality – the fraternization of the shared meal – between castes was impossible given the inviolability of the ritual boundaries. A Brahman, for example, was ritually polluted the moment someone from a lower caste observed him eating. However severely divided by questions of economy and prestige the Western guilds may have been, they in any event knew nothing of a ritual-religious line of separation. On the contrary, their fundamental difference from the Indian castes lay precisely in the fact that the Western guilds depended on fraternization in the fields of economy and even religion. The 'conception' of a European 'citizenry' occurred when, in early Christianity, the ritual boundaries between Jew and gentile were eliminated in common celebration of the Eucharist, and the 'birth' of that 'citizenry' took place a millenium later, in the Middle Ages, when the urban guilds united in the covenantal confederations, or 'oathbound organizations.' Commensality occurred precisely on important Saints' days, in the form of common celebration of the Eucharist. Thus castes were not professional associations but classes.

Castes, like Western classes, were based on distinctions in prestige and lifestyle. The difference between the two consisted in the first place in the fact that castes, unlike classes, were in principle always closed, being a matter of birth. The greatest difference, however, lay again in the area of religious magic and ritual. The injunction against connubium, or intermarriage, was not only carried much further by the Indian castes than it was in the West; it acquired an entirely different character as well. While in the West there were legal and social injunctions against connubium, the castes also placed severe religious sanctions upon it. The same was true of conviviality: not only what one ate and with whom, but also from whom one accepted food and drink and the manner in which it was prepared were regulated by laws of consumption that fell under religious magical taboos linked to the hierarchy of castes.

It is typical that Brahman rationalism thought through the *karma-samsara* belief consistently and linked it to the caste system.[57] This belief accepted two fundamental dogmas that determined the actual conduct of every devout Hindu, even if he did not always see all their implications himself. These two dogmas only, moreover, if denied, marked someone as heterodox.

Samsara, the doctrine of transmigration of the soul, holds that all beings – not just people or animals but spirits and gods as well – are mortal but that each has an immortal soul (which constitutes its 'ego,' whatever the further construction put upon the word 'soul' by the various schools) that migrates to another being after death. The world has neither beginning nor end, and man shall have neither everlasting reward nor everlasting punishment. Life can be likened to a wheel of constantly recurring rebirths turning perpetually on its axis. This doctrine was linked to that of *karma:* compensation. Whether after death someone returned as a king, spirit, farmer, or god, or as a worm in a canine intestine depended absolutely and exclusively on his good or evil deeds in this or earlier lives. Man's lot is deterministically, mechanically dependent on his good or evil deeds. They constitute a kind of running account, the balance of which automatically determines the destiny of the soul at rebirth; that destiny is always commensurate with the negative or positive balance. As a result, at least in part, of this proportionality, there could be no eternal reward or punishment: one's own acts could not obtain infinity. In the course of time, rebirth was absolutely unavoidable.

The *karma-samsara* belief is thus an indivisible whole. Socially it is of particular importance that this belief was carried through to its logical conclusions by Brahman rationalism, so that it applied not only to the cosmos and every form of life but also to organizations, notably the caste system. It is 'the most consistent theodicy ever produced by history.'[58] One was not born into another caste by chance; he had 'earned' this birth in a previous life. Strict fulfillment of the so-called caste *dharma,* the ritual and ethical duties of the caste into which one was born, determined one's future lot. Thus the fulfillment of caste obligations was subject to severe negative and positive religious sanctions. 'Let every man abide in the same calling' was the supreme and practically the only virtue. It was more redemptive to fulfill the obligations of one's own caste moderately well than those of another caste exceptionally well. In the latter case one risked rebirth at a lower level, while in the former case there was a chance of being reborn at least at the same level. This belief stimulated especially the lower classes to fulfill their ritual-ethical obligations: 'they have nothing to lose but their chains, they have a world to win.' Certainly they would not overthrow the established order: every renewal only brought them still greater future sorrow, but precise performance of duty could raise one 'into the womb of a queen and Brahman's daughter.'[59]

Thus Brahmanism had an extremely consistent 'organismic' social ethic: apart from a few duties that obtained for everyone (for example, not killing cows), there was nothing resembling a 'natural law' or universal 'human rights.' Every speculation in this field was fundamentally blocked by the recognition in principle of caste *dharma* as the essential way of salvation. There were likewise no universally pertinent sins: these too were particularized according to caste. Not only did the rights and duties of people vary according to caste; they could even be basically contradictory. 'In principle there could be a vocational *dharma* for prostitutes, robbers, and thieves as well as for Brahmans and kings. In fact, quite sincere attempts at drawing these extreme conclusions appeared.'[60] Thus for various castes there was often a caste *dharma* autonomously developed according to the caste's own regular requirements. The professional *dharma* for kings and warriors, for example, was a naked Machiavellism of power that condoned practically every means. That being the case, there also arose in India 'technical sciences' for particular professions or areas of life: construction technique, logic, erotic technique, and so forth.

Yet there were limits to these worldly teleological rationalizations, for by virtue of the *karma-samsara* belief one's primary interest was his own strictly personal salvation from this world.[61] The urgent question confronting everyone was: How can I be delivered from this meaningless, eternally revolving wheel of recurring rebirths? Or better, How can I be delivered from ever recurring death? For it was not so much the series of rebirths that inspired anxiety as it was death, ever returning and inescapable; death, which time and again plucked one away from everything and everyone to whom the heart was attached in this life. Philosophical and theological concern in India was accordingly focussed purely and simply on the answer to the question of deliverance from meaningless human existence. The answer to this question belonged to the class *dharma* of the Brahmans. The way in which they answered this question reflected their social position as a stratum of typical priestly intellectuals who were in principle independent of the profane authorities. In actuality the interests of the two castes were intimately linked. The Brahmans were the official interpreters of the caste *dharma* of the ruling powerholders, and it was a part of the caste *dharma* of the rulers to support the Brahmans financially. The last obligation was a duty of every caste, it is true, but it applied in a particular way to the bearers of profane authority. This *de facto* mutual economic dependence in no way compromised the fundamental independence of each caste. Entirely in keeping with their consistent organismic conception of society, the Brahmans advanced an answer to the worrisome question of deliverance that lay in the line of their own caste *dharma*.

Actually, this answer can be viewed as a form of rationalism with three distinct directions.[62]

First, logically speaking, this class of intellectuals consistently thought through the above-mentioned dogmas of the soul's transmigration and ethically compensative causality in a *metaphysical* direction. The ends and means of salvation hereby acquired a rational foundation. Of the six official orthodox schools of thought (orthodox because they all acknowledged the authority of the Vedas, the oldest sacred scriptures, and the position of the Brahmans) the most important were the Sankhya and Vedanta schools. Their metaphysics in particular concern us to the extent that it propelled the ethics of deliverance in a certain direction. The metaphysics of each school viewed the world as something perfectly meaningless in itself. The older Sankhya school, which was borne by Brahmans and knightly laymen, was a proud atheism. It proclaimed a metaphysical dualism. The material, 'psychic' and 'mental' events in the world are real. They are eternal processes of coming and going. In contrast, the soul is a heterogeneous and eternally immutable quality-less self. It is possible, especially through systematic schooling, to gain a deeper insight, to achieve a gnosis not subject to conceptual formulation whereby the soul is emancipated from the meaningless world process and whereby it sinks into an eternal, dreamless sleep. Through this knowledge – this gnosis as a means of salvation – the materialization of the 'ego' is abolished. It does not vanish, but it is withdrawn from the meaninglessly revolving wheel of rebirths and remains in a permanent, perfectly peaceful Nirvana.

The younger Vedanta school, mainly priests, proclaimed a metaphysical monism. The visible, perishable world is an illusion besides which the only authentic reality is an everlasting and immutable being, namely, the Brahman. The 'ego' as a separate independency belongs to the world of illusion. Authentic deliverance arises from gnosis in a special sense, which is not so much a 'knowing' as it is a 'having,' and which is to be found only in 'mystical reunion' with the divine World-Spirit, Brahman, the depersonalization of the original personal Brahma. Through this union with divine reality, the Self is withdrawn from the meaninglessness of the world of illusion.

From the standpoint of both schools of thought, the assurance of salvation gained through insight can already be acquired during this earthly life, and people can already enjoy this eternal bliss here on earth.

This metaphysical rationalism brings us directly to the two other directions of rationalism. Both are rationalizations of the means of salvation, or ways to attain this condition of 'eternal rest.' Namely, they are the rationalizations of asceticism and of meditation. The priestly class of genteel scholars, who by virtue of their position were tied to magic and ritual, purified both of all irrational, orgiastic elements. 'Knowing' became the cardinal virtue. The supreme means of salvation was gnosis. Not actions in this world but flight from it, through the practice of asceticism and meditation, brought salvation. Asceticism stood closer to the Sankhya school and meditation to the Vedanta school. Both asceticism and meditation had the attainment of gnosis as their ultimate goal, and both ways of salvation were practiced methodically and rationally.

For ordinary Brahmans, priests living in the world, this meant primarily the cultivation of a genteel and controlled pattern of life in keeping with which one avoided plebeian forms of breadwinning and every emotional imbalance. They maintained strict laws about food and drink.

Besides secular priests there were also *sramana,* hermits who withdrew (temporarily) from the world. Thus there arose countless

Brahman schools, ascetic communities, and cloisters. Here, through the study of sacred scriptures, people could train to be fully qualified Brahmans without having to be bothered about their daily livelihoods. Here especially asceticism and meditation were systematically and technically perfected as means to achieving gnosis. One of the most familiar techniques is yoga, a rationalization of the ecstatic practices of ancient sorcerers that the Brahmans used in order to achieve a methodical 'emptying' of consciousness and create room for an unutterable knowledge of the divine. The emphasis in Brahman yoga lay not so much on the cultivation of ecstatic emotional states as on more rational 'sacred knowledge,' which could culminate in mystical union with the divine. Countless other techniques were developed with a similar objective in mind. The matter was always one of gaining inner emancipation from psychic excitations, passions, and the purposes of ordinary life, etc., in order thereby to create the conditions for an ultimate situation of 'eternal rest.'

Brahmanism was extraordinarily tolerant. It recognized in principle a plurality of schools, of salvation objectives, and methods. In general, these were differentiated in keeping with the social position of those concerned.

We have already observed this to be the case in connection with the teachings of the Sankhya and Vedanta schools. A goal of terrestrial salvation leading to rebirth suited members of ordinary castes, while the monks pursued a timeless, eternal rest. That this link to social position should not be taken in an absolute sense is evident from the means of salvation involved.

The most classic means of salvation were the fulfillment of ritual and professional obligations and the attainment of gnosis via asceticism and meditation. Only the latter, gnosis, could ultimately deliver one from the eternal mechanism of compensation. This was also true for the non-monk, who while he acted in keeping with his caste *dharma* was nevertheless internally free of it, for 'one possesses as if he does not possess.'[63]

B. The Indian Rationalism of Jainism

Jainism[64] differed fundamentally from Hinduism in terms of social structures, because people could join this religion only by taking vows. Hence it was a sect in the Western sense. Intellectual professional monks formed the core of Jainism, and other members were laymen under their tutelage and discipline.

The duties of the laity did not differ in principle from those of the monks. In contrast to Hinduism, there was just one salvation objective and one form of perfection. The *dharma* of the laity consisted of striving to approach the *dharma* of the monks as closely as possible.

A third difference from Hinduism involved rejection of the authority, scriptures, and speculations of the Brahmans.

The religious basis of the sect was the classic Hindu *karma-samsara* belief. Deliverance from the wheel of rebirths could be achieved only by withdrawing from this perishable world and abstaining from inner-worldly actions and desires. Here too the ultimate goal was Nirvana, achieved mainly through meditation and insight, an intuitive, all-embracing knowledge. Their metaphysics greatly resembled that of the Sankhya school. The soul was an active principle of life existing in enmity with matter. The body was the source of all limitations, sin, and desire.

The great difference from the orthodox systems is that Jainism put much heavier emphasis on active asceticism, on ritualistic and ethical commandments and prohibitions as ways of attaining Nirvana (understood as 'emancipation from the body'). The extremely severe rules of the Jainist order were aimed above all at preventing untruthfulness, the enjoyment of wealth (the monks were permitted to live only from strictly voluntarily donated alms), unchastity, and every form of attachment to or love for anyone or anything whatsoever. Their 'atheism' was also devoid of anything resembling love towards God. Every emotion was sinful as such; in other words, it inevitably awakened *karma*. 'The heart of Jainism is empty.'[65]

The foremost prohibition, which applied to monks and laymen alike, was *ahimsa:* the absolute prohibition of killing any living creature whatsoever (with the single exception of oneself, in the case that one could not control one's passions or had already achieved salvation). This prohibition was systematically applied with all its consequences. A correct Jain burnt no lights during the dark periods of the year because the flames could kill moths; he kindled no fire, because the fire would burn insects; he wore a cloth over his mouth and nostrils to avoid inhaling insects; he did not shave but plucked his hair out by the roots to avoid killing lice, etc., etc.[66] Thus countless professions were closed to him: agriculture especially, but also countless crafts requiring fire or sharp objects. The only vocation open to a layman from a practical standpoint was trading.

The Jainist order, at least in so far as the laity were concerned, was a religion of reliable, ascetic merchants. Here then we have an economic rationalism which, as a result of *ahimsa*, restricts itself to commercial capitalism.[67] Furthermore, the rise of a methodically consistent rational way of life was precluded because their doctrine of salvation contained an inner contradiction. Besides meditation or contemplation, there was the equally radical ascetic means of attaining Nirvana. Thus the conduct of everyday life was never rationalized to a methodically consistent pattern, either in the direction of a purely contemplative mysticism or in that of a pure, active asceticism.

C. The Rationalism of Ancient Buddhism

The bearers of ancient Buddhism[68] were genteel, intellectual, professional monks. In contrast to later manifestations of Buddhism (i.e., *Mahayana,* or 'great ship to another shore: salvation"), to which laymen too belonged, ancient Buddhism was a religion exclusively of monks (the oldest form later acquired the name *Hinayana* or 'small ship' Buddhism). They did not settle down in fixed places but travelled about living from alms, which they accepted in a worthy manner to the extent necessary for their subsistence. Their community, which one was free to leave, was very loosely organized. Its structure was based on the seniority principle and especially on a strong bond between teacher (the guru) and disciple. This bond, which was governed by extremely strict rules of piety, was of course not unique to the Buddhist teacher-monk but was typical throughout India. It also existed between Brahman or Jainist gurus and their disciples.

The Buddhist lifestyle had only genteel class conventions. Every systematic ethical-ascetic or ritualistic method was missing in Buddhism. Strict asceticism, whether of the inner-worldly or monastic variety in orientation, was rejected in principle. In fact, Buddhist rationalism excluded in principle every form of rational behavior (that is, goal-oriented action) in every possible field of human endeavor, with the exception of the purely spiritual systematics of concentrated meditation. The Buddhist ethic was a meditation technique. It was not training for the attainment of higher moral perfection, nor was it aimed at the acquisition through study of theoretical, metaphysical knowledge. The Buddhist method restricted itself to the 'noble eight-fold path'[69] – general prescriptions indicating the various phases that would see a monk through to a strictly individual salvation and a definitive feeling of deliverance. Given meditation and disinterested contemplation, the Buddhist 'saint' was suddenly enlightened and transported into an attitude of equable, serene, and objectless mystical love.

The background of this ethic was the *karma-samsara* belief and the need for emancipation from the ever recurrent threat of death, which Buddhism too never called into question. According to the *karma* doctrine, every action performed in this world is ethically compensated. The basic cause of every action, in the Buddhist view, is belief in a soul as an enduring, substantial entity. In fact, however, this belief is a subjective, illusory investment of meaning in what is objectively only an aggregate of purely heterogeneous components and perceptions, strivings and imaginings. In fact, the 'ego' consists purely and simply of the 'will to live,' of the 'thirst for life.' Salvation consists in seeing through the illusory character of this 'thirst for life.' The 'will' to live, the 'thirst' for joy, satisfaction, power, social ideals, for science and metaphysics, for an afterlife, a god, or whatever else it may be – this 'thirst' produces *karma*. Thus this thirst must be destroyed. Salvation is accordingly not to be found in an eternal life but in an eternal death, the definitive end of existence as such. Salvation of this sort cannot be a 'divine gift of grace.'[70] Just the very question of the existence of a god is an expression of the thirst for life. According to the karma doctrine one must earn one's salvation oneself.[71] Through incessant meditation one can acquire practical insight into the truth via an 'illumination' in which one sees through the grand illusions from which the thirst for life springs. If one has achieved this insight, the 'ego,' which of course does not exist as a substantial, lasting unit, will have vanished.[72] With that, every subsequent reincarnation will have been rendered impossible as such and definitive salvation obtained.[73] Thus with no thought of any actual 'transmigration of the soul,' the socially self-evident doctrine of *karma* causality remains unimpaired, since after every death the thirst for life generates another 'ego.'[74] With its focus on the questions concerning the 'how,' 'from what,' and 'to what end,' Buddhism, according to Weber, is 'the most radical form of salvation-striving conceivable.'[75]

92

V. The Rationalism of Ancient Judaism and of Diaspora Judaism

A. Ancient Jewish Rationalism

The foremost bearers of typical Jewish rationalism were the Levites and the so-called 'scriptural' prophets. Independent of the secular authorities, at least in principle, the Levites were legal and ethical experts who might or might not also fulfill a cultic priestly function. Together, the Levites and the scriptural prophets influence the Jewish national community in a special way.

On the other hand, however, neither group's position and influence can be understood without reference to the unique character of the self-understanding to which the Jewish people owed their unity as a nation, under extremely diverse political structures. As a people the Jews were essentially a theocratic community: social cohesion was founded on a shared belief in God.[76] Or better: from an extremely heterogeneous complex of ethnic groupings, the Israelites became a nation through belief in a very concrete historical event. Namely, via Moses this ethnically heterogeneous community had, together and of their own free will, made a covenant with an already existing, distant and majestic God who had already showed his power over nature and nations by delivering Israel from Egyptian bondage. This God, Yahweh, had delivered the children of Israel by inflicting terrible natural catastrophes upon Egypt and destroying the Egyptian army. In a very remote past, moreover, this God had already promised the Hebrew patriarchs of Israel, particularly Abraham, that he would make them an innumerable and great nation. Thus Israel's covenant with Yahweh was mutual: both parties were freely covenanting partners pledging faithfulness to each other. Israel would not 'defect' and Yahweh would guarantee Israel's future. He was not only a 'God from afar' but likewise a God nearby who concretely intervened in history.

This mysterious and mighty God, just the sight of whom could be dangerous and even fatal, was for Israel both a God of salvation and promise and a jealous, wrathful God who watched carefully to see that Israel met its contractual obligations. Salvation and promise concerned not transcendental values or salvation from this world but actual intramundane political, social, and economic affairs. Yahweh saw to it that Israel defeated its enemies in time of war and that Israel could dwell in a 'land of milk and honey,' but he punished unfaithfulness with political debacles, poor harvests, etc.

The idea of the covenant was accordingly central. Yahweh was not some functional deity under whose external protection the Israelites had sworn a confederative covenant amongst themselves; nor was he a local deity, the lord and master of a certain territory to whom people were obliged on that account to offer sacrifices; nor was he a god of some everlasting and immutable ethical or cosmic order. No, he was the personal God of history, the God with whom Israel had made a mutual covenant. The bringing of sacrifices was important: 'no Israelite may stand before Yahweh with empty hands.'[77] More important, however, was the keeping of the intramundane social ethical obligations mutually agreed upon by the Israelite covenantal confederation: for these were obligations people had accepted together in the presence of Yahweh. Their violation meant personal unfaithfulness to God. The social order was thus not an immutable order: it could always be altered through a new covenant with God. Once agreement was reached, however, that which was 'unheard of' in Israel was an abomination subject to severe religious sanctions. Consequently, the Israelite nation was an association of free people who were communally responsible for keeping the divinely sanctioned commandments. Every member of the covenant was personally responsible before God for another's mistakes, yes, even for the mistakes of preceding generations. This conception of God was fraught with important consequences for the religious life and practical, everyday conduct of the Jew.

Weber points out that, depending upon the social position of those who held it, this conception of God could vary and even be internally contradictory. This was true both diachronically in keeping with the political structure of Jewry and synchronically in keeping with social stratification. Weber makes this observation while dealing with the question of whether the cult of Yahweh, given the very specific relation of Yahweh to Israel, is a form of monalatry (the exclusive worship of just one of a number of existing gods), henotheism (acting out of the conviction that only the god invoked is mighty), or monotheism (there is in principle only one god). For an Israelite warrior it is clear that the Yahweh he invokes is 'his' god and that the god of the enemy is therefore another. For a sedentary urban populace such as that of Jerusalem, for example, Yahweh dwells in the local city temple, and other cities have other gods that have to be worshipped in those places. For the semi-nomadic stock breeder, naturally, Yahweh is the God who is present everywhere, and the gods worshipped elsewhere are to be identified with Yahweh. For the schools of the professional prophets and visionaries with their international clientele, Yahweh does not exist for Israel alone, and he is also not the only god; rather, he is the mightiest of the gods, who are all 'nobodies' in comparison with him. For the prophets associated with the royal court, Yahweh exists for the salvation of the kingdom, and the gods of other peoples are his enemies.

In addition to Yahweh, various other deities were worshipped in Israel. These were the Baals: local or functional deities of certain high places, fields, cities, or of thunder, fertility, etc. This, too, could vary in keeping with the social position of the inhabitants of Canaan, who lived there prior to their 'conversion' to Jewry. The oldest and most typical Israelite God was probably the war god Yahweh, who demanded exclusive worship. This was characteristic of semi-nomads, who had a relatively undifferentiated culture and little need for various local or functional deities. The ecstatic war prophets and war chieftains were their typical representatives. The wars to conquer Canaan were holy wars fought in Yahweh's name.

Against the centrally important background of the covenant idea, we can locate the position of the bearers of typical Jewish rationalism and examine their teleological rationality of behavior more closely.

The first category we shall have a look at is that of the Levitical priests.[78] Given the situation of a covenantal community responsible for keeping Yahweh's commandments and in which the primary meaning of ritual sacrifice was making amends for mistakes committed, it is only appropriate that, traditionally, neither the bearers of profane authority nor the priests were able to demand a hierocratic monopoly for themselves. As a result, there was often competition between various lines of priests and between various kinds of prophets and seers, all of whom, like the bearers of profane authority, acted in the name of Yahweh, if not always of Yahweh alone.

While it is difficult to reconstruct the history of their actual origins and while their social position varied according to place and time, a priestly class did in fact develop, and they did claim for themselves, especially in the last period of Judah after the fall of the Northern Kingdom, the monopoly of being the only legitimate Yahweh priests. Their power was founded on the nation's need to be instructed in the Torah, the entire body of ritual and ethical duties attributed to Moses. Every war, catastrophe, or setback was attributable, for that matter, to transgressions against God's commandments, and he alone could help. Recurrent threats of war and the accompanying, heightened sense of sin contributed importantly to enhancing Levitical power over all who were 'under the burden.' The Levitical priests, having been schooled in the Torah, the knowledge of God's law, were thereby the obvious confessors and indispensable counsellors of the nation and also of the profane authority bearers. The professional bearers of Yahwehism, they gradually eliminated, as their power to do so grew, every irrational way of consulting or influencing God and developed a rational and systematized doctrine of Yahweh's commandments and of the way in which people could be reconciled with him again. They did not have some mysterious priestly doctrine; rather, they attempted by virtue of the covenant idea to probe deeper into the knowledge of God's law and into the methods of searching the conscience. Thus they trained themselves to pose rational questions and to find rational ways of answering them. They developed rational decalogues and a rational casuistry of sins. In this way they became the bearers of a religious ethic of intramundane actions divested of ecstatic and orgiastic elements, such as fertility, sexual, or alcoholic orgiasticism. These were 'folly'... the worst that could be said against an Israelite.'[79] Ethics was increasingly sublimated in the religious-ethical sense: it was not so much external deeds that were important but obedience, faithfulness, and reverence for God [*Gesinnungsethik*]. As a result, the teachers of the Levitical Torah opposed magic systematically. (While elsewhere – China and India – the priests developed magic systematically in order to preserve their power over the people, the Torah priests derived their influence primarily from the unique situation of chronic duress in which the Jewish people found themselves as a result of political and climatological circumstances.) Yahweh cannot be compelled by means of magic; although mighty and majestic, he is still ultimately an understandable ruler of the world and of human destiny. He does not enchant; rather, he works wonders. That is, he reacts to human actions meaningfully and with comprehensible motives. As a result at least in part of the openness of Yahweh's character to everyone's understanding, he was able to become a God of the common people in particular. Via the Levite's pastoral practices and their task of instructing the youth, the people here – more than elsewhere, where great value was attached to magic and to savior figures – became the bearers of a rational

96

(albeit not ascetic) ethic that motivated everyday conduct.

As a result of the absence of magic, Yahweh remained the lord of history, especially of the political and military history of Israel. He was a superhuman ruler whom people had to obey. Thus every metaphysical speculation about the meaning of the world was excluded. God could not be reached via mystical union or contemplation. Limits were likewise set to the mythologizing of Yahweh. In the theological rationalism of the teachers of the Torah, Canaanite mythological representations of god deriving from Babylon or Egypt such as those in which the god might wrestle with primeval forces became an abstract, majestic God whose word alone was sufficient to bring heaven and earth into being. The myth of the Fall of the first human pair and of their expulsion from Paradise, which would eventually assume great significance in Christianity, thus had no direct salvation significance as far as the Jew was concerned. The dominating significance of the covenant idea prevented this, and it put the Torah priests in a position to interpret the existing myths in an ethical sense. The ancient unmarried and imageless God who guaranteed the social-ethical order was not just some god of natural catastrophes, which he brought about personally on account of the unfaithfulness of his people. Paradise lost, death, and sweaty toil were the consequence of disobedience.

The pristine situation could be restored again by God in the future, however. The mythologies were accordingly interpreted not only ethically but also eschatologically. This future blissful state varied in hue depending on the social position of the Levitical clientele. For the peace-loving farmers, swords would be beaten into ploughshares. For warriors, the 'day of Yahweh' would be the great day of victory over Israel's enemies. For partisans of the monarchy, Yahweh himself or his anointed Messiah would establish a kingdom of peace.

The second category of the foremost bearers of typical Jewish rationalism, in Weber's opinion, is that of the so-called scriptural prophets (Isaiah, Jeremiah, Amos, Nahum, Zephaniah, etc.).[80] Weber deals with them at the beginning of the second part of his study of ancient Judaism, which examines 'the establishment of the Jewish pariah people.'

That the Israelites became a Jewish pariah or ritually segregated guest people who retained a confessional unity even after exile and the loss of their political unity and dispersal in groups throughout the Near East and the West is largely to be attributed to the activities of the prophets prior to and during exile. They added little of substance to Levitical rationalism. The ideas of the covenant and the Levitical Torah were for them self-evident facts and even occupied the central place in their prophesying. The prophets' significance is to be found primarily in the fact that they were able to fashion this rationality into a pattern of Jewish conduct that actually influenced everyday life.

Characteristic for the social position of the prophets is the fact that they occupied themselves purely as private persons, in a passionate and unconventional way, with the political and social lot of the nation. Their religious motivation was decisive for their activities and for the reason they meddled in politics: they were completely oriented towards faithfulness to Yahweh and the fulfillment of his law. Weber typifies them as 'emissary' prophets, as prophets with a 'mission':[81] they considered themselves chosen personally by Yahweh and charged with a special task. Psychologically speaking, they were 'emotional;' ecstatics, extremely diverse types of eccentric men subject to pathological states. In contrast to 'magical' ecstatics who trained themselves to evoke a state of ecstasy, they experienced ecstasy as something which overcame them – often against their will. What is of primary importance, however, is the fact that they interpreted their ecstasy as a state of being 'seized' by Yahweh; they 'heard' God's 'voice' and received a 'mandate.' In solitude they wrestled with themselves to understand the meaning and significance of their mission. They spoke not *in* ecstasy but *about* their ecstasy, after they had understood Yahweh's meaning and purpose. The 'pathos'[82] with which they approached the public stemmed from the self-confidence that they were the spokesmen and servants of Yahweh. Herein lay their legitimacy, both for themselves and for others. Moreover, this was tested still further against the Levitical Torah. The Law was ultimately the only criterion by which to distinguish them from 'lying prophets.'

Thus their prophesying was directed entirely towards fulfilling God's law. It was not so much the cult as it was social-ethical duties and faithfulness to Yahweh that occupied the place in the foreground. The difference from the Levites consisted above all in the fact that the prophets tended to deal less with individuals and never engaged in casuistry. In contrast to the more ordinary Levites, they spoke to the people in a passionate way. Most importantly, they sublimated the traditional ethic into an ethic of religious inwardness (*Gesinnungsethik*): the sacrifice is of no importance if the 'heart of stone' has not been exchanged for 'a heart of flesh and blood.'

Their concern was a change of conduct, especially of belief and trust in Yahweh, and the actual practice of righteousness. Further, in the prophets Yahweh acquired an incomparably greater majesty than he had had in the older Yahwehism and in the teachers of the Torah. He alone determined the course of the world. He is absolutely the only One: both blessing and curse upon the individual and the nation are his work. Yet however incomparable Yahweh's horizon was to that of mortal creatures, he was still never an object of metaphysical gnosis, of incommunicable contemplation, or of mystical union. The prophets preserved the rational character of Yahweh and of world events as a whole. Neither blind chance nor magical enchantment determine history; only Yahweh does that, and he acts on the basis of understandable and communicable motives. It was the task of the prophets as instruments of Yahweh to make the motives of this rationally acting God known.

Thus what was new in substance in the rationalism of the prophets pertained above all to the emphasis they put on the religiously inward ethic of intramundane action and to their absolutely monotheistic conception of God.

What was new and important about the prophets from a typically sociological viewpoint, however, was the way in which they played upon the actual state of the nation and prophesied future good and, especially, evil. Prominent in all this was the prophecy of doom. It was a product of the prophets' abhorrence of the 'defection' from Yahweh and his commandments. It touched kings who relied more on human allies than on Yahweh, patricians who preyed upon the poor, the 'idolatry' of priests and people who worshipped strange gods, in short, failure to fulfill the Torah. The prophets were the interpreters of the frightful anxiety that existed for the impending evil Yahweh would visit upon his people.

At the same time, the prophets testified to a Gibralter-like confidence in Yahweh, who would surely keep his promises. The terrible disasters the nation had to undergo were just the result of sin. Ultimately, the 'day of Yahweh' would be a day of salvation, if only for a 'holy remnant.'

Two factors account decisively for the great influence of these eschatological expectations. First, they always involved intramundane (*diesseitige*), perceptible, palpable, catastrophic events or astonishing deliverances and Godspeed. Secondly, the prophets did not project them into a distant future (as the Levitical Torah teachers so often did) but proclaimed them with great passion as current threats of imminent war or natural catastrophe or as impending victories or states of astonishing and sudden well-being that their hearers would certainly experience themselves.

Actual everyday conduct was hereby punished or rewarded with utopian premiums, and the people were fully captivated by these expectations. The 'day of Yahweh' was imminent. As in the past, so now, too, Yahweh would keep his word. By the word of the prophet, salvation or doom would be directly put into effect. The prophet's word was an almost irrational-magical power which effected the wonder or judgment, if only as an instrument in the hand of Yahweh, who punished his people for their sins or fulfilled his promises of salvation. The latter fact especially was a source of hope. It gave people strength to suffer and remain faithful to Yahweh and his law.

B. The Rationalism of the Jewish Diaspora

Modern Jewish Diaspora rationalism was borne by a sedentary, urban, burgher-intellectual stratum of the population. Its original bearers were the Pharisees (of about the last century before and the first century after Christ), and thereafter the rabbis. Weber still deals explicitly with the interlocal sect of the Pharisees and the earliest rabbis – an intellectual stratum who studied the 'law and prophets' in addition to their vocation. However, he makes only general and incidental mention of the doctrine of the later schools of the rabbis in Mesopotamia and Palestine, which finally became established in the Talmud.[83]

The most conspicuous feature of Diaspora Jews in the West is their capitalism. Weber supports Sombart on this point.

The Jews practiced various forms of capitalism and seized every opportunity to make a profit. This was already true in the Middle East and Europe in Antiquity and the Middle Ages. They engaged in commodity trade, currency exchange, purveyance and credit to governments, etc. The typical juridical and economic features of modern Western capitalism were not originated by the Jews, to be sure, but they were readily adopted by them and so spread across Europe and America. The modern juridical character of their capitalism is illustrated by the trade in stocks and by entrepreneurial structures such as the limited liability company. Economically, they were active in the stock exchange, the 'merchants' market.'

What is striking, however, is the almost total absence amongst the Jews of the organization of labor according to craft (there were no rationally exploited forms of cottage industry, no manufactures or factories), even though the highly concentrated Jewish population offered a potentially strong labor force. A Jewish industrial bourgeoisie never arose amongst them.

Weber refines Sombart's thesis by asserting that neither the specifically new element in the modern capitalist structure nor the modern economic attitude was typically Jewish. The basis for this is related to the Jews' religiosity and to the pariah character of the Jewish nation. Both were expressions of a typical Jewish rationalism. This led both to ritual segregation of the Jewish communities from the non-Jewish environment and to a double morality.

From the time of Israel's political collapse and dispersal throughout the entire world, the Jewish nation regarded itself as a confessional entity with Jerusalem as the religious center. This entity found its tangible expression in the possession of sacred scriptures, especially the Torah and the prophets. By tradition, as laid down in the law and the prophets, the Jewish nation regarded itself as God's 'chosen people' in an exclusive sense. Only the Jewish nation possessed God's law, and it regarded itself as universally rejected and despised on that account. Through faithful fulfillment of the law, a messianic kingdom would dawn in which God would reverse the world order. The coming of this messianic kingdom, which would be realized only through God's awesome power, had already been delayed for many generations; and generations to come would probably also have to persevere in their piteous existence, which stood in such an enormous contradiction to God's promises. And so the emphasis came to be placed more and more on knowledge of the law and exact fulfillment of it. It became the source of the devout Jew's sense of dignity. The lifetime ideal of the devout Jew was casuistic knowledge of the law. He desired to be a scriptural scholar who penetrated ever further into the 'law and prophets' and the commentaries on them. His method consisted of intellectual schooling in the law and the effect of such schooling on his conduct in everyday life. Already during his youth, the Jew's obligatory quantitative and qualitative knowledge of the law surpassed that of the Puritan. The law was comparable to the ritual laws of the Hindu, although it differed in content in that moral commandments occupied a larger place in it.

Nevertheless, one must not underestimate the ritual commandments. The fact of being God's chosen people in an exclusive way

101

brought with it the injunction against connubium with non-Jews. The Sabbath was strongly promoted. The obligation of the Sabbatical year (letting arable land lie fallow every six years)[84] and ritual slaughtering (only meat prepared by qualified, authorized butchers could be eaten) fostered the segregation of Jewish communities in urban areas. Living in widely dispersed homes or in the countryside made keeping the law practically impossible. That affected the purity of God's chosen people.

The most important content of the law, however, consisted of ethical norms. Since the Pharisees and first rabbis, these breathed the spirit of an ethical rationalism which was concerned not so much with the letter of the law as with the rationale of the things commanded or forbidden and which placed a positive value on the physical world (wealth, sexuality, etc.). Thus, far from being an abstract system of norms, the law was attuned to practical everyday life. This was appropriate to the social position of these burgher intellectuals, who combined their study and education with the practice of a profane vocation. Most notably, however, their conception of God excluded both magic and esoteric priestly mystery doctrines. Likewise excluded was the development of metaphysical speculation about the meaning of the world. Their mythological stories of God (e.g., the creation myth) were rational with respect not only to the story but also to the ethical drift, in the sense that they were understandable for a child. (The Talmud was the first book in which this practical ethical rationalism was developed into a more general and theoretical system.) Indeed, Jewish piety culminated not in concrete actions but in a religious 'feeling,' such as humility before Yahweh. God alone, after all, would bring about messianic salvation.

Jewish rationalism was consequently a lifestyle that combined study of the law with the fulfillment of ritual and ethical commandments. Ascetic practices and mystical love of God were secondary phenomena, conditioned by the permanent, conscious fulfillment of the law. For this reason it is understandable that the Jews were not the bearers of Western capitalism. Their voluntary ritual segregation alone was enough to hamper cooperation with non-Jews in industrial enterprises. Their mental attitude was intrinsically alien to a systematic ethos in which one's vocation could acquire significance for salvation. Success in business was a sign of God's blessing, but this blessing rested not on doing business as such but on keeping God's law. That the Jews nevertheless became capitalists in the pre-industrialist sense of the term is owing to an aspect of their ethic that still needs consideration, namely, the so-called double standard of morality.

A phenomenon that Weber considered universally observable – that ethically people assume a different attitude towards their own group than towards the alien group – was true of the Jews who lived in a pariah or ritually segregated guest situation down through the ages. This was in part religiously motivated. The pariah situation was God's will for the Jew, and he therefore accepted it voluntarily. The non-Jewish environment reacted to his sense of superiority (which was often interpreted as hatred of mankind) with contempt and hostility. Towards brothers in the faith the Jewish business ethic was traditionalistic, and it was founded on the standpoint of subsistence. Towards non-Jews, business conduct was tied to other norms as a matter of course. According to the rabbis, Jews should deal with their enemies in a sober and business-like manner free of love or hate. The law forbid taking interest from Jews, but taking it from non-Jews was permitted (and usually even required). Although usury was always regarded by the rabbis as impermissible, the quality of the prescribed legality (e.g., exploiting another's mistakes) was inferior with respect to non-Jews. Naturally, people eagerly took advantage of the situation. After all, it involved enemies who despised the Jews. That the Jew whose ideal was the study of the law should engage in commerce is understandable, for by doing so he freed himself of the necessity of being constantly engaged in a vocation.

CHAPTER FOUR

RATIONALIZATION AS A SOCIO-CULTURAL PROCESS

In the preceding chapter I described various forms of rationalism as more or less stable structures. From this presentation it was evident that rationality varied qualitatively in character from one time and culture to another. Indeed, Weber states this explicitly: 'In fact, one may – this simple proposition, which is often forgotten, should be placed at the beginning of every study which attempts to deal with 'rationalism' – 'rationalize' life from fundamentally different basic points of view and in very different directions.'[1] It is not yet possible to go on explicitly to compare and contrast the various forms of rationalism introduced thus far – that will be done in the next chapter – for in order to present such a comparative study in a responsible way, it is necessary first to have a look at rationalization as a process. In the course of doing that, one can hope to make the differences in rational patterns of behavior sociologically intelligible. Already in the preceding chapter it was evident that in this matter social positions, the balance of power or a competitive relationship, and the legitimacy of interests all play a role. Furthermore, it will also only be in the next chapter that I shall examine more closely the genesis of the concrete historical forms of rationalism here at issue. In this chapter I want to deal with the more general theoretical elements of the rationalization process.

In the first section I show that Weber regards the rationalization process as a 'dialectical' process. As far as possible, my abstractions are drawn from the substantive side of this dialectic.

In the second section I examine religious rationalization as a relatively autonomous process. I set about this in an ideal-typical way, abstracting from social factors, in order to gain as clear a picture as possible of rationalization as a cultural process.

In the third section I also investigate the social factors relevant to the rise, course, and consequences of rationalization. Here I discuss the socio-cultural rationalization process which the dialectic sketched in the first section reveals to us in its concrete empirical manifestation. Nevertheless, this discussion is still at the theoretical systematic level of analysis throughout.

I. Rationalization as a Dialectical Process[2]

A. The Externalization of Values

Rationalization is always a particularizing of the more general category 'meaning' or definition of reality, which according to Weber is constitutive for every sociologically relevant action. This particularizing consists, very generally speaking, in an actor's subjective intention somehow becoming conscious and consistently oriented to 'something.'[3] Thus rationalizing indicates that intending goes on consciously[4] in accordance with one criterion or another and that, as a result, it acquires a more or less systematic[5] character.

'Systematic' can be construed in both a horizontal and a vertical sense. That is, conscious intending is able both to coordinate mutually coherent meanings and to provide the basis or reason for a pattern. Scientific rationalization, as we saw in chapter two, is the analytical ordering of reality according to a criterion of 'truth.' Through scientific activity, reality in its internal coherence and basis is brought more clearly to consciousness. This systematization is never entirely successful. For the 'truth' itself is a value; as such, it is not subject to further grounding. Hence in that respect it too, according to Weber, is irrational. Of course, one can then still speak of value-rationality (*Wertrationalität*).

From a technical standpoint, the intentional activity of a scientist involves the deliberate application of means to reach a 'truth objective': teleological or instrumental, absolute goal-oriented rationality (*Zweckrationalität*).

Teleological rationality and value-rationality can therefore be distinguished analytically, it is true, but in actual scientific practice they permeate each other intrinsically. Teleological rationality manifests and realizes a value that is further not provable and in this sense irrational.

Science, however, is a typically Western form of rationality and not contained in the concept of rationality as such:

Magic, for example, has been just as systematically 'rationalized' as physics. The earliest intentionally rapid therapy involved the almost complete rejection of the cure of empirical symptoms by empirically tested herbs and potions in favor of the exorcism of (what was thought to be) the 'real' (magical, daemonic) cause of ailment. Formally, it had exactly the same highly rational structure as many of the most important developments in modern therapy... Furthermore, not every 'progressive' step in the use of 'correct' means is achieved by 'progress' in subjective rationality.[6]

Thus it is possible to speak of the rationalization process in a formal sense. Very generally speaking, it is evidently intending 'consciously and in accordance with one criterion or another' that renders this term ambiguous, albeit not without qualification. This criterion involves a value-orientation. Thus in China, for example, Taoism transformed the entire world into a grand magical garden. Just as in the case of Western scientific practice, this form of rationality was the result of a teleological rationalization process that was inspired by a fundamental value-orientation. Belief in magic functioned, according to Weber, as a kind of 'Magna Charta,' as an ultimate, irrational source of legitimation not subject to further grounding, from which sprang both the magical garden of vulgar Taoism and the Confucian system of norms. This example serves to show that while value-rationality and teleological rationality permeate each other intrinsically and motivate human behavior mutually, the analytical distinction between the two certainly makes sense sociologically. Namely, there is no suggestion of a determining influence of value-orientation on teleological rationality.[7] Other factors play a role as well, as I explain in the third section of this chapter.

What is of interest at this juncture is the fact that the rationalization process is a form of conscious and systematic intending in which value-criteria always also play a role.[8]

A number of additional examples will serve to make this even clearer. Thus the rationalization of work in ascetic Protestantism meant not only the fact that work was done consciously and methodically but also that it was done to the greater glory of God. Here work was made a 'calling' or 'vocation' in two senses of the term: it was methodically made a trade on account of a 'calling' from God.

The same is true *mutatis mutandis* of the rationalization of work in modern capitalism. Here the 'divine call' is replaced by 'man's goal in life' or by some sort of 'ethical duty' incapable of further grounding. To the Buddhist, rationalization meant striving for salvation: the methodical and consistent rejection of every form of goal-oriented work, with a view to total elimination of the 'thirst for life.' To him, this was the supreme and ultimate value attainable.

Thus it is typical of all the forms of rationalism described in the preceding chapter that the criterion in terms of which conscious and systematic action was measured always also entailed a value. It was realized by teleological rationality. We can accordingly regard teleological rationality too as a form of the externalization of values. That brings us to the second moment of the rationalization process, namely, the objectification of values.

B. The Objectification of Values

Sociologically, the rationalization of religion involved the emergence of a normative pattern of behavior in terms of which a particular concrete society can be characterized. In the preceding chapter, in order to facilitate a grasp of the central value-orientation of the various forms of religious society, I always described that normative-practical pattern of life at the outset. I did so in the cases of modern man, the ascetic Calvinist, the Chinese mandarin, the Indian man of caste, and so forth. This societal normative pattern of behavior must be viewed, according to Weber, as a form of human collective self-objectification. In other words, it constitutes an objectified intention that now comes to confront the individual, who must subject himself to it. Here people speak of a 'tragedy,' Weber comments, 'which always accompanies the realization of ideas.'[9]

This objectification must be construed as a product of historical collective society; Weber says this explicitly with reference to the modern capitalist's lifestyle: 'In order that a manner of life so well adapted to the peculiarities of capitalism could be selected at all, i.e. should come to dominate others, it had to originate somewhere, and not in isolated individuals alone, but as a way of life common to whole groups of men.'[10] The 'way of life' of modern man, including the capitalist social-economic structure, could sometimes be such a one-sided process of externalization of values that the normal reciprocity between 'idea' and social-economic structure was lost, to the advantage of the former. Weber observes, for example, that in Massachusetts, the country of Benjamin Franklin's birth, the capitalist 'spirit' was present earlier than the 'capitalistic order.'[11]

However, this does not detract from the fact that, according to Weber, the value once externalized, or in other words the normative-practical lifestyle, is objectified in this sense, that as a quasi-independent magnitude it comes to confront man as a kind of second nature. The generation that is born and bred in this society has to bow before this objectified, stone-hard 'spirit.' The manufacturer who in the long run acts counter to the norms of the market 'will just as inevitably be eliminated from the economic scene as the worker who cannot or will not adapt himself to them will be thrown into the streets without a job.' 'The capitalistic economy of the present day is an immense cosmos into which the individual is born, and which presents itself to him, at least as an individual, as an unalterable order of things in which he must live.'[12]

The more the enormous power of the given order of society is rationalized, according to Weber, the greater that power is. This is true for both material and immaterial culture. Weber speaks of the machine as 'objectified mind.' It is precisely because of this quality that the inanimate machine has the power to determine people's working lives coercively, as it actually does in the factory. Yet bureaucracy as 'animated machine' is likewise 'objectified intelligence' (*geronnener Geist*), and equally so. It is a highly rationalized form of administrative organization featuring the specialization of trained experts, delimitation of 'competencies,' general rules, and hierarchically articulated obedience relationships. Together with the inanimate machine, according to Weber, bureaucracy is better able than any other power relationship to construct for the man of the future a 'shell of bondage' in which the individual will have little or no living space.[13]

What Weber says about capitalist society is also true of the other forms of societal structures I have described. They too are products of a collective historical process; and here too the social order, a product of human design, is objectified into a coercive power external to the formers themselves, as it were. Weber describes at length how the mandarins of China won their power position in history and how their lifestyle became the typical Chinese lifestyle, persisting in spite of all imperial dynastic changes. The same was true for the Brahmans of India. The consistently 'organismic,' strictly traditional caste system was the product of their systematic thought and of their need to dominate the masses. Through a long process the caste system became strongly anchored structurally throughout India. In Weber's day it offered powerful resistance to the rise of Western capitalism in India after British colonization.

To Weber this last fact demonstrates that the objectified rational system remains – whatever difficulties are encountered – a human product. The social system can be altered by the introduction of another system of norms and production. This can occur when a particular social system comes into contact with a different one, as in the case of British colonization in India. Yet it can also occur as a result of factors intrinsic to a system, as we shall soon see in a number of cases. Here I wish only to note that modern Western society, in which the rationalization of life is rushing onwards in increasing measure and in ever more fields in a mechanistic sense, is no exception to the principle that a society remains the product of human collective intentionality and that it can be altered by people. Weber states explicitly that this is possible in principle. 'No one knows who will live in this cage [namely, of capitalism – ML] in the future, or whether at the end of this tremendous development entirely new prophets will arise, or there will be a great rebirth of old ideas or ideals, or, if neither, mechanized petrifaction, embellished with a sort of convulsive self-importance.'[14]

In his discussion of bureaucratic state administration, too, Weber entertains the possibility that it could be carried so far that man would be doomed to utter slavery. However, he goes on directly to ask how man can be spared this "inescapable' fate' and how the society of the future will have to be structured politically in order to 'save *any remnants* of 'individualist' freedom.'[15]

Thus we can say that the rationalization process, as it has assumed a concrete form in the normative structure of a particular society and come to confront members of this society objectively as an inescapable actuality, is viewed by Weber not as a determined and unilinear development but as a reality that stands in a dialectical relation to the society's intending, or meaning-giving, actors.

This conclusion agrees with Weber's methodological views as I explained them in chapter two: Weber denies science the possibility of foretelling the future in a deterministic way, or he describes structures as the 'chance that a particular intention will persist.'

C. The Internalization of Values

Rationalization as a dialectical process implies still a third moment, namely, internalization. It can be described as the phenomenon whereby a particular society's objective, rational socio-cultural pattern of norms is assimilated by the members of the society via the socialization process. The rational objective social reality becomes the intellectual property of the individual. It becomes a component of his consciousness. Usually the individual is not aware of this, and to him the pertinent way of thinking, feeling, and acting seems natural. That Weber is familiar with the phenomenon (not the word) internalization in this sense is apparent from numerous loci in his writings. In his foreword to the *Gesammelte Aufsätze* [see *GAR I*, ET (1)] he attacks the notion that the typically Western rationalization of the ethos could be attributable to particular inherited characteristics of Western man. He does not deny that particular hereditary factors may have been co-determinants, but that they actually were so, he says, is in any case not yet scientifically demonstrable. What is certain, however, is that sociology and history can show in a satisfying way that socio-cultural influences were (co-) determinative for the rise of the Western rational ethos.[16] In other words, Weber implicitly acknowledges at this point the currently generally recognized fact that so-called human nature is in some measure a product of culture.

Weber repeatedly expresses this implicit standpoint explicitly. It is in this light, for example, that he views the typically Western 'man of calling,' who can be designated as rational 'personality' in a very special sense as the result of a lengthy educational process. At least in his work the 'man of calling' regards achievement-directedness as something self-evident. Yet this mentality is 'by no means a product of nature.' Even less is it to be construed as an indirect reaction to wage incentives. On the contrary, in traditionalistic regions wage manipulations fail to achieve the desired effect. In industrialized areas the recruitment of male and female workers is relatively easy, whereas elsewhere there is considerable resistance.[17] This means that the capitalist spirit with its pattern of norms has been internalized: 'willingness to work' and 'duty to work' have become socially self-evident and are not normally the subjects of reflection. The rationalization process therefore penetrates into the motivational sphere of human existence and leads to a commitment that is relatively independent of the more superficial mechanisms of positive and negative social control.

We can say even more about this standpoint. The polar opposite to this 'personality' in the Western sense is the Confucian 'personality.' The Confucian was inwardly and outwardly a 'man of harmonious adjustment.' His rationality consisted of systematically adjusting to 'propriety': the requirements of the established order. If the Western (capitalistic or Protestant) personality was an identity 'from the inside out,' Confucian personality was an identity 'from the outside in.'[18] Thus externally given norms were assimilated and integrated into a certain unity. The Chinese can accordingly be characterized in terms of such traits as patience, lack of 'nerves,' controlled politeness, strong attachment to habits, insensitivity to monotony, and slow reaction to unusual stimuli, especially in the intellectual sphere. This psycho-physical habitude or bearing was also observable in the gestures and facial expressions of the Chinese. Where such externally imposed norms were lacking, however, character traits appeared which contrast sharply with those just mentioned. In their place one finds strong distrust of the Chinese for one another, dishonesty, remarkable unreliability in business, etc. The Chinaman's was not a 'unified personality' in the Western sense; his life as a whole remained as it were a 'series of consequences.'[19]

Weber asserts there is a possibility some traits mentioned here as belonging to the Chinese race as such are indeed racial qualities but claims the possibility also needs to be taken seriously that these so-called innate traits may be purely historically and culturally determined.[20] As the most important argument, he relates that eminent sinologists confirm that the further back in history one goes, the more the characteristics of the Chinese and their culture resemble what is found in the West.

Weber speaks even more resolutely about the so-called 'national characters'[21] of countries or regions influenced by either Lutheranism or Calvinism. Religious forces were of decisive significance in the formation of those national characters. Here Weber rules out hereditary factors. What the Germans experience as 'good nature' (*Gemütlichkeit*) or 'naturalness' in contrast to the 'narrowness, unfreeness, and inner constraint' in the atmosphere of the English and Americans with their 'disillusioned and pessimistically inclined individualism' which finds expression in Anglo-American institutions 'even to-day' (that is, Weber's day), can be accounted for from the fact that the latter were and the former were not influenced by Protestant ascetic rationalism.

Besides hereditary factors, Weber also expressly rules out climatological factors as a basis for explaining the national character. The proposition that the Indian is contemplative by nature as a result of the climate, which would cause a certain 'enervation' or 'passivity' Weber rejects out of hand as 'completely unfounded.' After all, no land in the world has been so chronically engaged in so many barbarous wars and witnessed so much pitiless, unrestrained lust for conquest as India.[22]

Now, it should not be concluded from all this that Weber distinguished the various depth-levels at which it is possible to pose the

111

problem of man's being influenced by factors external to himself.[23]

To close this discussion of internalization, I want to observe that Weber was aware of the phenomenon of the internal dialogue or internal dialectic between the socialized personality and the creative 'I.'[24]

Quantitatively speaking, most human social action approaches ideal-typical 'traditional action' (*durch eingelebte Gewohnheit*).[25] This is so not only in traditional forms of society but also in Western rationalized society. For the progress of rationalization through science and technology does not mean, according to Weber, that modern man acquires more insight into the conditions that determine his everyday life. An American Indian or a Hottentot knows more about the tools he uses than the modern man does about the streetcar he steps into or the money he spends. Only the physicist or the economist, respectively, has theoretical insight into these matters. For the ordinary man or, more accurately, for those who do not play the special role of the physicist or economist, the only difference from the primitive person is that they are aware that in principle it is possible for them to know how a streetcar functions or why money gains or loses purchasing power. For the modern man there are no longer any mysterious powers. The world is disenchanted and man is able in principle to 'master all things by calculation.'[26] Where the modern person has no special role to play, he frequently lives in a 'traditional' way, which is to say according to the unconsciously internalized pattern of norms or expectations of society. He lives in conformity to the customs (*Sitte*) of his society, that is, in conformity to the actual practices, with which he has become inwardly fused.[27]

The person can now enter into dialogue with this internalized social self, via the rationalization process:

> One of the most important aspects of the process of 'rationalization' of action is the substitution for the unthinking acceptance of ancient custom, of deliberate adaptation to situations in terms of self-interest. To be sure, this process by no means exhausts the concept of rationalization of action. For in addition this can proceed in a variety of other directions; positively in that of a deliberate formulation of ultimate values (*Wertrationalisierung*); or, negatively, at the expense not only of custom but of emotional values; and, finally, in favor of a morally sceptical type of rationality, at the expense of any belief in absolute values. The many possible meanings of the concept of rationalization will often enter into the discussion.[28]

The 'many possible meanings' (*Vieldeutigkeit*) of the concept of rationalization obviously pertains to the substantive side of the rationalization process. What interests us here is that via the rationalization process a person can re-orient himself, and that he can do so in any direction: to new or old values or to interests prejudicial to emotional, traditional, or value-oriented action. Rationalization means in that case a re-defining of the situation. With that, the inner dialectic of the rationalization process has been closed, at least in so far as the logic of it is concerned.[29]

From what has now been said it is evident that Weber regards the rationalization process as a dialectical process, although he nowhere uses the term 'dialectic' in this sense.[30] The moments of externalization, objectification, and internalization are not simply separate phenomena in Weber's view but evoke one another in a relationship of mutual opposition; I shall illustrate this by way of summary with a quotation on the sociological genesis of Western capitalism:

> The Puritan wanted to work in a calling; we are forced to do so. For when asceticism was carried out of monastic cells into everyday life, and began to dominate worldly morality, it did its part in building the tremendous cosmos of the modern economic order. This order is now bound to the technical and economic conditions of machine production which to-day determine the lives of all the individuals who are born into this mechanism, not only those directly concerned with economic acquisition, with irresistible force. Perhaps it will so determine them until the last ton of fossilized coal is burnt. In Baxter's view the care for external goods should only lie on the shoulders of the 'saint like a light cloak, which can be thrown aside at any moment.' But fate decreed that the cloak should become an iron cage.
>
> Since asceticism undertook to remodel the world and to work out its ideals in the world, material goods have gained an increasing and finally an inexorable power over the lives of men as at no previous period in history. To-day the spirit of religious asceticism – whether finally, who knows? – has escaped from the cage. But victorious capitalism, since it rests on mechanical foundations, needs its support no longer.[31]

II. The Rationalization of Religion as a Cultural Process

In this section I shall undertake an ideal-typical study of the rise, course, and consequences of the rationalization of religion. In doing so, I regard the rationalization process as a cultural process in the abstract. I abstract from the social context as much as possible in order to cast as clear a light as possible on the rationalization process as a meaning-giving, or intentional process.

At the outset, I show that the rationalization process is relatively autonomous.

I go on to examine the consequences of that for society. At issue is the rationalization of 'ethics.'

Finally, I examine the legitimation of the pertinent ethics: the course of the theoretical rationalization of religion.

A. *The Relative Autonomy of the Rationalization Process*

Religion, according to Weber, arises naturally and constantly from some human 'psychological' need. Often the salvation that people strive for in religion is entirely this-worldly (*diesseitige*) in nature: health, length of days, affluence, etc. Even when the religious person construes the salvation he seeks as purely other-worldly (*jenseitige*), however, the object of the quest is still in the first place, from a psychological standpoint in any case, a (permanent or incidental) this-worldly frame of mind as such, sought for its own sake. Thus, psychologically considered, all religious salvation consists first and foremost of intrinsic and concrete emotional values. The Puritan *certitudo salutis*, the feeling of assurance of one's election, was accordingly of primary importance, psychologically speaking, in Puritan ascetic religiosity. The matter was no different in the case of the acosmic love of the Buddhist monk who felt certain of his entry into Nirvana, or in the cases of the more popular extraordinary states of mind which, in the form of magical intoxication, were widely experienced as consecrated or divine.[32]

By the same token, however, in the most primitive religions too the rational element was never entirely lacking. Even in its earliest forms, religiously and magically motivated action is at least relatively rational action. True, it need not yet be action that consciously applies means to ends, but it is at least based on certain rules of experience.[33] People act, in that case, on the basis of regularities learned from experience, although they may have no insight into the reasons for the regularities. Often this rational moment is studied in depth and systematized by the religiously more talented. This rationalization has a typical inner regularity of its own, which is relatively independent of the psychologically sought salvation benefits.

This rationalization is accordingly not to be regarded without qualification as rationalization in the psychological sense of the term – that is, as someone's interpretive but unconscious transformation of a personally undesirable situation into a desirable, or at least apparently desirable, one.[34]

> At the present time, it is widely held that one should consider emotional content as primary, with thoughts being merely its secondary expression. Of course, this point of view is to a great extent justified. From such a standpoint one might be inclined to consider the primacy of 'psychological' as over against 'rational' connections as the only decisive causal nexus, hence to view these rational connections as *mere* interpretations of the psychological ones. This, however, would be going much too far, according to factual evidence.[35]

In this context, Weber's position should be seen in contrast to Friedrich Nietzsche's theory of resentment. The ethics of 'duties,' in Nietzsche's view,[36] would be the product of 'repressed' and ineffectual vengefulness harbored by a disprivileged stratum (*Banhauser*) condemned to hard work, in contrast to the lifestyle of a privileged stratum (*Herrenstand*) living without obligations. Ethical esteem for mercy and brotherhood would in fact be only a 'slave revolt in morality' of social strata thwarted in their expectations of life. Weber acknowledges the merits of this psychological explanation of feelings of resentment, but he warns against applying it imprudently to religious ethics. Resentment is totally absent in various religions, most notably in Hinduism, where the lower castes in particular accept their position consciously and positively. Jewish religion, in contrast, was supremely a religion of vengeance and retribution. Yahweh was a God with an unprecedented thirst for vengeance. Nowhere in the world was anything comparable to be found in a universal deity. The Psalms are full of vindictiveness. It is often treated as morally justified and legitimate. That that should be the case is understandable, too, according to Weber, given an almost permanently threatened pariah people.[37] Yet it would be erroneous to account for Jewish religiosity exclusively in terms of resentment. The rationalism of the rabbis, as it found expression in the Talmud, not only recognized a psychological rationalization of vengefulness but also understood the core of this mechanism. This vengefulness was rejected by the rabbis: 'For nothing is more impressively emphasized than the commandment: not to will the 'shaming' of others.'[38] Here we have a concrete example of how the *ratio* is relatively autonomous with respect to the inner emotional state and how rationalization can function, directing and correcting, with respect to behavior, which in that case no longer allows itself to be led by sentiments alone.

The fact that the rationalization process is in principle an autonomous process influencing concrete human actions is stated by Weber repeatedly. Surely, 'not ideas,[39] but material and ideal interests, directly govern men's conduct. Yet very frequently the 'world images' that have been created by 'ideas' have, like switchmen, determined the tracks along which action has been pushed by the dynamic of interest.'[40]

One can regard the rationalization process, as the preceding quotation shows, neither as a rationalization in the psychological sense nor as an unqualified 'ideology' in the sociological sense of the word: as an unconscious distortion of reality inspired by interests. As far as religious action was concerned, "from what' and 'for what' one wished to be redeemed and, let us not forget, 'could be' redeemed, depended upon one's image of the world.'[41] As the product of a rationalization process, this image of the world could assume extravagantly varied forms, it is true, but the facts show that the *ratio* always played a role of its own in the matter:

> The rational elements of a religion, its 'doctrine', also have an autonomy: for instance, the Indian doctrine of Kharma, the Calvinist belief in predestination, the Lutheran justification by faith, and the Catholic doctrine of sacrament. The rational religious pragmatism of salvation, flowing from the nature of the images of God and of the world, have under certain conditions had far-reaching results for the fashioning of a practical way of life.[42]

The fact that the rationalization process is a relatively autonomous process also finds expression in Weber's perception that often the process is the consequence of a 'metaphysical' human need, an actual inner need for metaphysics, which compels people to systematize their world picture.

116

B. The Ethics of Magic, the Religious Ethic of Inwardness ('Gesinnungsethik'), and Society

I wish now to proceed in an ideal-typical way to examine the rationalization of religion in its relation to society. Such an ideal-typical approach is in principle nothing more than a technical means of gaining orientation, the better to study the rationalization process as it actually takes place concretely. Because the *ratio* itself still exerts an influence on the pattern of practical human life, however, it is at the same time more than a means of gaining orientation. It indicates as well how the rationalization process has at times actually appeared.[43] Given the enormous power of other societal factors, this is of course only rarely the case.

Weber advances two criteria for measuring the degree of rationalization:

> To judge the level of rationalization a religion represents we may use two primary yardsticks which are in many ways interrelated. One is the degree to which the religion has divested itself of magic; the other is the degree to which it has systematically unified the relation between God and the world and therewith its own ethical relationship to the world.[44]

The greatest chance that the actual course of the rationalization process will follow the book is represented by the people Weber calls 'virtuosi.' He notes the empirical fact that from the beginning of the history of religion people have been unequally qualified in a religious way. Accordingly he distinguishes between 'virtuoso' religiosity and 'mass' religiosity. Hence by 'mass' he does not mean those situated lowest in the social stratification but those who are religiously 'unmusical.'[45] In this context Weber emphatically warns people to avoid the evaluative connotations of these terms. He would prefer to use the term 'heroic' religiosity if it were not so inadequate with respect to the enormously varied kinds of religious virtuosi (magicians, holy dancers, eremites, monks, ascetics, devotees of sects, etc.).[46]

The word society is a global term for indicating that to which the process of religious rationalization can be related. Against the background of the original 'unbroken' enchanted society, Weber examines the conflict relation between religion and various other sectors of life in a rationalized society. Namely, the rationalization process fragments the original undifferentiated world ever more into a relatively autonomous religious sector beside relatively autonomous other sectors of life, each of which possesses its own typical inner rationality. This gives rise to a differentiation of value spheres within society that can become involved in latent or open conflict with religion. Weber analyzes the origin and meaning of possible conflicts between the rationalization of religion and five other rationalized spheres of value. He deals with the economic, political, artistic, erotic, and intellectual spheres, respectively. In order to provide a somewhat manageable synopsis, I shall deal with the practical-ethical rationality of magic and religion first. Then (under *c*) I shall go on to examine theoretical rationalization, which legitimates practical-ethical rationality. Naturally, the two aspects are distinguishable only in the analytical sense; there is a mutual causal relation between theoretical rationalization and practical-ethical rationalization.

1. Magical ethics and the stereotyping of social behavior[47]

The person who practices magic distinguishes in the first instance and as a rule only between the lesser or greater extraordinariness of the effect of his behavior. Not every stone can serve arbitrarily as a fetish, for example, nor can every person achieve an ecstatic state or produce effects of a meteorological, therapeutic, divinatory, or telepathic character. This extraordinary power, this 'charisma,' is ascribed to certain objects, animals, events, or persons directly (naturalism) if it inheres in them naturally, or indirectly (symbolism) if these have acquired a 'supersensual' meaning. We alone, according to Weber, have the capacity, given our view of nature, to distinguish between objectively 'correct' and 'fallacious' causal ascription and then to view the latter as irrational and to adjudge corresponding acts as 'magic.'

One who practices magic always has in mind the realization of this-worldly (*diesseitige*) objectives, as does all religious action, for that matter, in its most elementary form. Magical action too may therefore not be viewed in isolation from everyday economic life; it is at least relatively rational action that finds a basis for its calculations in the rules of experience. Should the experience of the magician or his clientele indicate that the extraordinary power of a natural object, an artefact, or a person is no longer operative, or in other words should this object or this person have lost its magical

118

charisma, then that would mean the end of that particular sort of magical action.[48]

Now, a striking feature of all magical action is its strong tendency to exercise a stereotyping effect on the pattern of life: action that has been found to work once must always be repeated in precisely the same way; the slightest deviation can condemn it to ineffectuality. This relatively rational behavior can, where symbolic magic is concerned, be further rationalized: (magically) appropriate means are employed in ever more fields of life. Thus a 'magical ethic' can develop, as a complex whole of (as we would see it) extremely heterogeneous significant and insignificant norms the violation of which would immediately entail concrete evil consequences. Weber also speaks of (rationalized) 'taboos'; observing them is magically motivated, and violations are followed by evil spells. It is usually symbolic magic that is involved in such cases: objects or persons are brought into association with supersensual forces which effect these evil consequences.

It is typical of magical ethics that these supersensual beings can be directly influenced by human activities. Weber speaks in this connection of magical coercion (*Gotteszwang*) as opposed to religion (*Gottesdienst*). Here in fact lies the difference between magic and religion, although Weber often uses the terms without distinction while maintaining expressly that in reality the one flows into the other. Magic appears even in the most highly developed religions (for example, in the Catholic religion in the consecrating power of the priest):

> The relationships of men to supernatural forces which take the forms of prayer, sacrifice, and worship may be termed '*cult*' (*Kultus*) and '*religion*,' as distinguished from '*sorcery*,' which is magical coercion. Correspondingly, those beings that are worshipped and entreated religiously may be termed '*gods*,' in contrast to '*demons*,' which are magically coerced and charmed. There may be no instance in which it is possible to apply this differentiation absolutely, since the cults we have just called 'religions' practically everywhere contain numerous magical components.[49]

Through magic with its taboos, limits are set in principle to a rationalization of ethics. Magical taboos always pertain to stereotyped rules of behavior bearing on concrete matters of everyday life. Magical taboos are a case of an extremely practical rationalism that orients action only incidentally, and always ad hoc. The practical rationalism of magical taboos does not lead to a permanent pattern of life methodically oriented to an ultimate purpose. There is in other words no gap between magic and the immediate interests of everyday life, between magic and the 'world.' Magic protects the interests of life's 'natural' relationships (sib or tribe)[50]. Magic esteems wealth as a self-evident good. Art, in the form of images, paramounts, edifices, song, and dance occupies an important place in magic ritual. Sexuality, too, often plays an esteemed and important role in magical orgiasticism.[51]

2. The religious ethic of inwardness, and society

In contrast to magical ethics with its ritualistic attitude towards the world, religiously rationalized ethics lead to a pattern of conduct which in conflict situations can extend to various sectors of social life, the more so as these in their own turn are the more strongly rationalized and thereby conspicuous in their intrinsic value[52]. Now, the better able an ethic is to bring human conduct systematically to a conscious and enduring inward unity, the more highly rationalized that ethic is. Weber speaks here of the ethic of inwardness (*Gesinnungsethik*). This ethic breaks through 'the stereotypization of individual norms in order to bring about a meaningful total relationship of the pattern of life to the goal of religious salvation.'[53] In place of any 'sacred law' comes a 'sacred inner religious state' which is inherently dynamic in its operation and at odds with the realities of life. Depending upon the pattern of life this sacred inner religious state 'engenders,' the conflict with reality that it entails will assume various forms.

Weber distinguishes two diametrically opposed directions within a religiously rationalized ethic, namely,

> ... the active *asceticism* that is a God-willed *action* of the devout who are God's tools, and, on the other hand, the contemplative *possession* of the holy, as found in *mysticism*. Mysticism intends a state of 'possession,' not action, and the individual is not a tool but a 'vessel' of the divine. Action in the world must thus appear as endangering the absolutely irrational and other-worldly religious state.[54]

This conflict is the more fundamental whenever on the one hand active asceticism has an intramundane, or inner-worldly, character (*innerweltliche Askese*), as it does in the case of ascetic Protestantism, which seeks via 'vocation' to change not only man but

120

also the world in a rational way, and whenever on the other hand mysticism draws the consequences of total rejection of the world (*weltflüchtige Kontemplation*), as in the case of ancient Buddhism. The inner-worldly ascetic proves himself precisely by being active in the world, while in the view of the mystic, the created world must be silent so that God can speak. The mystic is in the world accommodating himself externally to its structure, but he proves himself to the world via a kind of religious incognito: by rejecting action in the world. To the inner-worldly ascetic, the conduct of the mystic is a form of lazy self-indulgence; for the world-fleeing mystic, the active ascetic is someone who, in all the vanity of self-justification, is entangled in a worldly hustle and bustle that is estranged from God.

The fundamental tension within the ethic of inwardness is ameliorated if the active ascetic restricts himself to concentrating on his personal self-protection and avoids acting in the world (*Weltflüchtige Askese*), as in the case of a Catholic monk, for example; or if on the other hand the mystic does not draw the consequences of world rejection but instead remains within its structures (*innerweltliche Mystik*), as in the case of the Brahmans.

The religious ethic of inwardness always fosters a fraternal ethic (*Brüderlichkeitsethik*). The first power with which a religious ethic came into conflict was the tribal community. Where a community arose on a religious basis, its brotherhood would obviously have more intimate mutual bonds and weightier obligations to each other than towards those to whom they were bound by ties of blood, kinship, or marriage. 'Whomsoever cannot hate his father cannot become a disciple of Jesus.'[55] The ethic of religious inwardness is accordingly a supreme fraternal ethic. Its psychological tone and rational indication can vary somewhat between the ascetic and the mystic, but the ethical requirement always tends in the direction of a universal brotherhood that transcends all restrictions and social barriers. The more the sacred objective is rationalized into 'salvation' from a situation of fundamental extremity common to the whole of humanity, the more the fraternal ethic becomes an unrestricted love of man, including the enemy: it becomes an ethic of universal love (*Gesinnung der Caritas*). It is now feasible to illustrate the conflict situation alluded to above by discussing successively the political, economic, artistic, and erotic spheres in the light of this caritative inward ethic.

a. The modern state can be viewed as a consistent rationalization of the guarantee of justice that a community requires. The au-

121

tonomy of this institutionalized value is sharply underlined in the modern state, and it contrasts strongly with the rationalization of ethics. The state, which by definition monopolizes the legitimate exercise of power and the sword on Weber's view, must (and can), by virtue of its immanent order and in spite of all 'social politics,' meet force with force. This is true both for domestic and especially for foreign political affairs. The bureaucratic state apparatus and the rational political man (*homo politicus*) who is a part of that apparatus must be able to employ power, even to punish injustice, without respect to persons – *sine ira et studio*, 'without hate and without love.'[56] The 'resist not evil with violence' of the Sermon on the Mount stands here, of intrinsic necessity, in contrast to the 'by virtue of your responsibility towards injustice you must assure even by violence that justice triumphs.' The more the state methodically and calculatingly employs power in its domestic and foreign relations, setting power against power, the more inwardly estranged it becomes from the fraternal ethic. The estrangement between the two spheres [of ethics and politics] can come to sharp expression in war, because there politics can appear as the direct competitor of the religious ethic. War as the actualization of violence can unleash in modern political communities a pathos and feeling of togetherness that brings with it a readiness for unconditional sacrifice and surrender. It arouses a massive feeling of love for all who are threatened, and it breaks through all natural ties. Moreover, war brings a unique commitment to death, which becomes a meaningful event in that the individual feels he now has something to die for. It is precisely this extraordinary feeling of fraternity, which war has in common with the sacred charisma of the religious ethic of fellowship with the divine, that raises the level of its competition with the religious fraternal ethic to its highest pitch. The religious fraternal ethic finds in war nothing more than technically sophisticated cruel conflict; the inner-worldly devotion to death in war is to this ethic nothing but a glorification of fratricide.

The ethic of inwardness has only two consistent solutions to this conflict relation. These solutions are to be found in the ascetic and mystical extremes this ethic engenders. The radical, world-fleeing mystic consistently withdraws from all politics, with its unavoidable resort to violence, and 'turns the other cheek' – unworthily from the standpoint of a self-assured worldly heroic ethic. Radical inner-worldly asceticism can in certain instances accept war as the means to a rational transformation of the world, since the world must be transformed in any case, by its own means, and these means in-

122

clude violence. In this case a limit is placed on fraternal loyalty for the sake of God's own cause. This ascetic Protestantism accepted revolution for the sake of faith and the obligation to resist tyranny in defense of faith.[57]

b. The conflict between the fraternal ethic and society is revealed particularly clearly in the economic sector. Virtually every caritative ethic has upheld some form of prohibition of usury,[58] which has been regarded as embodying an interhuman commercial attitude inconsistent with a relationship of personal love. The modern rationalization of economics brings this tension to a head, for modern economics is a commercial affair oriented to prices that arise in a market as the result of conflicts of interest. Without estimates in money and without conflicts of interest, a modern economic calculation is impossible. Money is the most abstract and most 'impersonal' thing there is. Now, the more the modern capitalist economy obeys its own rationality, the more it becomes a cosmos totally inaccessible to every caritative ethic. This cosmos of purely commercial relations requires rational social action totally divorced from concrete persons. Fraternal considerations are in that case bereft of all meaning; relationships between masters and slaves are deprived of any inward ethical norm; and the relationships between shareholders and workers, between tobacco importers and plantation laborers, etc., become not only in fact but also in principle inaccessible to caritative norms. Someone who acts in a purely economic way acts, needless to say, in an impersonal-rational way and therefore, from the viewpoint of fraternal ethics, in an ethically irrational way.

Here again it is only the two diametrically opposed forms of the ethic of religious inwardness that have led to consistent solutions to the conflict at issue. Radical mysticism flees the world, in the form of an objectless surrender to anyone at random, not for the sake of the other personality but for the sake of the surrender itself, in what Baudelaire called 'the sacred prostitution of the soul' – a phrase Weber invokes repeatedly in this connection. Here, brotherhood becomes an acosmic love. Radical asceticism commercialized, via its vocational ethic, every relationship to the world, and of course it regarded the impersonal economic cosmos, too, as a God-ordained work terrain. Asceticism hereby relinquished the universalism of love. In ascetic Protestantism, for example, the prohibition against usury came to be limited to clear-cut cases of selfishness, and it became legitimate in principle for businessmen to charge each other interest. Charity for the able-bodied was rejected on ethical grounds. Support for those incapable of work became a 'rationalized 'enterprise"[59] bereft of personal love or transformed into its opposite.

c. The third area in which the fraternal ethic could come into conflict with socially relevant sectors of life Weber calls art. Viewed substantively, the aesthetic sphere can contribute to building up a community, but to the extent that the specifically aesthetic is consciously discovered as an autonomous sphere and then rationalized in keeping with its own inner order, it cultivates a scale of values that is disparate to religious ethical values. The beautiful form as such becomes the object of artistic enjoyment in that case, and aesthetic responsibility is regarded as a threat to the creative and most personal element in man. Ethical value judgments are metamorphosed into aesthetic ones: it becomes the fashion to speak of the 'tasteless' rather than of the 'reprehensible.'[60] From the standpoint of religious fraternal ethics, such enjoyment without a sense of responsibility is a form of latent lovelessness. Moreover, it is always a flight from an ethical stand, and it impedes an ethical systematization of the conduct of life. Here the most radical forms of rationalized ethics of religious inwardness reject art completely as inconsistent with the goal of religious salvation. Inner-worldly asceticism regards art as a flight into the irrational at the expense of rational work in the world; world-fleeing mysticism is hostile to any attachment to (aesthetic) forms, which it regards as impediments to union with the divine All-One, transcending as that does all temporal-spatial creation.

d. Weber also mentions the erotic sphere as a possible point of conflict with the fraternal ethic. Sexuality has always strongly influenced social life. It belongs (together with economic interests and those of power and prestige which we have yet to discuss) to 'the most fundamental and universal components of the actual course of interpersonal behavior.'[61] The greater the intellectualization of culture, the greater, too, the conscious sublimation of sexuality to 'eroticism'; in other words, the more sexuality too is rationalized, the more sharply the conflict with the fraternal ethic comes to the fore.

Erotic intercourse appears to be the culmination of a loving relationship because it is socially constructive in its operation and is experienced as a perfect union. This complete, mutual surrender to each other's irrational individuality stands in the most radical imaginable opposition to all that is routine or rational. It becomes an inner-worldly value that transcends all this. In erotic relationship people mysteriously experience being 'meant' for each other; it is a being 'destined' in the highest sense of the word, and it is self-legitimating.

From the standpoint of the fraternal ethic, the meaning of this mysterious destiny is simply a purely incidental flare-up of passion, and eroticism is at core an exclusive and subjective relationship diametrically opposed to religious brotherhood and authentic neighborly love. It is a form of conflict, not only because of the quest and desire for exclusive possession of each other as over and above third parties, but above all because of the inward rape of the soul (unnoticed by those concerned), which in a sophisticated way and in the guise of human surrender seeks self-gratification in the other.

For radical asceticism there is the added consideration that this irrational eroticism entails the loss of self-control and of orientation to the rational ordinances of God. Only an institution of sexuality within marriage that is oriented towards procreation and the nurture of children falls within the framework of God's ordinances.

For radical mysticism, eroticism is an even greater threat, because psychologically speaking there is such a close kinship between the two that mysticism can at times be exchanged for eroticism, however much the two may differ from each other in meaning and importance. Eroticism resembles mysticism because lovers feel themselves caught up in an inexhaustible, in every respect ineffable, authentic life. Like the mystic, lovers transcend not only the chill skeleton of every rational order but also the absurdity of ordinary routine life. To have the mystical experience as an 'objectless' experience is from the standpoint of the erotic, which feels itself directly tied to what is 'most vital,' merely measured and inauthentic. From the standpoint of the mystic, however, eroticism is a fundamental impediment to union with the divine and to the abolition of limited individuation.

e. It is obvious from all this that the religious ethic of inwardness, too, contains a deep, internal tension, for it apparently has no way of answering the initial question of whether the ethical value of an act is to be measured in terms of its consequences or in terms of the value inherent in the act itself. In other words, is one responsible for the consequences of one's actions and to what extent does the end justify the means, or are good intentions so important that no heed need be paid the consequences? The religious ethic of inwardness usually tends towards the second alternative: 'the Christian does what he ought to do and leaves the consequences to God.'

Radical inner-worldly asceticism emphasizes the ethics of responsibility so strongly that it sometimes entails revolutionary consequences. Under the motto 'We ought to obey God rather than men' [Acts 5:29] there have been typically Puritan revolutions.

Radical world-fleeing mysticism can so strongly emphasize the religious state as such that it results in total anomie. If 'possession' of the divine flares up into 'divine possession,' all is permitted, and the commandments no longer hold.

C. Theoretical Rationalization of Magic and Religion

The practical, ethical rationalization of magic and religion is comprehensible only if its cognitive aspect, too, is given explicit consideration. Thus the rationalization of ethics means substantively a rationalization of the quest for 'salvation.' It is time to examine this theoretical-substantive dimension more closely.

1. Theoretical rationalization of magic

The rationalization of the cognitive aspect of magic runs from naturalism via animism through incarnation to symbolism.[62] In naturalism certain objects, events, animals, or persons are viewed as directly endowed with some kind of 'extraordinary power.' In other words, certain objects or persons are 'charismatic.' This magical charisma simply adheres to such an object or person. It can also be acquired by them by extraordinary means, but they must in that case already possess it in the germ at least. Charisma can never simply be developed or learned; it can at most be awakened, by asceticism, for example.

An initial and only apparently simple form of abstraction appears as soon as people imagine that some kind of hidden 'being' is 'behind' such a charismatically qualified thing, animal, or person, influencing its activity: 'the belief in spirits.' Here 'spirit' is in the first instance a still totally indeterminate 'something' – it is still not clearly a 'soul,' 'demon,' or 'god' – that endows a concrete and visible thing or person with the power distinctive to it.

It is possible to go on to conceive of such a 'spirit' as 'soul': as an entity differing from body but near or in natural objects 'even as the human body contains something that leaves it in dream, syncope, ecstasy or death.'[63] This is animism.

A further phase of abstraction occurs when these 'spirits' are imagined to be beings capable of temporarily dwelling in plants, animals, or people, 'incorporating' themselves into them, as it were.

The highest phase of abstraction is reached when 'spirits' are construed to be invisible essences – 'souls,' 'gods,' or 'demons' – subsisting according to their own laws and at most 'symbolized' by plants, animals, or people. This is symbolism.

Essential especially for this last form of abstraction, which occurs in countless transitional forms and combinations, is the fact that here 'suprasensual' forces are projected as having real power to influence the destinies of people in a way comparable to that in which man himself influences the world. Besides these things 'that are and that happen,' there are also powers that play a direct role in life because they 'mean' something. People react to these powers with behaviors that 'mean' something in return, that have meaning. People no longer consort exclusively with 'realities'; rather, they begin to think 'symbolically' and to address themselves to an invisible world. Like naturalistic-magical activity, this symbolical activity has a stereotyping effect on human conduct, because symbolic acts always have to be repeated in precisely the same form in order to guarantee the fresh achievement of the previously observed effect. Any alteration of the ritual might provoke the wrath of a god or of an ancestor's soul.

This thinking in symbols can be rationalized still further. In that case it comes to be known as 'mythological' thought, the special importance of which in the present connection consists of the fact that it involves a form of analogical thinking in which resemblance plays a great role. The syllogistic concept formation of logical rational thought is not yet present here.

The latter has its inception only with pantheon formation, in which the chaos of the deities (and their cults) becomes a systematic whole through the specialization and characterization of specific divine forms on the one hand and their investment with fixed attributes and jurisdictions on the other hand.[64] Here there is the possibility of a delimitation of jurisdictions according to systematic rational principles. Besides, the *ratio* in that case demands the primacy of a universal god. Meanwhile, it must be remembered that in so far as practical life is concerned, this does not mean that the theoretically 'highest' god exercises the greatest influence. In prac-

127

tice the matter is one of which god intervenes most forcibly in the everyday interests of an individual or group. If it should be 'lower' spirits that do so, then everyday life will be determined principally by the relationship to them, regardless of the appearance of the official god concept of the rationalized religion.

The supreme god of the pantheon is not yet a universal world deity, but all advanced thought about gods desires in increasing measure that the existence and quality of a being like god be established everywhere and for everyone and that it be in this sense 'universal.' The greater the preponderance of the supreme deity of the pantheon becomes, or in other words the more monotheistic features this deity acquires, the greater becomes the tendency to regard it as 'universal' in the sense of its being a general god of the world.

2. Theoretical rationalization of religion

With the increasing universalization of the concept of god and with his growing personal power over man, 'magical ritual' and 'magical ethics,' which coercively influence the god in some way or another, come in principle to be exchanged for a 'religious cult' and 'religious ethic,' which attempt to acquire the god's favor by means of prayer, sacrifice, and the keeping of the god's commandments. Naturally, such a more universal and more powerful deity can refuse to acquiesce to human desires. This is true not exclusively but certainly in a particular way when this deity is not subject to a higher power but instead has created the world himself. It is in that case not the powerlessness of god but the shortcomings of man, or in other words his ethical 'sin,' which is the cause of evil. The keeping of the god's commandments can in that case lead man to holiness and 'salvation.'

At the outset the disparity to magic is not great, and the matter remains one of preventing evil or acquiring 'this-worldly' goods, with which this god 'punishes' sin or 'rewards' virtue.

The increasing rationalization of the concept of god is accompanied, however, by the decline of this practical rationalism, which seeks to achieve directly observable advantages for everyday life. This must now yield to the rationalization of the conduct of life as a totality (the religious ethic of inwardness, or *Gesinnungsethik*), whereby sin becomes simply that which is against god while 'salvation' likewise pertains to the 'being' of man as such. The goal of religious conduct is increasingly 'irrationalized' in this sense, that it is steadily less goal-rational with respect to the external advantages of everyday life and increasingly a specific value as such. The quest for 'salvation' comes to be focussed more on 'other-worldly' ends, in which case it is regarded as specifically religious activity.[65]

In itself, the idea of salvation from peril, hunger, drought, disease, suffering or death is ancient, and it also appears strongly in magical religiosity. Given the increasing rationalization of the idea of salvation, it was however less and less possible to view it in isolation from the conception of the world as a totality. To explain suffering was a matter of central importance. Undeserved suffering occurred all too frequently while those who ethically speaking were the worst seemed to fare the best. How could this unequal apportionment of happiness be explained? The explanation of 'sin' and divine chastisement was unsatisfying. Thus salvation came increasingly to be viewed as part of a systematically rational 'world picture' intended to account for what seemed 'senseless' in the world. The world in its visible and invisible totality must be or must become a meaningful cosmos, in one manner or another. Now, this meaningful 'cosmos' is the core product of genuine religious rationalism.[66]

This religious rationalism went ever further in its devaluation of the *diesseitige* world, whereby not only that which was without value, humanly speaking, but also precisely that which was humanly valuable came to appear fleeting and valueless in contrast to the eternal.

From this vantage point it is clear why even at the theoretical level tension arose between the religious ethic of inwardness and the various sectors of worldly life. This tension increased in proportion on the one hand to the degree of rationalization of the conception of salvation in an increasingly unworldly sense and, on the other hand to the degree the world itself became more goal-rational in its external organization and more sublimated in the conscious experience of its irrational value. In the theoretical sense, too, the world became increasingly 'disenchanted.' The rational political cosmos, the economic cosmos – routinized and rational and indispensable to meeting the world's material needs – aesthetics, and the erotic: these came to appear not only transient but even as laden with a special guilt, since they, precisely, created the illusion of conjuring a solution for people. This was true of the apparent meaningfulness of war and devotion to death on the field of battle, for inner-worldly aesthetic enjoyment, or for the salvific sensation in erotic relationships. The final value to which all culture seemed to be reduced, namely, the cultural self-perfection of man, brought to light at the same time the absolute meaninglessness of all inner-worldly active creation of culture or passive absorption of culture. For the more culture became differentiated and multiplicitous, the more human self-perception was confronted in principle with the infinite. This accented more sharply the meaninglessness of death, for there was no guarantee that a 'meaningful' end to this self-unfoldment would coincide with the 'fortuitous' moment of death.

Weber now mentions four types of religious rationalism that have attempted to work out a meaningful theoretical solution to the problems of the imperfection of the present world and of deliverance from suffering. These four 'rationally pure types of theodicy' are messianic eschatologies, Zoroastrian dualism, the Puritan belief in predestination, and the doctrine of *karma* or the transmigration of souls.[67]

Messianic eschatologies solve the problem of present suffering by believing that matters will be set right in a future kingdom of salvation in this world. Present suffering is a consequence of one's own sins or of the sins of one's ancestors. The salvation to come will at least accrue to one's posterity. The messianic event is a political and social transformation in this world, and it is guaranteed by an omnipotent Creator God, as in Jewish rationalism, for example.

In Persian Zoroastrianism this Jewish creator-creation dualism is replaced by eternally opposed forces of light, truth, purity, and goodness on the one hand and of darkness, lies, contamination, and evil on the other. Here suffering can be explained in terms of man's spirit participating in the realm of light while whatever is corporeal and material is identified with the realm of darkness. God is not the Almighty Creator but someone wrestling with a satanic, independent power.

According to Weber, this dualism was an inconsistent form of the most prevalent popular theodicy. The sovereignty of God would be restored in that the power of light would ultimately vanquish the power of darkness or in that the evil demon would become his creature. The existence of a devil and hell set a limit to God's goodness in that case.

The puritan belief in predestination carried the creature-Creator dualism through so consistently that the all-powerful God and his decrees were thought totally inaccessible to man, so that human suffering was inexplicable in principle and concealed in God's providential governance of the world.

The Indian doctrine of *karma* advanced the most consistent solution to the problem of suffering. 'Guilt and merit within this world are unfailingly compensated' by an ethical retribution mechanism. 'Each individual forges his own destiny exclusively, and in the strictest sense of the word,' in that only his own deeds determine his future rebirth in another being. 'Sin' in the strictest sense of the term does not exist. There are merely 'offenses against one's own clear interest.' Nor does a personal, omnipotent god exist. The creature-creator dualism is replaced by an ontological dualism between the transient course of the world on the one hand and, on the other hand, the 'serene and perduring being of eternal order – immobile divinity, resting in dreamless sleep.'

The concept of 'legitimation' can serve as a link between the practical-ethical and the theoretical rationalization of religion. Namely, the ethic of inwardness that directly motivates behavior is legitimated by the 'theoretically meaningful cosmos.'

Social action in Weber's view is usually motivated, at least in part, by the notion of the existence of a legitimate order. Only seldom is social behavior ruled exclusively by tradition or convention (*durch eingelebte Gewohnung*) or exclusively by subjective interests. It is of course correct that economic interests in particular, such as modern economic actions oriented to market prices, generate rational regularities in human social behavior that are often more stable than actions oriented to norms or duties. Yet usually, even in the case of rational economic actions, considerations arising from motives of legitimation play some role. People act in that case because they regard a particular order as 'obtaining,' as something that must be followed as an example or duty. The idea of legitimation need not be based explicitly on value-rational considerations; tradition, affectual surrender, or positive legislation can of course also be regarded as 'obtaining' and as having to be taken into consideration.[68] This idea of legitimation reinforces the stability of tradition or of rules oriented to the pursuit of interests. It can influence conduct profoundly and even be effectual where prejudicial to the one concerned or where there is an absence of all external sanctions whatsoever. This is the case, namely, when a particular order is religiously guaranteed. What concrete behaviors are positively or negatively sanctioned in respect of religion depends heavily on the religious world picture. In this way, theodicy functions as a source of legitimation for practical-ethical behavior.

The connection between this ethical-motivational aspect of human behavior and the cognitive aspect is not determined, but there is a certain affinity between the two. Thus the ascetic ethic will usually be associated with belief in a personal, transcendental God and be inclined towards a messianic-eschatological theodicy or a theodicy of predestination. Mystical ethics are usually associated with an impersonal, inner-worldly divine original ground, and they usually incline towards the dualistic type of theodicy, be it a spiritualistic dualism à la Zoroastrianism or an ontological dualism along the lines of the *karma* theodicy.

Until now I have dealt mainly with the rationalization process associated with religious virtuosi, who of course constitute a small minority and whose activity is in a certain way ethically-religiously motivated. To Weber it seems obvious that the religiosity of the masses (*Massen religiosität*) is largely pre-theoretical.[69] Here was a level of legitimation that accounted for the order of a society *in toto*, in terms of a theoretical worldview (*Weltanschauung*).[70] Moreover it is, for Weber, a frequently observed fact of experience that mutually contradictory 'orders' may obtain within one and the same group of people. Even an individual can orient himself to mutually contradictory norms, not just successively but in a single action. Fighting a duel, for example, he may orient himself at once to a code of honor and to a code of criminal law, by either concealing his action or surrendering to the authorities.[71] Only seldom will the four types of theodicy be encountered in their pure forms. Why that is so is the subject of the following section.

III. The Rise, Course, and Consequences of Rationalization as a Socio-Cultural Process

In the preceding section the rationalization process was presented as an intentional, or meaning-giving process that is relatively autonomous in its relation to both religious behavior and religious ideas. Formally speaking, this meant that man attempted to make empirical, opaque (irrational) and therefore unpredictable reality ever more intelligible as a 'meaningful' cosmos in order to bring his behavior into greater harmony with it and so to give form to his autonomy, whatever this autonomy might mean (in this case: the goal of salvation).[72] Naturally, this cultural process never transpires *in abstracto*, in a socially empty space, but always in a concrete, social-historical situation, through the effective intentions of concrete historical persons. In so far as the persons involved are concerned, "consistency' has been the exception and not the rule' – there are often whole series of motives involved that interest and even contradict each other, so that no one would be found to follow any one such series consistently.[73] While psychologically determined 'inward' interests thus always play a role where actors are concerned, the social situation always corresponds to 'outward' interests, of which Weber discusses mainly economic interests and power. Now, such inward and outward interests are often incorporated into the rationalization process as irrational and self-evidently accepted assumptions, thereby leaving their mark on that process. This is true both for the theoretical rationalization of the world picture and – in stronger measure – for the practical rationalization of the conduct of life.[74]

Interests function in social reality only if people have the power to pursue them. This means that social positions possessing power to pursue their interests will play a large role in the sociocultural rationalization process. By 'power' (*Macht*) Weber means 'the probability that one actor within a social relationship will be in a position to carry out his own will despite resistance, regardless of the basis on which this probability rests.'[75] It may rest, for example, on custom or on goal-oriented consideration. The 'probability that a command with a given specific content will be obeyed' Weber calls domination (*Herrschaft*).[76] The concept 'master' indicates a 'leader' whose power to command is not derived from someone placed above him.[77] The concept 'obedience' means as such only that people's conduct conforms to the command regardless of their personal judgment about the behavior commanded, 'as if the ruled had made the content of the command the maxim of their conduct for its very own sake.' Sociology, however, proceeds from the fact that the actual powerholders who issue commands pretend to the superaddition of a normative power of command 'by virtue of law.' In other words, their commands have a 'factual' character and possess legitimacy.[78] Amongst the psychologically determined 'inward' interests that control the rationalization process, this need for legitimacy plays an extremely important role.

With respect to this basis of legitimacy, Weber goes on to distinguish three ideal-typical forms of domination, namely, legal, traditional, and charismatic domination.[79]

The first is found in its most fully developed form in a bureaucracy, the specifically modern way of exercising authority; one commands and another obeys by virtue of belief in impersonal, formal norms; there is a routine delimitation of 'jurisdictions' and a hierarchy of 'higher' and 'lower' channels of appeal (*Instanzenzug*). This form is encountered in a modern capitalistic enterprise, in the state, but also in a hierocratic community like the church. There the pastor or priest has his well-defined competency, which is laid down in formal rules. This is true also for the highest authority in the church; the 'infallibility' of the Pope, for example, is a jurisdictional idea: there is a distinction between the official vocational sphere of competence (definition 'ex cathedra') and the private sphere, precisely as in political and other vocational agencies or enterprises.

Traditional domination is based on piety, on belief in the sacredness of what has been inherited from the past. Here, besides a totality of norms considered absolutely inviolable on pain of magical or religious sanctions, there is also a terrain within which the 'patriarch' (*paterfamilias*, husband, leader of the sib, etc.) can act arbitrarily. Here considerations of personal loyalty or fairness play a predominant role. This terrain is in principle never abstract and formal, and hence it is to that extent always irrational in character.

Charismatic domination exists where authority is based on belief in and submission to a person possessing special qualifications of some sort. Because of his supranormal, supernatural or at least extraordinary competence he is esteemed as a 'leader.' He can be an unopposable warrior hero, a sorcerer, a leader of hunting or looting expeditions, a genial artist, a scientist, or a demagogue. Here authority is not exercised according to rational or traditional norms; instead, it is strictly personal and in this sense always irrational (value-rational or emotional). It is not bound to what exists, and is accordingly always 'revolutionary' in this sense: 'It is written – but I say unto you.'

The purest type of charismatic domination associated with the rationalization process in the sociology of religion is that exercised by the prophets: their revelation always contains the conception of the world as a 'cosmos,' as an in some way or another meaningfully 'organized' whole to which human behavior must be oriented if blessing is to be expected. In keeping with the assumption of an essentially positive stance towards the world, human behavior in all its expressions is intended to be brought into a systematically meaningful unity. The confrontation of the prophetic message with empirical reality can evoke strong tensions both for the prophet and for his disciples.

Weber distinguishes two types of prophets, the exemplary and ethical types, which determine the direction of the rationalization process. The clearest example of the first type is Buddha. It pertains to prophets who, by their example, personally present the way to religious salvation and appeal to others to follow the same way for their own sakes. As the clearest examples of ethical or emissary prophecy Weber names Zoroaster, Mohammed, and the so-called Jewish scriptural prophets. They act in the embassy of a God whose instruments they consider themselves to be. They proclaim a message that expresses the will of God in the form of a concrete imperative or an abundant norm. They require obedience.[80]

The realization of a prophetic message triggers the mechanism Weber calls the 'routinization of charisma' (die Veralltäglichung des Charisma). This is a special case of the general law of value-externalization and the objectification and internalization that accompany it.

In this section I shall in the first place explain the nature and function of this mechanism in a general sociological way. Then, turning to the area of sociology of religion, I shall examine its role in the rationalization of both magic and religion.

A. The 'Routinization' of Charisma[81]

1. Charisma

To obtain insight into the process of 'routinization' of charisma it is first necessary to have a look at charisma itself. A charisma is no purely individual affair. It is not sociologically amorphous; rather, it has a certain structure and arises only in particular situations. Charismatics, Weber says, were once the 'natural' leaders in terms of psychic, physical, economic, ethical, religious, or political exigency:[82]

> Charismatic rulership in the typical sense... always results from unusual, especially political or economic situations, or from extraordinary psychic, particularly religious states, or from both together. It arises from collective excitement produced by extraordinary events and from surrender to heroism of any kind.[83]

The charismatic structure will correspond to this situation of inner or outer need or hope. At the appearance of a charismatic leader, people and things will be 'organized' in a specific way. This does not occur according to any criteria of ends. In other words, there is no question of organization in the technical sense of the term, nor of the force of tradition; rather, a new group arises having mutual personal relations, together with an apparatus of services and goods, that is suited to the mission of the bearer of the charisma. Within this group the personal aides of the charismatic leader comprise a subgroup which likewise has a pattern of personal relations. Moreover, they are recruited on the basis of personal qualifications. They constitute a 'charismatic aristocracy'[84] of faithful disciples. For the group as a whole it can be said that the adherents' 'recognition' of their charismatic leader is not a purely psychological reaction of enthusiasm born of exigency or hope; rather, they experience it as a 'duty,' given the new or the valuable qualities conspicuous in the charismatic leader. He who fails to obey is simply worthy of contempt.

In this basis of legitimation lie the reasons for the revolutionary power of the charismatic structure of domination.[85] A change (*metanoia*) takes place: there is a radical alteration of mentality that finds expression in deeds. In other words, a fundamental reorientation is brought about by an internally strong, coherent group who feel themselves bound to no established institutional order whatsoever. This group, gripped by and subject to the compelling force of the 'mission' (*noch nie Dagewesene*), is even anti-institutional by definition. In pre-rational, tradition-bound times, charisma was the supreme revolutionary force, and virtually all actions could be characterized as traditional or as charismatic actions.

In modern times, too, the rationalization process has become a revolutionary force of the first order. In contrast to charismatic belief, which motivates and revolutionizes 'from within,' the rationalization process is a revolutionary force imposed 'from without.' Namely, in the first place it deals effectively with the external circumstances and problems of life by technical means, and then it goes on to influence man, too, indirectly. It shifts or perhaps enlarges the conditions for his adaptation to the situation. In this sense the modern economic system and the modern bureaucracy are forces that revolutionize 'from without.'

Weber states explicitly in this connection that the contrast between 'from within' and 'from without' must not be understood incorrectly, and that the meaning of 'rationalism' in particular must not be misapprehended. From a psychological standpoint, all 'ideas' arise in precisely the same way, however fundamentally the spheres to which they pertain may differ from each other. Religious, artistic, ethical, scientific, and especially political and social-organizational 'ideas' involve time-bound, subjective value-judgments (*ein 'der Zeit dienendes,' subjektives 'Werten'*). These valuations are attributed to 'understanding' by some and to 'intuition' by others, but that is not where one should seek the difference between the 'from within' and the 'from without.'[86] The mathematical fantasy or 'imagination' of an innovative mathematician, for example, is 'intuition' in precisely the same sense as in the fantasy of the artist, prophet, or demagogue. The distinction lies not at all in the person or psychic experiences of the 'creator' of these ideas but in the way in which a group 'experience and internalize' these ideas.[87]

Now, in a rationalized society the masses appropriate only the technical results of the rationalization process, which are important for practical workaday life. They 'learn' to employ them just as they learn 1 x 1, or as all 'too many' jurists 'learn' the techniques of law. They inevitably find the content of the 'ideas' of the 'creator' of the process irrelevant.[88] In this sense the rationalization process works in a revolutionary way 'from without.' A charismatic group, in contrast, appropriates the ideas of the charismatic leader and is thereby revolutionized 'from within,' to oppose the established order.[89]

2. The institutionalization of charisma

a. The institutionalization process
Structurally, a charismatic movement is extremely unstable. It vanishes if in the long run the charismatic leader is unable to prove himself (if he is forsaken by God or loses his magical, demagogic, or heroic powers, etc.), but especially when his leadership fails to have the desired effect on the group. In that case the movement loses its only source of legitimation, which of course by definition is not based on belief in either official competence or tradition. The effectual force of a charisma always lies ultimately in the belief of the group in the new and intrinsically valuable.

If the movement not only arises but also endures, however, then it undergoes an internal change of structure:

> ... the faith of the leader himself and of his disciples in his charisma – be it of a prophetic or any other kind – is undiminished, consistent and effective only *in statu nascendi*, just as is true of the faithful devotion to him and

137

his mission on the part of those to whom he considers himself sent. When the tide that lifted a charismatically led group out of everyday life flows back into the channels of workaday routines, at least the 'pure' form of charismatic domination will wane and turn into an 'institution' (*ins 'Institutionelle' transponiert*); it is then either mechanized, as it were, or imperceptibly displaced by other structures, or fused with them in the most divine forms, so that it becomes a mere component of a concrete structure. In this case it is often transformed beyond recognition, and identifiable only on an analytical level.[90]

The reason why charisma can exist in pure form only *in statu nascendi*, why it institutionalizes itself, and why it thereby changes in structure is to be found in the last instance in charisma's need to maintain its existence. This need is usually a concern of the leader himself, but it is in any case a concern of his disciples and other adherents. They seek to realize as a permanent possession the charismatic salvation belonging to extraordinary times and persons. Thus the mechanism of 'routinization' comes into play in connection with the objective demands of everyday life. These everyday demands are of an administrative but more especially of an economic nature. Charisma was a specifically anti-economic force. This is not to say that the possession of money and of goods was repudiated. On the contrary, a warrior hero and his band were out precisely for booty, while the prophet and his followers rejected profit and remuneration as a matter of principle. Charisma was antieconomical because it rejected the normal, generally accepted (traditional or rational) occupational provision of needs and all the entanglements that accompany workaday life. People lived instead from occasional incomes, in a caritative monastic communism or a warrior 'spoils' communism featuring communal possessions and consumption.[91] The quest for permanence of course brought with it rising everyday demands for guaranteed and stable incomes. In extreme cases this led as far as the transformation of caritative or war communisms into unrestricted freedom to acquire incomes in the normal manner.

Thus ideal and material interests of the members of the charismatic movement and especially those of the administrative 'personal staff' (an aristocratic inner circle) are responsible for the transformation of the structure of charismatic authority. Weber views these interests as exponents of the force of the factors that remain determinative for the normal course of social life.

The transformation of the charismatic structure may lead either to a traditional or to a rational structure of authority.

138

Naturally, the traditional structure is more likely to appear in a less rationalized environment, increasingly so the more the traditional form of domination resembles the charismatic form; and indeed, their structures are sometimes only distinguishable in 'spirit.' Structurally, for example, the commensality of a patrimonial leader and a charismatic warrior chieftain appear highly comparable, since both cases feature personal bearers of authority and the pious submission of subordinate figures. Both forms of domination also bear religious adherence. The 'spirit' or, in other words, ground on which the domination rests is actually totally different, however, in the two cases. The revolutionary character of charisma is transformed into its opposite and makes way for a Gibralter-like sacred tradition. All who claim a privileged economic or social position now legitimate themselves by appealing to 'a charismatic, and thus sacred, source of authority.'[92] The charisma functions as a legitimating legal basis for 'acquired rights.' While charisma as a creative force thus vanishes via the process of institutionalization, it nevertheless remains a highly important moment in the structure of domination.

Charisma is transformed in an analogous way when the institutionalization results in a rational or legal rather than traditional structure of domination. The charismatic warrior hero with his followers may become a state, for example; a church or sect may grow out of the charismatic movement of a prophet; from the admirers of an artist may arise an academy; from a cultural movement there may grow a party, or an organization with newspapers and periodicals. There appear officers and officials, priests, teachers, party functionaries, editors, publishers, secretaries, etc. The charismatic followers become tax-paying subjects or disciplined soldiers, dues paying members, etc. The charismatic 'spirit' becomes dogma, doctrine or theory, rule or legislation. Once again the forces of everyday life, especially economic interests, are often the most important explanatory factors. In this case, however, the privileged social positions need more emphatically explicit legitimation than they do in a traditional environment.

In a traditional society the position of a head of family or, in a more extended family connection, the position of a patriarch is legitimated self-evidently, by inherited sacred rules. In the broader social connection there arises in this way a 'cosmos' of self-evident, acquired rights, which legitimate and sanctify the actual power relations of the politically, socially, or economically privileged strata. For the same reason, charisma as a legitimating function continues to play an important role even in modern times. Thus the maintenance of inherited monarchies, for example, is in large measure dictated by the thought that all inherited positions would be shattered if the sanctity of the throne should vanish. It is accordingly also no accident that this view has more appeal to the propertied class than to the proletariat.

Legitimation in rationalized social systems reveals the most fundamental transformation of charisma. Here the legitimation of the highest powerholder is crucial, and charisma is totally transformed. In a pure ideal-typical form of bureaucracy with appointed officials whose only function is to carry out orders received from a superior, there must be 'an authority (*Instanz*) which has not been appointed in the same fashion as other officials.' 'Even the head of a bureaucracy might conceivably be a high official who moves into his position according to general rules.' However, as it turns out, 'this is usually not the case,' for such an official 'is not selected according to the same norms as the officials in the hierarchy below him.'[93]

b. The problem of the succession of the charismatic leader and its importance for the institutionalization process

The question of finding a successor for the charismatic leader has always been a problem for every charismatic movement. The question goes to the core of charisma, namely, the person of the charismatic himself and of his legitimation. The way in which this problem is resolved is naturally of great consequence for the process of institutionalization, which usually has its inception at that point.[94]

The most obvious and prevalent form of bestowing the function of a new leader was through belief in the transferability of charisma through blood ties. Charisma was thereby made an inheritable 'something,' and thus routinized. This approach lies at the basis of the development of royal and aristocratic power. Here the meaning of charisma is transformed into its very opposite. Whereas personal courage was what ennobled originally, legitimacy now derived from noble birth or the deeds of one's forefathers. This development followed the same pattern everywhere. The typical American (Puritan) mentality originally esteemed the 'self-made man' who had created his own wealth, while the heir, in contrast, did not count. This mentality is transformed into its exact opposite 'before our very eyes.' Now one enjoys social prestige by virtue of birth or of membership in an established family with relatively 'old' wealth.

A second way of accrediting a new leadership figure is to regard

140

charisma as personally acquirable (*persönlich erwerbbar*).[95] Weber means by that that the new charismatic leader is appointed not automatically, by birth, but by artificial, technical means, such as oracles, divine judgments (for example, duels), lots, selection, and the like. Here there appears a kind of routinization in which the ascertainment of the correct successor is made according to (traditional or rational) rules. This person is subsequently confirmed in a definitive and inevitably winning way. The 'manipulations' at the consecration of a bishop or priest and the anointment or coronation of a king derive from the more simple 'techniques' mentioned above.[96] Moreover, they reveal clearly the transition to the third, most routinized manner of indicating a leader.

The 'manipulations' at issue become formalities at a given point. The accent in that case falls upon the office acquired by anointment or the laying of hands on the head. Here charisma acquires a typically 'institutional' character: the office and the social structure as such gain sanctity. The office as such becomes the source of legitimation. Again, there is a reversal of charisma into its exact opposite. Thus the authority of the pope, bishops, and priests in the Catholic church is legitimated and derived from the sanctity of the church as the bearer of all grace. The charismatic office stands entirely apart from personal capacities. Theologically, the priestly office is based upon a *character indelebilis*, an ineradicable quality fully distinct from the personal worthiness of the priest as a private person. 'The charisma of office – the belief in the specific state of grace of a social institution – is by no means limited to the churches and even less to primitive conditions. Under modern conditions, too, it finds politically relevant expression in the attitudes of the subjects to the state.'[97] Any talk of charisma under these circumstances is justified only by the fact that not everyone is admitted to such an office. From the vantage point of the subjects it appears to be something extraordinary, exalted, and different in principle from their own personal qualities. On the other hand, however, it has meanwhile become an office or capacity that can be prepared for through a rational system of education, although charisma can only be 'awakened' and 'tested,' not 'taught.'[98]

Finally, conferment of the function of the new leader can occur in a way whereby the meaning of charisma is so fundamentally altered that the idea of domination vanishes completely. That being the case, Weber deals with this approach not in his exposition of the routinization of charisma but in his introduction to democracy.[99] The earlier charismatic leadership function is here converted into a 'business.'[100] The demands made upon it are different from those made on subjects, true; but every trace and remembrance of religious devotion is missing. The leadership position is now regarded only as 'functionally necessary,' and the attitude of subjects towards the leader is now purely 'naturalistic and rational' (*a naturalistisch rationale innere Haltung und innere Stellingnahme*).[101] Here we have the ideal-type of 'legal domination' that one encounters in more or less pure form in a modern bureaucratic state or factory. The authority is in that case just a component of a 'mechanism' made by and for people, which leads Weber to say charisma 'is often transformed beyond recognition, and identifiable only on an analytical level,'[102] all thought of actual domination having disappeared. 'The personally legitimated charismatic leader becomes leader by the grace of those who follow him...'[103] Thus some link to the charisma remains, because the notion of legitimation remains: 'The basically authoritarian principle of charismatic legitimation may be subject to an anti-authoritarian interpretation.'[104] Charisma still functions, but only as a source of legitimation. 'In this function, which is alien to its essence, charisma becomes a part of everyday life,' and in doing so, satisfies 'universal needs.'[105]

This last transformation of the meaning of charisma naturally accompanies the increasing rationalization of social relations. For example, if the political system is viewed as man-made, obviously the thought will arise that the citizens can appoint or remove the leader of that system of their own free choice. Hence the leader has no authority by virtue of his personal qualities, as a charismatic leader does; he has authority, rather, solely by virtue of his selection. His legitimacy is thus not a consequence of recognition of a natural leadership which people would have to obey. *Formally* free acclamation by the people is the basis of his legitimacy. Weber accordingly speaks of 'democratic legitimacy.' The psychological pressure felt in recognizing a true charismatic does not exist here, where there is no longer 'only one correct decision' to be arrived at as a duty. The 'nimbus' of sanctity disappears completely in the ideal-type of leadership here at issue.[106]

At first glance there could be mention here too – even outstandingly so, it might appear – of charismatic leadership. For example, 'every modern conduct of war weighs – precisely the morale factor in troop effectiveness' (*die 'moralischen' Elemente der Leistungsfähigkeit der Truppe*). The troops are taught, by every conceivable emotional means, to be obedient to the military leadership, in order to enhance their capacity and will to achieve a given end. The great difference from charismatic leadership in the authentic sense, sociologically speaking, is that these irrational 'imponderable' factors are 'calculated' in a rational way that in principle differs not at all from the rational exploitation of a coal mine; even the case of 'personally tinged devotion' to a 'fascinating leader' (*Führer*) is somewhat 'routine,' involving as it does devotion to a common 'cause' aimed at achieving results in a rational way.[107] This is especially clear in the business world, where rationalization has attained its most formidable triumphs in the American system of 'scientific management.'[108] There is no element of devotion to a person as such. A uniformly habituated, disciplined and thus 'uncritical and unresisting mass'[109] can be brought to bear on a routine objective, and hence also on whatever objective the leader commands. It needs finally to be emphasized again that in social reality these ideal types never occur as such. Thus a church with its institutionalized charisma of office may be found to make use of emotional means, as in the case of 'the most sophisticated techniques of religious discipline, the *exercitia spiritualis* of Ignatius Loyola.'[110] Meanwhile, in a parliamentary state numerous positions – and most certainly the highest: *Le roi règne mais il ne gouverne pas* ('the king reigns but he does not interfere in government')[111] – are charismatically legitimated as acquired sacred rights.

c. Institutionalization and conflict

Usually, the institutionalization of charisma began with the problem of finding a successor for the charismatic leader. The nature of the solution was determined in part by the course of the process. Naturally, this process was often accompanied by conflicts – a point that we now need briefly to examine. By 'conflict' (*Kampf*) Weber means a social relationship 'insofar as action is oriented intentionally to carrying out the actor's own will against the resistance of the other party or parties.'[112] This conflict can be carried on by peaceful means (that is, without physical violence), whereupon it is called 'competition': 'a formally peaceful attempt to attain control over opportunities and advantages which are also desired by others.' Such competition can be institutionalized; in which case Weber speaks of "regularized' competition to the extent that its ends and means are oriented to an order.'[113] Examples would be a modern market or a modern election campaign. Finally, there can also be mention of conflict between people that is neither intentional nor even conscious but whereby the advantages for participation in social intercourse are divided unequally. However, in this

143

case Weber prefers to speak not of 'conflict' but of 'social selection.'[114]

All the above-mentioned forms of conflict result in 'social selection.' What criteria control this selection depends not only on personal characteristics (physical strength, slyness, intelligence, or education) but more especially on the institutionalized order providing the pertinent frame of reference. The criteria vary with the requirements of the position at stake, such as husband, official, contractor, or managing director. In this last sense of 'social selection,' from an empirical standpoint, conflict is a structural element of all social relations. 'It is only in the sense of 'selection' that it seems, according to our experience, that conflict is empirically inevitable... Selection is inevitable because apparently no way can be worked out of eliminating it completely.'[115]

The above applies not only to individual actors but also to structures, in an analogous way. These, too, can be consciously bent or destroyed through conflicts (for example, a domestic revolution or the annihilation of a state through war). They can also be repressed by other institutional frameworks as an unintended and even unnoticed secondary effect. Hence in Weber's view one may speak of 'social selection' only if one keeps in mind that structures are not in themselves independent entities and that it is always necessary to inquire further to get to the bottom of their disappearance or transformation. Very often the reasons will be found to be of a purely historical-accidental nature, allowing one to conclude directly that 'unfitness' produced the result in question and that the 'strongest,' or in other words fittest, structures would always survive.[116]

That conflicts often arise precisely with respect to the problem of finding a successor follows from the fact that charisma is then often routinized and detached from the person of the charismatic leader. Certainly, in the opening phase of 'routinization' people are mindful of the high demands that must be made of the successor. The conflict between official or hereditary and personal charisma is thus an ever-recurring phenomenon in history, too.

Hereditary succession[117] often reveals a conflict between the sons of the previous leader or, in their absence, between other pretenders. One encounters this amongst primitive peoples, but also in the Middle Ages and in modern times. The fortuitous dying out of the German Carolingians and of the royal lines that succeeded them 'just when hereditary charisma might have become strong enough to prevail over the electoral claims of the [feudal] princes, has been highly significant for the decline of royal power in Germany,' in contrast to the strengthening of royal power in France and England.[118]

Personal charismatic succession[119] often involves the use of technical means as a touchstone whereby the new charismatic leader must prove his qualities. Among these means are divine judgment by duelling, and magical or oracular techniques. Yet the matter in such cases is never one of election by the majority. It is rather one of making the right choice. There can be only one right choice, and it is just as possible for a minority to be right as it is for an overwhelming majority to be wrong. Conflict is ever likely.

The problem of the right choice also plays a role in the third form of succession, which is based on belief in the transferability of office, or office charisma.[120] All norms for the choice of a pope, for example, are aimed at achieving unanimity. The election of two popes or charismatic kings corresponds to a church schism or political revolution.

Succession conflicts are common in modern rational systems as well. In a state and in labor unions the revolt of charismatic leaders against official powerholders is not uncommon. 'The more highly developed the interdependence of different economic units in a monetary economy' becomes; the greater the numbers of people that are involved; the more pressing the need is for stability in everyday life, the greater will be the tendency towards 'routinization' and the less room there will be for charisma. Charisma is typical of the early stages of the exercise of power, although the assertion may not be reversed to say that every new process of institutionalization must have a charismatic inception.[121]

3. 'Routinization' as a dialectical process

From what has now been said it is clear that the 'routinization of charisma' is a dialectical process.

At the beginning of this process of institutionalization there stands a weakly structured but authentic group with strong social cohesion and a certain collective consciousness. This group spirit arises via a process of identification with the group's leader, who represents some value. Here one could speak of a combination between a psychic group and a social group, since the interaction between the members is based both on mutual feelings and a common goal. Because of the latter of these factors, the group is also hierarchically stratified, and it consists of a leader, an inner circle, and more peripheral adherents. Because the group desires to realize an ideal,

145

it must necessarily be made permanent, that is, 'objectivated,'[122] at the inception of the process of institutionalization. This collective self-objectivation takes place at all levels of the initially weak structure and hence pertains to the adherents, the inner circle, and the leader. Meanwhile, the culture of the group is transformed in the process, so that at the end of the process it is often the exact opposite of what was originally intended. The members of the group may be more or less profoundly transformed, without consciously desiring or even being aware of the fact. Weber alludes, for example, to how Puritanism 'unintentionally' led to 'a *civic* and *methodical* way of life...* This strange reversion of the 'natural', which is strange only at a first, superficial glance, instructs us in the paradox of unintended consequences: i.e., the relation of man and fate, of what he intended by his acts and what actually became of them.'[123]

Now, in the first place, this confirms the correctness of my position, presented in the first section of this chapter, concerning the dialectical character of rationalization. The collective consciousness; the normative socio-cultural order which assumes of itself a quasi-independent position vis-à-vis the members; and its internalization are elements of the 'routinization,' or in other words, of the process of institutionalization. These elements are not detached from each other but necessarily evoke and oppose each other. In this formal sense the dialectical process is actually inherent in every socio-cultural event. It is necessarily present in every form of human society.

In the second place, the mechanism of 'routinization' as the substantive concretization of this – in the formal sense – ever present dialectical process, is at the same time something more than a mere confirmation of my original position. As an empirically observable, historico-social event the institutionalization likewise occurs dialectically, but now in a less singular sense requiring a more complex description. The substantive aspect raises the question of the pertinent dialectic in a more concrete way, revealing, for example, the diversity of meaning of the concept of rationalization. The unbreakable coherence between collective consciousness, socio-cultural order, and internalization leads necessarily to institutionalization, to be sure, but this does not actually take place according to a concretely predictable pattern of continuity or discontinuity. The ever recurring dialectical pattern of radical reversal (*Umschlag*) of charisma into its opposite, as we observed it in hereditary, personally transferable and office charismas alike, and, finally, as in the reversal of charisma into a rational-routine leadership, *can*, indeed, occur in exactly the way described, but this is never empirically verifiable except in retrospect. The radical reversal is an ideal-typical construction of the qualitative transformation of meaning that takes place in the process of institutionalization. The shifting of meaning can in principle occur, however, in an infinite variety of ways. Concrete situational factors, the interests and power of the pertinent mutually involved social positions, always require examination. Conflicts in the strict sense may perhaps not be necessary in a given theoretical model, but empirically speaking, there has never been a society in which conflicts did not occur in some form or another:

> Even the most strictly pacific order can eliminate means of conflict and the objects of and impulses to conflict only partially. Other modes of conflict would come to the fore, possibly in processes of open competition. But even on the utopian assumption that all competition were completely eliminated, conditions would still lead to a latent process of selection, biological or social, which would favor the types best adapted to the conditions, whether their relevant qualities were mainly determined by heredity or environment.[124]

In summary, it can be stated that the dialectic in this second sense of the term furnishes a model for the analysis of concrete empirical phenomena. It shows which externalizations of value are objectivated and how this happens.[125] I shall now examine the matter as it pertains to the rationalization processes of magic and religion.

B. The Rationalization of Magic as a Socio-Cultural Process[126]

If the magical charisma of a person, animal, or thing is not terminated at some point by the failure of its extraordinary power in crisis situations, then magical actions can be institutionalized and rationalized. I have already discussed how the rationalization process takes place as a cultural process. There arises in that case a mythological cosmos that leads to a supremely practical rationalism with rules of behavior directly oriented to acquiring things important to everyday life. Violations of this magical ethic are sanctioned by a pattern of taboos, which immediately bring about evil consequences. They stereotype everyday life and block virtually every renewal. From a socio-cultural standpoint, this rationalization process takes place dialectically in reality. This is evident from a closer examination of the social positions relevant to the course of the process, together with their 'inward and outward interests.'

The first to be considered is the position of the 'sorcerer.' The sorcerer is someone who is permanently qualified charismatically, in contrast to the 'layman,' in the magical sense of that term. The fact that the charisma – in this case mainly ecstasy – is not accessible to everybody comprises the basis of the possibility of the rise of 'the professional necromancer.' The sorcerer is the oldest practitioner of a religious vocation. A layman can achieve ecstasy only occasionally. He requires all manner of means to do so, such as alcohol, tobacco, or similar narcotics, besides music, dance, and so forth. The social form in which this happens is the orgy, the 'primordial form of religious association.'[127] This 'occasional association' contrasts sharply to the rational 'enterprise' of the wizard, which is a permanent form of teleological activity or, in other words, a 'continuous rational activity of a specified kind'[128] that institutionalizes itself within a society. The task of the magician's enterprise is mainly to influence the 'spirits' rationally on behalf of the clientage. Moreover, it is the 'initiated' sorcerers who must teach the laity how to celebrate orgies. Now, in interaction with their actual practice, the sorcerers rationalize magic, making a mythology of it in the theoretical respect and a magical ethics of it in the practical respect.

Whether they succeed or not depends mainly on the power position and on the strength of the organization they have been able to construct within a social group. This depends in turn upon the secular powerholders who may or may not protect their practice, but more especially on the needs of the laity. In general the masses have a strong need for certitude in the coercion of suprasensual forces. This is produced by means of palpable and immediate magical techniques and by the exact formulation of magical rituals of proven efficacy. Agricultural folk in particular have a need for magic. The peasant's entire life is heavily dependent on natural forces. Sorcery as the means of coercing the spirits controlling these natural forces seemed the obvious solution. Coercion could be by magic ritual or by simply purchasing divine favor according to the *do et des* pattern (although the latter is no longer purely magic from a conceptual standpoint).[129]

Thus the central point in the rationalization process of magic is the power position of the sorcerer's enterprise, whereby a magical-rational world picture can be constructed. This in itself unstable suprasensual realm of souls, spirits, and demons is able to continue to exercise real influence on everyday life by virtue of this power position. It is a dialectical process in which the power of the sorcerers, the power of the secular authorities, and the needs of the laity are the leading, mutually influential forces.

C. The Rationalization of Religion as a Socio-Cultural Process

Rationalization of religion, culturally speaking, means the disenchantment of the world picture in favor of a meaningful 'cosmos.' Thus various types of 'rational theodicy' can arise.

In the process, magical ritual and magical ethics were in principle replaced by a religious cult and an ethic that led to a consistent pattern of religious conduct, to a systematic-rational striving for salvation consistent with the postulate of a theoretically meaningful cosmos. Magical activity was thereby rendered irrational. Practical-calculating rationalism based on stereotyped and magically tabooed rules of conduct vanished. The original magical unity of the experience of the world gave way to conflicts with the realities of the 'world' (world flight, rejection of the world, transformation of the world), which was now disenchanted in the practical as well as in the theoretical sense.

The actual course of this process of rationalization as Weber presents it again turns out to be a dialectical movement. Three factors play an important role in determining whether the three conflicts will all work in the same direction, or impede or compete with each other, or remain latent or break into the open. The process of rationalization will follow a different course depending on the nature and strength of these factors, their mutual interaction, or the absence of one of them. The pertinent 'factors' are again social positions, and more specifically the revolutionary force of the prophets, the power and interests of the priesthood, and the needs and interests of a lay congregation upon which prophets and priests would like to exercise some influence but the influence of which they undergo themselves in the meantime.

1. Priests, prophets, and rationalization[130]

In normal situations the priests are the most important bearers of the process of rationalization. Sociologically, they are the reverse of the sorcerers and the mainspring of the transition from magic to religion. They can be characterized as a particular group of persons whose vocation consists in attending regularly to the service of certain ethical deities (functional gods, local gods, or a monotheistic God) on behalf of a religious congregation.[131] Both the priesthood and the congregation may have developed gradually from the sorcerer's enterprise, but usually they are the result of the 'routinization' mechanism of a prophetic movement of either the ethical or the exemplary type. This is the case, certainly, when they are the bearers of a religious rationalization process. In contrast to the prophets, whose inward-ethical rationalization is meant mainly to engender a consistent pattern of conduct consciously opposed to the world in terms of some adopted value, the priests are mainly interested in hammering their (old or new) doctrine into a systematic-rational whole of a scientific or practical-ethical character. The difference between prophetic and priestly systematics is obvious from the fact (among others) that the sacred writings containing the revelation are now 'canonized' – which expresses the awareness that the prophetic revelatory strife is now definitely a matter of the past. Moreover, it is a priestly task to formulate dogmas that interpret the meaning of the canonical books authentically. In a casuistic, rational way the old doctrine and ethics are accommodated to the habits of life and thought of the priests themselves and the laity whom they guide, and defended against attack. More thorough-going systematic rationalization of orthodox doctrine and practice is induced especially by the competition of groups with ideas and ways which are different from those of the priests' own congregation. The concern for orthodox doctrine leads to a proliferation of dogmas; the concern for orthodox practice leads to the development of a rational method of salvation.

The difference between priestly and prophetic rationalization is closely related to the fact that priests always have ties to a congregation.

By religious 'congregation' (*Gemeinde*) and 'congregational' religiosity Weber means the phenomenon of the laity's being institutionalized into a religious group and actively involved in some way in the religious enterprise.[132] The formation of the congregation is of great importance for the priests because it is essential to the security of their ideal and material interests. And it is important sociologically because it is only within a congregation that there can be any thought of real influence by the laity on the process of rationalization. It is through their relation to a congregation that priests differ from sorcerers and prophets. Sorcerers are (sometimes organized) practitioners of a free profession that they carry on for the sake of a clientage that are not mutually united in a specific religious congregation. They serve a particular region or a particular political community. Prophets too are not directly oriented to group formation. They attempt rather to influence the conduct of everyone, by their word or example. The formation of a congregation occurs only when sorcerers become priests and attempt to influence people on behalf of their office, or when an ethical or exemplary prophecy is institutionalized and a permanent priestly enterprise arises. The fully open community around a sorcerer or prophet becomes a more or less closed religious congregation. The traces of its origin, however, remain evident as a rule.

A priesthood deriving from ethical prophecy is oriented more towards the delimitation of dogmas in confrontation with competing systems of doctrine, while in keeping with the nature of exemplary prophecy the emphasis of priests in that line tends to be on more practical-ethical matters or on ritual concerns. The congregational community is looser because the individual salvation event is more conspicuous. In that case the exemplary prophet also often tends to become a mystagogue in the second generation: a servant of sacraments, someone who performs magical activities as a guarantee of the benefits of salvation. Only gradually do mystagogues become differentiated from sorcerers. The difference is that the former gather a group around themselves and share with them the benefits of salvation and derive from them their own economic subsistence. As in the case of sorcerers, here too there can be a strongly developed rational secret lore, but this magical knowledge and craft are of secondary importance at most for the laity.

The typical priestly rationalization is meant for the laity in principle and, in contrast to that of the sorcerers, it is permanently nurtured by their professional practice. In contrast to magical help in distress, one accordingly finds within congregational religiosity preaching and pastoral care as typical, new rational instruments for influencing the masses.

Preaching is 'specific to prophecy;... and the importance of preaching stands in inverse proportion to the magical components of a religion.'[133] Its influence on the laity is especially great in times of 'prophetic excitement,' and it declines proportionately as the prophetic movement is transformed, via institutionalization, into a priestly enterprise. The simple fact that the charisma of preaching is bound to an individual can lead to the decline of its influence to zero, given increasing 'routinization.'

Pastoral care, 'the religious cultivation of the individual,' is the typical means of priestly power. Its influence parallels the ethical character of a religion and the growth of the power of the priests over the masses. The pastor of souls is asked for advice in all manner of situations, by private persons and official functionaries alike. Jewish rabbis, Catholic father-confessors, Pietist pastors, Reformed spiritual leaders, Brahmanic *purohitas* at the courts, Hindu *gurus*, and Islamic *muftis* and sheiks have influenced the everyday lives of the laity and the attitudes of the powerholders in a permanent and often decisive way.

Preaching and pastoral care are the most important, permanently operating factors to have influenced the casuistic systematization of religious truths and commandments. Time and again they forced the priests to solve problems not dealt with as such in the revelation. Hence priestly rationalization is more rational than prophetic rationalization in the sense of constructing a casuistic systematics, but it is less rational in the sense of a clear deduction of an ethical 'must' from a 'distinctive 'meaningful' relationship to one's God.'[134] Rather than being concerned about the external forms of particular actions, the prophet cares more about their inward significance in a total relationship of man to the divine.

The source of the material of conflict between prophets and priests lies in this difference in rationalization, as well as in the resistance of the prophets to every form of magic (for Buddha, knowledge of the Vedas and the ritual was of no significance for salvation; and the God of Israelite prophecy required not sacrifices but obedience). Here prophetic charisma stands juxtaposed to the technicians of the everyday cult; the sacredness of a new revelation stands diametrically opposed to the sacredness of tradition. Consistent with the results of the clash of the two forms of demagoguery, the priesthood compromises with the new prophecy, adopts the new teaching or surpasses it in casuistic systematic rationality, hounds it to death and makes a martyr of the prophet, or is hounded to death itself.

2. The lay congregation and rationalization

The priestly rationalization of religion is not influenced exclusively by prophetic rationality, as the preceding discussion will have made clear. The lay congregation – the source, for that matter, of prophets and their adherents – is at least as influential a factor. That is true not only with respect to folk traditionalism but also with respect to lay rationalism, which, historically speaking, usually originated in priestly circles.

Lay traditionalism influenced the systematizing work of the priesthood in exactly the opposite direction as prophecy did. The more intensively the priest attempted to influence the people and the more economically dependent upon them the priests were, the more this was so, for in such cases the priests had to take the people's needs more into account. The tremendous variety encountered here can be reduced to two types, that is, to magic and the need for a personal savior.

Pervasive popular devotion to magic lent the priestly cult in ever greater measure the character of magical-sacramental coercion of the gods.

The second type of need led to countless incarnations of gods and goddesses or to prophets becoming apotheosized saviors. An inward, devout, and edifying relationship to these savior figures was in such cases a prerequisite to religious salvation. Thus Buddhism had Bodhisattvas who would consciously forego their personal salvation and not enter *Nirvana* in order to save their fellow men.[135] In Hinduism the gods Shiva and Vishnu with their countless incarnations were worshipped, and there were apotheosized gurus and the like. Confucianism has the Taoist pantheon. Islam and Catholicism have their countless saints of specific places, for specific needs, or for particular vocations. It is to them that the real devotion of people goes.

Lay rationalism is likewise a factor that influences priestly rationalism. This rationalism varies greatly from one social stratum to another.[136] A warrior nobility and feudal powers are not very receptive to a rational religious ethic. Concepts such as 'sin,' 'salvation,' and religious 'humility' conflict with their sense of personal dignity. To believe in divine providence does not suit them, accustomed as they are to facing death and the irrationalities of fate courageously. Yet in periods of strong prophetic or reformist religious tumult the nobility in particular have often been swept along by the new movement, because the entire social order is shaken and the nobility are generally the first bearers of lay education.[137] With the 'routinization' of the prophetic religiosity, the nobility quickly vanish again from the circle of the religiously enthusiastic.

The sober, routine rationalism of the world of bureaucratic officials with its ideal of order and rest and its deep-seated contempt for all irrational religiosity is by nature even less congenial to the typical religious rationalization of the priests. Bureaucratic rationalism values religion mainly as a means of 'domestication' to keep the masses under control.

The middle classes 'evince striking contrasts'[138] and are hence the most atypical stratum insofar as their affinity to religious systems is concerned. This is not a result only of the strongly heterogeneous composition of these classes. There are, after all, 'merchants' who belong to the most privileged social strata, and there are 'peddlers' who have nothing and are pariahs. In between, there are strata that possess real economic power but negative social prestige. In general, it can be said that the more privileged the bourgeoisie are, the less disposed they appear to be to accept a salvation religion. However, in the case of the 'real 'middle' strata'[139] and especially of the less privileged bourgeoisie, the atypical character increases: here pure magic may be found side by side with the religiosity of the ascetic sect.

Yet exactly here it is possible to speak of a typical affinity. This stratum is particularly accessible both to congregational religiosity and rational ethical religiosity as compared to the peasantry. Many reasons may be adduced for this.

This stratum is less dependent on unpredictable natural forces, and its economic existence is more subject to rational influence. Predictability and goal-oriented considerations play an important role in trade and craft activities. Specialized craftsmanship leads to a rational way of life. However much every such specialized 'art'[140] may once have been taken as a manifestation of magical charisma, and whatever the extent to which technology may have been magically stereotyped, the petty-bourgeoisie show a strong affinity to prophetic or priestly rationality as a consequence of their specialized artisanry.

They are also sensitive to justice, in the sense that faithful labor 'deserves' its reward; hence they are open to an ethic of compensation.

The merchant and artisan also have more time for reflection during their work, and upon their work, than a peasant has.[141]

Added to all this is the fact that in general the non-privileged strata derive their social prestige not from their 'being' but from their 'mission.' The most highly privileged can gain their sense of dignity from a 'being' that does not transcend their situation. They need religion at most only to legitimate their privileged social position. The lowest classes, however, must find their sense of self-esteem in something that remains to be done, in a 'function, mission, or vocation,' in a better future here or in the hereafter.[142]

Finally, the intellectual strata are the most congenial to the phenomena of rationalization. This is the case, namely, when, whether voluntarily or not, they are isolated from military and political responsibilities and their existence, in the economic sense, is assured. Their rationalization can be skeptical of religion, but it can also follow the same course as religious rationalization, especially as regards the question of a meaningfully ordered cosmos and the need for emancipation from inward distress through mystical enlightenment. It is to this layer, then, that the monks and priests themselves often belong. 'Proletaroid [quasi-proletarian] intellectualism,' too, can be mentioned as being pertinent to religious rationalization, although it operates in a more prophetic direction than the better established priestly intellectualism.[143] It involves autodidacts from the lower classes and people who have perhaps enjoyed a secondary education but who, economically speaking, live on the periphery of the established order. They are congenial to religious and ethical enthusiasm and open to a new and original stance towards the 'meaning' of the cosmos.

This sketch of the field of forces within the religious community concretizes in some measure the social factors which, in mutual coherence with it, definitively influence the dialectics of the process of the rationalization of religion.[144]

CHAPTER FIVE

MODERN WESTERN RATIONALITY AND RELIGION

Max Weber's sociology of religion seeks to illuminate and explain the origins of the specific character of modern Western rationality. Having shown in this connection that Protestant ethical rationality was already closely related to the capitalist ethos and that it was, indeed, one of the factors causing it[1], he went on to examine other forms of religious rationality. In doing so he sought both to refine and explain this causal coherence with greater nuance and to clarify the typical nature of Western rationality through comparison.[2]

In this chapter I want to look into both these aspects – the genesis and nature of Western rationality – in a concrete historical way without, however, 'lapsing' into the role of a historian.

To this end I shall in this first section compare and contrast the various forms of religious rationality and explore the sociological basis for explaining these points of difference. Hence this section includes both a rounding off of chapter 3, which dealt with the various forms of rationalism as structure, and a more exact concretization of chapter 4, which examined rationalization as process.[3]

In a second section I shall look more closely at the question of whether religion plays a role, and if so, what role, in today's rationalized society.

I. Comparison of the Various Forms of Religious Rationality

In this section I shall first examine the various forms of religious rationalism. Then I shall deal with the sociological genesis of each in turn. Finally, I shall describe the sociological genesis of capitalistic rationalism.

A. The Various Forms of Religious Rationalism

The best way to compare the various forms of religious rationalism is to design a chart showing clearly the basic religious attitude each form takes both towards magic (which it rejects) and towards the world. Such a presentation meets the criteria for determining the level of rationality of a religion.[4] The religious attitude towards the world is expressed in the world picture, which establishes, or helps to establish, what it is people want to be saved 'from' and saved 'to' and which thereby orients social behavior. This orientation can be rationalized in various directions, depending on the world picture involved. In going on to examine the matter from case to case, I shall make abstractions from the corresponding world picture as required.

Weber characterized these directions with the help of two ideal types, which can be viewed as variables; that is, asceticism versus passive mysticism, and inner-worldly or intramundane as opposed to other-worldly.[5]

Now, it is possible to represent the differing orientations of the rationality of religious conduct as points on a geometric graph, the abscissa of which indicates the degree of other-worldly or inner-worldly character of the pertinent religious orientation, and the ordinate the measure in which that religious orientation follows a more mystical or more ascetic direction. Magic is located at the intersection of the axes.[6]

At the extreme corners of the system of coordinates are located ancient Buddhism, Western monasticism, and ascetic Protestantism. They alone have both totally rejected magic and rationalized conduct to a consistent pattern. Buddhist and Western monks accomplished this by withdrawing entirely from the world. Buddhists fled the world in order to quench the 'thirst for life' as consistently as possible, thereby attaining mystical emptiness. Western monks rejected all worldly encumbrances in order to subdue the 'flesh' and enter fully into the service of their salvation. The Catholic system of sacraments, which was a magical means of salvation in the eyes of the Catholic laity and which therefore had the effect of atomizing the pattern of life, had no magical character whatsoever in the experiential world of the monk. To him, the ethic of inwardness and strict self-control was all-important, and the sacramental means of salvation served to edify this religious personality. Magical lore and ritual had no saving importance at all for the Buddhist monk, for

157

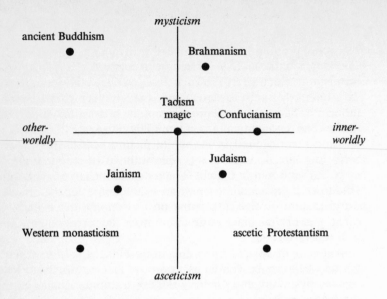

whom all that counted was the practical, systematic death of all desire for personality in the Western sense. The Protestant burgher rejected every form of magic, just like the Oriental and Occidental monks. In contrast to the Catholic recluse, however, he was never satisfied with self-control but considered it part of his vocation to intervene actively in the world around him in order to subdue it in a systematic, professional way. In doing so, he found the assurance of his election.

The only other religion that rejected magic and sacramental means of salvation in principle was Judaism. Yet neither the Israelitic Levite or prophet nor the Jewish rabbi or urban burgher withdrew from the world. Even less did they arrive at a consistent ascetic relationship to the world. Surrender in trust to Yahweh and obedience to his commandments were at the center. Their rationalism consisted more of a methodical, systematic studying and keeping of the law (in a more casuistic-rational than inward-ethical sense of the word). Asceticism and mysticism were, at times, secondary effects of this principal concern. The commandments pertained largely to active engagement in the world, which was positively esteemed in principle, without yet being considered the best place to work out one's salvation. On the geometric graph, the Jewish attitude (be it that of ancient or diaspora Judaism) must therefore have a clearly

158

inner-worldly abscissa with a less far-reaching ascetic ordinate.

Even more pronounced in its inner-worldly character was the attitude of the Confucian civil servant, who believed in a radical world optimism in which wealth as such had positive value for salvation. The supreme virtue was pious submission to all higher bearers of authority. The rationalism of the Confucian consisted in his consciously and systematically perfecting his personality in all its aspects and adapting himself harmoniously to the established order in society and the cosmos. Yet this open-minded attitude towards the world was anchored in magic. Hence the Confucian knew nothing of an inward systematic orientation of life, either in the direction of mysticism or in that of asceticism. Every need for salvation was absent, and his 'religious' basic orientation was simply opportunistic. It was in no respect at all a methodical whole set under a transcendent goal. Graphically, Confucianism must therefore be placed in a decidedly inner-worldly position. It does not qualify for the final, consistent degree of inner-worldliness in its rationality of conduct, however, because it accepts magic as self-evident even though it does not cultivate it and may despise it. The popular Taoism of the Chinese obviously leads to a religious habitus that focusses life in its totality on a transcendent goal in the case neither of its priests, who are trained in magic and divination, nor of the masses, who employ their services. Given its supremely practical rationalism, I identify Taoism graphically with magic.

In contrast, the privileged and intellectually trained Brahman priests rationalized magical salvation to a permanent religious orientation in the directions of asceticism and mysticism. To them, asceticism as a systematically rationalized way of life was a means of concentrating on the authentic property of salvation that could issue, via the individual, salvation-bestowing magical gnosis, in a mystical union with the divine. The Brahmans and their clientage remained as a rule within the established world order, to which they meekly adapted themselves, living incognito, as it were. Magic ritual and the practice of a profession, however, were for them ultimately merely means to a salvation that lay behind the established inner-worldly order. Brahmanism must accordingly be given an inner-worldly position on the geometric graph, provided it be kept in mind that from a subjective standpoint, it can hardly be said to belong there.[7] On the other side it clearly takes the mystical direction.

The basic religious orientation of Jainism does not lead to an inwardly closed and consistently rationalized pattern of conduct. Not only is this prevented, as in Brahmanism, by magical elements – here the rationalization actually takes two mutually contradictory directions. The highest salvation benefit was only attainable via meditation, but active asceticism in its most radical form of methodical world rejection was held in at least equal esteem as a way of salvation. The localization of Jainism at a single point on the geometric graph is therefore even more hazardous than comparable placement of the other religious attitudes. Because Jainists knew a higher degree of asceticism than was familiar in other Indian circles, and especially because Jainists viewed this as their distinguishing characteristic in contrast to what they regarded as 'worldly' Buddhists, I have assigned them to the ascetic ordinate. World-rejecting professional monks, together with lay members remaining in the world though in a cloistered way, must be regarded as other-worldly.[8]

Only ascetic Protestantism, together with capitalism, to which it reveals an inward affinity, can be characterized as typical Western rationality. This rationalism alone implies systematic domination of the world. All other forms of rationalism are by comparison 'traditionalistic,' because in principle they tolerate the world for what it is.

B. *The Sociological Genesis of the Various Forms of Religious Rationalism*

I shall go on now to discuss rather concretely how religious rationalism is always the dialectical result of power positions which have managed to uphold their ideal and material interests in the face of competing positions.

1. The rationalism of the Chinese mandarins

The mandarins, the leading 'intelligentsia' who gave the Chinese pattern of culture its typical ethos, were able to establish their power position definitively only with interruptions and an often fierce struggle.[9]

As the oldest sources of history show, there were always literati in China who, through their knowledge of tradition and their technical administrative skill, were able to support the secular power-holders. In the period of the warring states before the unitary empire, they helped the kings to establish and consolidate their power over the great feudal families. The royal courts competed with each other for the services of these literati, whose distinctive characteristic was a supremely courageous political rationalism. They were intent upon strengthening their own influence and power by acquiring the most attractive positions at such courts. They received their training at various schools, which were in competition with each other. Disposed towards political renewal, they became important stimulators of the rise of the unitary Chinese empire. As this empire was consolidated and pacified in the course of time, partly as the result of conquests by foreign dynasties, the rationalism of the literati underwent a dialectical reversal: their charisma of the independent thinker was transformed into that of the loyal interpreter of a traditional, orthodox doctrine of unity. Even the heroic charisma of the emperor and kings was transformed into a long-standing 'seemly' way of life. Both charismas came to function as means of magical legitimation upholding the established order. This resulted in a shifting of the struggle. The struggle between the magnates and the emperors for the best mandarins now became a struggle between individual mandarins for the emperor's favor. The examination system precluded their developing into a closed front against the imperial power. The examination system provided them, too, with a means of power useful both for making their own careers and for monopolizing all available prebends for their own class.

In 'normal' situations reasons of state and their own magic-oriented position required that they be tolerant towards the Taoist priests, of whose services they availed themselves from time to time – as did the emperor himself. Yet whenever – and it happened again and again – the Taoist hierocratic power became a political power, they stigmatized it as heterodoxy, and extirpation of the 'heretics' became a sacred duty. They intervened sharply whenever Taoist congregations arose that incorporated laymen or whenever sects arose in which members had to prove themselves personally, for in such cases the exclusive saving character of the caesaropapistic church-state was directly impaired and the cardinal virtue of piety underlying the entire bureaucratic system was 'sinned' against.

Historically, such Taoist or Buddhist organizations were exterminated with fire and sword time after time. They were always able to reappear because they satisfied popular needs. (The Buddhism imported into China was Mahayana Buddhism, which had a strong appeal since in China its migration of souls was interpreted as immortality.)

Moreover, Taoists and Buddhists were often supported by the sultanism of emperors, who with their harems and eunuchs sought to shake off the power of the mandarins. In the absence of insight into this constantly recurring conflict, Chinese history is, Weber believes, incomprehensible. The mandarins triumphed time and again, however, by interpreting every disaster, defeat or setback as a magical consequence of 'incorrect' conduct by the emperor. Having once succeeded (at about the turn of the Christian calendar) in deposing a popular usurper from the throne in favor of their own 'correct' candidate, their prestige in this respect was permanently assured.

Besides competing with such political power and these forms of lay traditionalism, the mandarins had to struggle with lay rationalism, which reared its head again and again in the form of craftsmanship or of speculation concerning life- and worldview.[10]

Their position of power enabled them to prevent the rise of an emancipated (and hence politically subversive) religiosity of salvation. That is, they successfully resisted the rise of an ethical prophecy, which by proclaiming a personal and transcendental God would have dashed to pieces the magical picture of the world. The imposing success of the T'ai P'ing Rebellion (1850-1864) is proof, according to Weber, that such a 'religious structure' is not at all alien to the 'natural disposition' of the Chinese:[11]

> Hence, the culture of this [Confucian] bureaucracy can be considered an experiment which approximately tests the practical rationalism of government by office prebendaries and its effects. Orthodox Confucianism resulted from this situation.[12]

2. The rationalism of the Indian Brahmans

In India too there was a social stratum which unified the culture and lent to its ethos its characteristic features. It can be said that 'this well-integrated, unique social system could not have originated or at least could not have conquered and lasted without the pervasive and all-powerful influence of the Brahmans.'[13]

In contrast to China, there was in India from the most ancient times a distinction between profane and priestly powerholders. Indian kingship arose from the purely worldly politics of erstwhile charismatic warriors. The Brahmans were originally magical priests, and that is what they continued to be throughout the whole of Indian history. Unlike the Chinese literati, who left what they considered parasitic and barbaric legerdemain to the Taoists, the Brahmans cultivated basic magic and rationalized it into asceticism and mysticism. In doing so they had to recognize the autonomy of the development of the secular power.

Following the dialectical reversal of the originally personally qualified magicians and warrior heroes into hereditary, genteel priestly lines opposed to secular priests and kings, the jurisdictions of both spheres of power remained reciprocally delimited in principle, and tightly institutionalized.

Although the Brahmans, like the mandarins, were retired from the public forum temporarily from time to time as the powerholders had recourse to heterodox Jainists and Buddhists, they were nevertheless able to enhance their position of power systematically in the long run. This contrasts to the political power which, while in principle likewise hereditary, was subject to sharp shifts. India was, after all, a land typically vulnerable to foreign invasions and domestic conquests. Accordingly, the demographic map showed conspicuous racial differences, on which were based acute social-economic contradictions between ruled and ruling tribes. The social divisions of labor and commerce did not follow geographical boundaries and urban markets; they were structured ethnically. People were familiar with the phenomena of 'foreign workers' and 'pariah peoples,' marginal groups who virtually lacked a home or country of their own, as the case might be.

As a result of this political and social situation, the Brahmans were able to establish and maintain their power. For all these groups knew that the so-called 'genteel charisma,' that is, the qualification to practice a certain craft, engage in a trade, and above all to hold certain positions of authority did not depend on individual qualities but was bound primarily by heredity to a tribe, clan, or sib. This ubiquitous phenomenon of the 'routinization' of charisma was nowhere in the world carried as far as it was in India. The explanation is to be found in the Brahmans. (In China, for example, this principle of genteel charisma was broken through by the mandarin examination system.)

In the first place, the genteel charisma was followed most consistently by the Brahmans themselves because, from ancient times, they had monopolized the magical charisma and because they fell outside every totemist form of organization. They were thereby a 'genteel charismatic guild' or, in other words, a caste. Castes are hereditarily distinguished closed status groups of practitioners of certain professions and holders of certain positions of authority, the

163

boundaries between which are legitimated by magic.

The Brahmans, furthermore, were the only ones who could bestow this legitimacy. The acceptance of guest workers and alien peoples into the Hindu community involved the Brahmans' supposing they had a remote Hindu origin, so that they belonged *ipso facto* to this 'birth-religion.' The Hinduization of India was actually a process of acculturation and assimilation of new peoples and tribes.

Assimilation meant that the pertinent alien, guest, or pariah people became a caste, or castes. Weber speaks of 'conversion' and 'transformation' (*Umschlag or Umwandlung*) to caste. Genteel charisma and the caste system reciprocally strengthened each other. Brahmanic thought brought them both into association with the *karma* theodicy (which was present elsewhere as well), and thus forged the unique Indian social structure.

The driving motives in this process were, insofar as the Brahmans themselves were concerned, the extension of their sphere of influence and the enhancement of their income; for the social recipients, the motive was the need for social recognition and legitimation. Political powerholders in particular found legitimation by the Brahmans to be beneficial. Foreign conquerors, such as the Musselmen, after an initially fierce conflict with the Brahmans and slaughter of the Buddhist monks, used the former as a means of domesticating the masses, who looked to them for refuge. Weber observes that this is a recurrent phenomenon with political powerholders elsewhere as well. In contrast to the Buddhists and Jainists, both of whom were in principle a- or anti-political, the Brahmans could meet the needs of the rulers and the ruled alike. They religiously legitimated the positions of both. It was precisely the caste segregation of guest workers that guaranteed them permanent employment opportunities.

It was ultimately to this need for legitimation that the Brahmans owed their enduring authority, which was increasingly beyond dispute. Social revolutions accordingly occurred with greater frequency in the higher strata because the need for social acceptance was not as strong there as it was in the lower castes or with the princes and kings whose power position depended on social acceptance. As a rule, religious-magical and secular powers therefore worked together.

Hence it is also not merely fortuitous that prophetic Buddhist and Jainist movements arose precisely in intellectual circles. However, political and hierocratic powers acted conjointly to destroy

164

both of these anti-Brahman forces. Yet Buddhism expanded enormously outside India. In doing so it turned rather rapidly (even in India, after several generations) from a prophetic movement of peripatetic mendicant monks into resident, studying, land-controlling monastic communities, which were in fact strongly hierocratic powers with slaves and predials. Sometimes this originally anti-political movement even changed into a political power with tax-paying subjects.[14]

3. Jewish monotheistic rationalism

The Jewish ethos, too, was the result of an ever-shifting conflict between various priestly groups amongst themselves, between priests and prophets, and between religious leaders and secular powerholders.[15] Here too the 'morals' of the laity co-determined the 'morality' rationalized by the priests. Again and again, the power position of the dominating status group had an especially dominating influence on the character of Jewish rationalism. Thus the 'spirit of prophecy' vanished not by virtue of 'some mysterious psychological regularity'[16] but as a result of the priestly power, which took over the reins with the assistance of secular politics. This priestly 'birth-aristocracy' had to yield in turn to the 'development-aristocracy' of a sedentary urban bourgeoisie in the diaspora, which again profoundly altered Jewish rationalism.

The coincidence of 'church and state,' which in the Jewish covenantal confederation guaranteed the inward unity of an otherwise quite unstable inter-ethnic community in the midst of a hostile situation, continued to exist more or less clearly down through the centuries, but while it had been a dynamic factor at the time of the conquest of Canaan and the Pharisaic diaspora, it became in later 'pariah Judaism' a 'caste' devoted to self-perpetuation.

Although I will not explain the further unfolding of this dialectic, it seems desirable to indicate the social factors that contributed to the rise of the conception of a transcendental creator-God, as well as to the character of the Jewish rationality associated with that conception. Jewish rationality acquired a typically ethical character. Only in the Middle East did an ethical prophecy arise. Although transcendental ethical deities were also known in India and China, they appeared there only in a popular, magical-sacramental form. There were specific ethical commandments, but there was not a consistent ethical way of life. The rational, transcendental God immune to magical coercion and accepted also by intellectual circles, as that God is found in the Middle East in Judaism and Zoroastrianism in particular, is unique in world history.

Besides strictly historical and individual factors there are also sociological and general causes to be indicated in explanation of the rise of the conception of a transcendental creator-God and the Jewish rationality associated with it. Specifically, there is the marginality of Jewish culture:

> Rarely have entirely new religious conceptions originated in the respective centers of rational cultures. Rational prophetic or reformist innovations were first conceived, not in Babylon, Athens, Alexandria, Paris, London, Cologne, Hamburg, Vienna, but in Jerusalem of pre-exilic, in Galilaea of late Jewish times, in the late Roman province of Africa, in Assisi, in Wittenberg, Zurich, Geneva and in the marginal regions of the Dutch, lower-German, and English cultural areas, like Frisia and New England. To be sure this never occurred without the influence and impact of a neighboring rational civilization. The reason for this is always the same: prerequisite to new religious conceptions is that man must not yet have unlearned how to face the course of the world with questions of his own. Precisely the man distant from the great culture centers has cause to do so when their influence begins to affect or threaten his central interests. Man living in the midst of the culturally satiated areas and enmeshed in their technique addresses such questions just as little to the environment as, for instance, the child used to daily tramway rides would chance to question how the tramway actually manages to start moving.
>
> The possibility of questioning the meaning of the world presupposes that capacity to be astonished about the course of events.[17]

The mighty, exclusive kings who with their rational bureaucratic administration reigned over the nearby Egyptian and Mesopotamian world empires, executing laws and creating justice, regulating water or artificial irrigation to bring forth harvests from the emptiness of the desert sands and permanently threatening Israel – such kings must, according to Weber, have made an enormous, awesome and fascinating impression on the stratum of independent thinkers and on the weakly organized peasants and shepherds with their relatively undifferentiated material culture, both of whom had been present in Palestine since the beginning of historical times. Given this culture, they were capable of developing the idea of a divine king who had not 'begotten' people and the earth – the prevalent idea elsewhere – but rather had 'made' them from nothing.[18] 'The Yahweh of Moses and the ancient war prophets simply never was the primitive fiend into which, in the interest of a theory of unilinear evolution, attempt has been made to cast him.'[19] Nor did he ever become this in the course of history. The great wars of conquest, the appearance of kingship, the rise of the monarchical state and of the sedentary urban culture, the imperilment by the great powers, the collapse of the Northern Kingdom and the conspicuously similar lot of the Southern Kingdom, and finally the Exile, led this people to question permanently the course of the world.[20]

C. The Sociological Genesis of Capitalistic Rationalism

Directly at the cradle of the capitalist ethos stood Protestant ethical rationalism. In order to evaluate its causal influence correctly, in Weber's spirit, one must place it, however, within the broader perspective of the development of Western society as a whole. Here, namely, there were two phenomena running more or less parallel which reciprocally supposed and fructified each other and influenced the culture and structure of the West in a decisive way. These phenomena were the expansion of Christianity and the rise of an autonomous urban bourgeoisie.

1. The urban bourgeoisie

The city plays a great role in Weber's sociology. His treatise on the sociological foundations of Chinese Confucianism commences with 'city, prince, god.' The city is also prominent in his studies of India and Palestine. To Weber the differences in the nature and development of cities are symptomatic for the entire politico-economic structure of the pertinent societies.[21]

In China, with its ancient centralized bureaucratic state apparatus, the cities were mainly a rational product of the central administration. They served as centers from which the state assured itself, via mandarins temporarily stationed there, of the governmental revenues it required. Most of the inhabitants of the cities continued to be bound, religiously and socially, to their tribal or sib relations dwelling outside the walls. The central administration, which was not intensive, needed to take account of strong local 'self-administration,' to be sure, but that was to be found in cities and villages alike. It needed also to take account of the trade and craft guilds, which were localized mainly in the cities. Socially and economically these guilds often had considerably more power over their members than their counterparts in the West ever did. The character of the cities was such, however, that they never confronted the central administration with the challenge of a systematically executed economic policy aimed at gaining a power position.

In India the situation was analogous. There too the urban guilds had succeeded in establishing a strong position, so that, for a while, a bourgeois plutocracy was able to compete with the secular and religious nobility. Eventually, however, they had to give way before the power of princes and Brahmans, the latter of whom employed religious sanctions to effect, finally, the non-urban, stratified caste organization. As a result, India never experienced urban autonomy.

In contrast to the extensive interior regions of China and India and, in fact, everywhere else that a state bureaucracy arose before there were urban power centers, the coastal regions of Palestine, ancient Greece, and the Roman Empire had cities which, politically speaking, were autarchic entities. Economically, they oriented themselves to maritime trade or to the surrounding tributary countryside. The Hellenistic and Roman Empires arose because such city-states succeeded in expanding their territories. The pillars of these world empires were formed by widely scattered cities. These were in the first place politico-military centers that dominated the surrounding region. Indirectly, they thereby likewise became economic entities with urban markets. The core of the urban populace was comprised, however, of a politico-military nobility whose livings were supplied by their estates outside the cities.

The fall of the Roman Empire and the appearance of early medieval feudalism resulted in part from the fact that such landed nobility re-established themselves on their rural domains. A structural shift ensued that led to a decline in the importance of the city, and a landed feudal aristocracy began to rule Western Europe. Yet this aristocracy remained interested, in the long run, in (founding) cities – no longer for political but instead for economic and fiscal reasons. The European Middle Ages saw the development of a new type of city which was an economic center and only secondarily a military power in service of the economic function. People of the free professions formed its core. The focus of its interest was no longer the subjugation of the surrounding countryside but a juridically guaranteed autonomy vis-à-vis the feudal nobility and the extensive and intensive expansion of commercial and craft activities. Urban power thereby gained in importance.

The bearers of this process of economic rationalization were the urban guilds. What was typically new in all this was that the crafts were now involved in the process of rationalization – something which, given the nature of traditional political capitalism, had never previously been possible. Any rather one-sided, specialized large enterprise would previously have had to run too great a risk, since there was no regular, predictable market.

In the West during the High Middle Ages an independent peasant class arose, although owing tribute to feudal lords; and an urban 'industrial' capitalism appeared that even bore all the marks of modern capitalism. It was an organization of free labor that distinguished family income from venture capital and was economically oriented towards peaceful conquest of the market.[22]

2. Christianity

According to Weber's view of things, this typically Western socio-economic structure could not have arisen without the influence of Christianity. Weber emphasized that the reverse is also true.

Without the urban community, in the profane sense with its compulsory organizational (*Anstalts-*) character, its concept of office, the absence of religious dividing lines between sibs, and the like, Christianity probably never would have developed into the organized form of congregational religiosity with an official priesthood that it became in the Middle Ages. The importance of Christianity increased at that time *ceteris paribus* with the size of the city. A bishop was supposed to reside in the city. Primitive Christianity was already a typically urban religion. Namely, there was a strong affinity between this ethical religiosity and the mentality of the petit-bourgeois sedentary or wandering traders and artisans.[23] Christianity would have found it difficult to take root amongst the ancient slave proletariat.

Even in the absence of a direct relation to the cities, Christianity contributed to the rise of capitalistic rationalism. Already in its earliest form, as a charismatic movement, when the irrational 'gifts of the Spirit' were considered the distinguishing marks of holiness, Christian apologetics pointed to its fruits, that is, to its influence on concrete moral behavior, as the trademarks of its divine origin. 'No Hindu could make this kind of statement.'[24]

Weber advances five reasons why Western culture, given Christianity, developed in an entirely different direction than the cultures of China and India.[25]

The difference lay first in the concept of a transcendental creator-God. Christian mysticism was thereby prevented from issuing in an absolute union with the divine; at the same time, a radical rejection of the world, ever God's creation, was impossible.

Further, metaphysical speculation about the 'meaningfulness' of the world could never in itself effect salvation, since intellectual command of the world did not lead to saving insight into the divine. The paradox of an imperfect creation and a perfect God actually carried every consistent metaphysics further away from him.

In the third place, the combination of Christianity with rational, Roman law[26] led to a juridically defined 'relationship of subjection' between man and God and to a conception of salvation as a legal procedure.

Beyond that, the sober and practical rationalism (partly of Roman, partly of Jewish origin) of the leading Christian congregation, that of Rome, resulted in a permanent rejection of ecstasy. One sign of this is the Latin translation of 'ecstasy' as 'superstition.' Later, in the cloisters, this rationalism would lead to a relative esteem for work, which could be regarded as a hygienic-ascetic means to holiness.

In the fifth place, finally, the disciplined, cloistered, rational way of life was linked to a consistent, rational church organization with a monarchical top. In addition to a transcendental God there was now also an inner-worldly ruler with unprecedented power who could commit the cloistered ones like so many troops to the service of a rational, official bureaucracy. In this way, at least in principle, the possibility was created for the method of an active rational and systematized lifestyle to gain a foothold in the ordinary world. In ascetic Protestantism, this actually happened.

Protestant ethical rationalism found in the traditional industrial capitalism which had developed in the High Middle Ages a socio-economic structure particularly suited to expressing its religious enthusiasm within the world; meanwhile, on the other hand, this socio-economic structure itself received the religious dynamic that allowed it to develop into a 'rational industrial capitalism.'[27] Weber states that

> the religious valuation of restless, continuous, systematic work in a worldly calling, as the highest means to asceticism, and at the same time the surest and most evident proof of rebirth and genuine faith, must have been the most powerful conceivable lever for expansion of that attitude toward life which we have here called the spirit of capitalism.[28]

Thus the impulse to modern capitalism came from a religious movement that appealed to the petty and middle bourgeoisie in the first instance. In their own spirit they bent the original salvation doctrine of the great Reformers into a psychologically strongly motivated feeling of being God's elected instruments if only they would relinquish every unqualified pleasure and all joy in possessions. Profit was to be employed to expand the enterprise. In this way there could develop, in all good conscience, a class of calculating and daring entrepreneurs who had come up through the hard school of life and whose whole being was committed to the 'cause.' Moreover, the power of religious asceticism put at their service a class of sober, conscientious, supremely competent workers who regarded their own labor as being likewise the realization of God's will.

Considerations of justice arising from the unequal distribution of the goods of this world, a result, after all, of God's unfathomable decree, placed no limit on the entrepreneurial fervor of individuals. On the contrary, honest exploitation of work was legitimated as the entrepreneur's religious vocation. Begging, which in the Middle Ages had still been ethically idealized in the form of mendicant orders or even of licensed secular beggars, was abhorred.

In Weber's view the rise of capitalism is thus not primarily a consequence of scientific and technological progress, which in many cases was hardly even discernible in the opening phase; nor is it the quasi-automatic result of capital accumulation, which existed in all times and places in history. Clearly the basis must be sought in a fundamental change in the pattern of religious values which finally won the day only after a fierce struggle with traditionalism. The first capitalistic entrepreneurs encountered grim resistance, suspicion, and moral indignation. Only as a result of their absolute integrity were they able in the long run to win the confidence of their workers and customers. Gradually, a process of socialization got under way in society and produced a specific bourgeois work ethic.[29]

This bourgeois rationalism, after the high point of pure religious enthusiasm was over, turned via the 'routinization' mechanism into the purely this-worldly oriented, serious vocational ethic of capitalistic rationalism. This happened, Weber states expressly, via the same law to which the predecessor of inner-worldly rational asceticism, namely, that of the medieval cloisters, so often fell victim. As soon as the rigid regulation of life and the sober consumption or, in other words, the rational economic pattern of life, began to bear fruit in the form of increasing wealth, the possessions that had been acquired were feudalized and one of the many monastic reforms was required in order to destroy its 'secularizing' effect. This relatively autonomous dialectical development was usually not foreseen and certainly never intended, since often it was diametrically opposed to the original intention. Religious leaders naturally were aware of the dangers wealth posed to their ideals.

The comparison of the consequences of Protestant and monastic rationalization has certain limits, in that the former entailed an inner-worldly process of such far-reaching scope that no one was any longer able to escape it.[30]

II. Modern Rationalized Society, and Religion

Modern rationalized society, itself a product (in part) of the rationalization of Western religion, no longer has any need of this religion, finds Weber. This religious rationalization had its cradle in ancient Judaism, as will be clear from what has been said thus far, and it reached its acme in ascetic Protestantism, which 'radically disenchanted' the world. Once 'disenchanted,' the world had no need of religion.

Given the fact that many present-day writers who deal with secularization see in this modern rationality one of the fundamental causes of the secularization process and thereby rely to a greater or lesser extent on Weber's train of thought,[31] it will be worthwhile to examine Weber's own view of the relation between rationality and religion.

In his essay on the North American system of sects, Weber mentions several aspects of secularization. I shall begin by looking at this system of sects, since it is a suitable point of departure for going on to examine the secularization process, which in its own turn is an appropriate starting point for analyzing more closely the connection between modern rationality and religion. Hence the three subdivisions of this section.

A. Protestant Sects and Capitalism

One of the reasons why ascetic Protestantism with its extremely heavy ethical demands on the individual was still able to develop into a (non-traditionalistic) 'mass religiosity' is to be found in the sectarian character of this religion.

From a structural standpoint, the ideal-typical 'sect' is the polar opposite of a 'church':

> Indeed, a church is a corporation which organizes grace and administers religious gifts of grace, like an endowed foundation. Affiliation with the church is, in principle, obligatory and hence proves nothing with regard to the member's qualities. A sect, however, is a voluntary association of only those who, according to the principle, are religiously and morally qualified. If one finds voluntary reception of his membership, by virtue of religious *probation*, he joins the sect voluntarily.[32]

A church makes universalistic claims. It seeks general acceptance of its dominion and offers its salvation benefits to all. Naturally, it strives for recognition by the state, and it minimalizes its ethical demands. In contrast, a sect accepts only members who are found worthy and adheres to 'separation of church and state' as a structural principle. In principle the sect as an organization of 'charismatics' also has no internal official bearers of authority. At the core, a sect is a local, sovereign and self-governing congregation.

To Weber it is obvious that this ideal-typical distinction is never fully present in social reality, but he emphasizes the fact that from the very outset Protestant asceticism wrestled with the conflict between these two structural principles. In studying the system of sects, which appeared in its most extensive and pronounced form especially in North America, Weber's main concern is thus with the consequences of this 'voluntaristic principle' of the sect, the so-called 'believer's church,' of which adult baptism is the symbol.

The voluntary principle arises from the concern to keep the congregation pure and to admit only 'saints,' or true Christians, especially to the celebration of the Lord's Supper and to prayer meetings. This concern acquires form in a way fundamentally different to the rules of discipline known also to the churches. Church discipline is in the hands of the spiritual office, it employs authoritarian means, and it rewards or punishes specific good or evil deeds. In contrast, sect discipline is at least partly and often entirely in the hands of the laity, usually of the local congregation. They know one another personally, so that the member of a sect can be accepted only by proving himself within the circle of his companions and – most importantly – by showing himself open to the constant and self-evident scrutiny of his personal characteristics. If the substantive side of ascetic Protestantism led of itself to the cultivation of ethical professional qualities, this social structure was an extremely well-suited means to the formation of people who experienced the Puritan ethic authentically and inwardly. Their self-respect and their entire social existence stood or fell, even without strictly supernatural sanctions, with a methodical rational attitude towards life, which found expression mainly in the conscientious practice of a vocation. Besides these internal sanctions within the circle of companions in the faith, the conduct of the member of a sect was also subject to external sanctions. The integrity, reliability, and creditworthiness of members of the sect was guaranteed, as far as the outside world was concerned, which did their enterprise or business good, often to the extent of being the *sine qua non* of their success.

This internalized social control within the sect, together with external business success, created the modern autonomous professional person acting according to his own conscience. Weber makes clear that this was not attributable to the sect structure alone by drawing a comparison to the medieval guild system. These organizations of free labor were, certainly, as I have indicated,[33] already a form of 'bourgeois rationalism,' but they still breathe a traditionalistic spirit. Like the sects, the guilds too controlled their members in ethical matters, but they did so for the sake of a (traditionally established) just division of incomes, which led, among other things, to restrictive regulations with respect to mutual competition. The sects, however, were not primarily vocational associations like the guilds but associations of fellow believers whose conduct of life was sanctioned exclusively in terms of formal justice without reference to a substantive division of incomes and without any restrictions on competition. On the contrary, the capitalistic success of a brother in the sect was a sign of his having grace, and it was beneficial to the prestige and drawing power of the sect.

It is unnecessary to elaborate on the fact that the sects were a very important source for the inception and diffusion of the bourgeois Puritan ethic and thereby also of the specific capitalistic ethos:

> The ascetic conventicles and sects formed one of the most important historical foundations of modern 'individualism'. Their radical break away from patriarchal and authoritarian bondage, as well as *their* way of interpreting the statement that one owes more obedience to God than to man, was especially important.[34]

The term 'individual' must be understood here, as this passage reveals, in the sense of an autonomous person deciding according to his own conscience, resisting all authoritarian arbitrariness on the basis of a sense of religious duty. Individualism is here virtually synonymous with modern rationalism.

B. The Secularization Process

Weber observed during his trip to America (1904) that membership in a sect was still indispensable to one's economic success and, indeed, to one's being able to participate in social life. This was particularly the case in Anglo-American middle class circles and in socially unarticulated regions where the church 'congregation' was the only goal-oriented association, so that someone lacking 'church membership'[35] was subjected to a virtually absolute boycott, also socially. One need not on that account speak denigratingly of the religious character of these sects and call this 'hypocrisy.' Weber calls it 'his personal opinion' that 'strong religious convictions,' whatever external form they assume, always and everywhere intermingle with political, economic, and other societal interests, whether people are aware of it or not. This does not mean, however, that in that case the religious character would have disappeared. In this regard, 'cooking is always done with water, but – people like to overlook it nowadays – not with water alone.'[36]

Despite the fact that in America religious church life permeated the whole of social and economic life in much greater measure than was the case in Europe, 'closer scrutiny revealed the steady progress of the characteristic process of 'secularization', to which in modern times all phenomena that originated in religious conceptions succumb.'[37]

Weber repeatedly uses the term 'secularization,' without expressly defining it and without describing systematically the phenomena indicated by it.[38] Yet something can be said about it if his scattered references to it are considered together. These point to the processes of change in society at both the structural and the cultural levels and even suggest the possibility of expressing certain expectations regarding the future of religion.

The previous citation pertained primarily to structural changes in society as a whole. Weber's point is that the social and economic functions which once were fulfilled de facto by the sects alone now in increasing measure – specifically where the Anglo-American middle class is concerned – are being carried out by numerous culturally diverse but structurally similar exclusive clubs. The members co-opt one another by ballot; one can become and remain a member only by 'proving' his qualities in some way. These clubs are artifacts and have the same structure as the sects, but they have no religious purpose nor do people aspire to affiliation for religious motives. Even during the last generation every typical Yankee who wished to be thought worthy and to have a career as a businessman, commercial traveller, technician or physician needed to belong, in the course of his life, to a respectable number of such clubs – for example, the Boys' Club at school, the Athletic Club or the Greek Letter Society at university, or one of the clubs of notables in the business world.[39] Moreover, the 'specifically American democracy... did *not* constitute a formless sand heap of individuals' – only a bureaucracy, says Weber, could do that – 'but rather a buzzing complex of strictly exclusive, yet voluntary associations.'[40] Anyone who was not a member of such a club (*'Gesellschaft'*, in Tönnies' sense) was until recently a 'pariah,' socially speaking. Now, according to Weber, even this system of secular clubs is undergoing change. Many Americans 'disdain' them as 'backwardness' or 'humbug,' or even deny them or know nothing about them.

What interests Weber in this connection, he writes, is mainly the fact that the role this system of worldly clubs (*Klubs und Gesellschaften*) plays in American society 'is largely the product of a process of *secularization* of the prototype of these voluntary associations (*Verbände*), to wit, the *sects*.'[41] Thus he calls the universal suffrage of American democracy and the (official) separation of church and state achievements of the recent past, since 'during the colonial period... especially in Massachusetts, full citizenship status in the church congregation was the precondition for full citizenship in the state,' and that was determined by the church alone.[42] Hence the conclusion is justified that by 'secularization' Weber meant the process whereby religious associations lost their power position in public life and had to give way to profane organizations.

The secularization process also took place at the cultural level. 'We modern, religiously 'unmusical' people can hardly imagine or even simply *believe* what an enormous role religious moments played in these periods, in which the characteristic features of the modern nations were formed. These moments overshadowed everything in a time when concern about the 'hereafter' was more real to people than anything else.'[43] Church membership in Germany, Weber observes, is often a purely formal matter, a simple question of convention, albeit prerequisite to a career in certain categories, such as those of officers and officials. With the Europeanization of America, one sees the same phenomenon appear there, with this difference, that there such membership is beneficial especially for commercial success. The 'captains of industry' need no such support, however, and their membership serves only their personal, social legitimation and not their commercial legitimation.[44]

Weber also provides other indicators for this cultural secularization. One example would be the phenomenon, common in America, of interdenominational[45] cartel formation. Originally it was meant to obviate unethical competition between the sects. The dangers of this were real and grew, among other factors, from the material interests of the preachers, who benefited from an increasing number of souls. Yet the criteria of selection for admission to the sects were thereby automatically reduced to a lower level; cartel formation served to prevent that. Such cooperation was made possible by the minimal emphasis on dogma in practically all American sects and the virtually exclusive emphasis on civic, professional, and business morality. If such cartel formation thus originally derived from considerations of a religious nature, it is 'now,' Weber observes, at least in part a symptom of the religious 'indifferentism' linked to the Europeanization of America.[46]

A particularly clear example of cultural secularization is provided by Weber's observation that ideas that were originally religious in nature can acquire a purely profane meaning:

> Calvin himself had made the much quoted statement that only when the people, i.e., the mass of labourers and craftsmen, were poor did they remain obedient to God. In the Netherlands (Pieter de la Court and others), that had been secularized to the effect that the mass of men only labour when necessity forces them to do so.[47]

Weber goes on directly to state that this formulation became a 'leading idea of capitalist economy' and eventually entered into the stream of 'theories of the productivity of low wages.'

This transformation of meaning whereby originally religious ideas acquire a purely profane content in a later phase is not a typically modern phenomenon in Weber's view. In this respect I noted earlier how wealth had a 'secularizing' effect in the medieval cloisters.[48] The matter involves a general mechanism of the sociology of knowledge. Referring to the above-mentioned transformation of meaning from 'obedience to God as the result of poverty'

into 'willingness to work under the compulsion of necessity,' Weber states, 'Here also, with the dying out [*Absterben*] of the religious
root, the utilitarian interpretation crept in unnoticed, in the line of
development which we have again and again observed.'[49] As I see
it, this 'line' or scheme of development must be interpreted thus: at
a given moment, values or interests realized and objectified by religious inspiration become autonomous. Then they develop a compelling social force and so come to be regarded as ends in themselves. In other words, social structural changes are accompanied by
changes at the level of consciousness. In that case the originally religious motivation to realize these values or to pursue these interests has no relevance or is even a nuisance.

While at the cultural level the secularization mechanism must
thus be viewed as a particularization (in terms of the sociology of
knowledge) of the general socio-cultural dialectic[50], it is likewise the
case that it must be viewed as having been in Weber's eyes a typically modern phenomenon as well. The summary I presented of
statements by Benjamin Franklin[51] that were meant to illustrate the
modern pattern of norms were also selected by Weber because of
the absence in them of any direct relation to religion.[52] According
to Weber, modern rational society is typically a-religious. Where
religion does still continue to play a role in modern business life,
this role is usually – according to Weber, at least in Germany – of
a dysfunctional, or negative, nature. Entrepreneurially zealous and
practically effectual figures tend today to be hostile or at least indifferent to the church. To them religion seems to be 'a means to
drawing people away from labour in this world,' and the capacity
to escape this religious tradition in favor of a liberal 'Enlightened'
mentality provides a more suitable basis for today's modern business approach to life.[53] However, even this Enlightened optimism,
the 'laughing heir' of Protestantism, seems to have faded 'irretriev-
ably.' In any case, modern capitalism no longer needs the support
of a religiously motivated asceticism 'since it rests on mechanical
foundations.' The correct interpretation of this has to be that capitalism has now become a system developing according to principles of its own, without any intrinsic reference at all to religion. This
social mechanism is kept running by the normative 'idea of duty in
one's calling' that 'prowls about in our lives like the ghost of dead
religious beliefs.' Subjectively, this calling is sometimes simply experienced as 'economic compulsion,' and sometimes it is impossible to relate its fulfillment to higher spiritual values directly. In either case, 'the individual generally abandons the attempt to justify

it at all.' In the United States, where this development of doing business without any religious-ethical motivation is the most advanced, there is a tendency to associate it with the 'mundane passions of a contest between life and death' so that there the calling often actually assumes the character of sport.[54]

As far as the future is concerned, 'genuine' religiosity (by which Weber means that religiosity which is experienced subjectively as such and which also has an effectual influence on the actual conduct of life)[55] will be forced to retreat steadily into the private sphere and in doing so to become either a purely individual affair (as in mysticism) or something which is played out in small, face-to-face communities. A person who is genuinely religious nowadays is no longer so in a socially relevant way, as part of a genuine 'religious community.' The 'sect,' the most adequate structure for socially relevant religiosity, thus no longer has a chance. The religious individual must accordingly have recourse to the 'church,' which he may ignore if he desires. This fact and a growing indifferentism, which drain the ecclesiastical confession of its religious meaning and make church membership a purely conventional affair, favor the future of the 'church.' Thus it is precisely the 'weakness' of the 'religious' motives that favors the 'future' of the church in the foreseeable future.[56]

C. Rationality and Religiosity

Given the preceding, mainly descriptive section on the secularization process, I want to examine at a more interpretive level, to the extent Weber's writings permit, the relation between modern rational society, and religion.[57]

Modern society is a 'disenchanted' society – which must not in the first instance be interpreted to mean an 'irreligious' society. Disenchantment means first, negatively as the word implies, the repudiation of all sorcery, so that there are in principle 'no mysterious incalculable forces that can come into play' to break a spell or set a limit to man's control of the world. Ascetic Protestantism, which rejects every form of magic, has in this sense, according to Weber, thoroughly disenchanted the world. The world may still be defined in religious categories, but the Protestant God so transcended man and the world that He was totally inaccessible to understanding, making it senseless to try to discover His mysterious purposes.

The sole ground for knowledge of human salvation lay in vocational mastery of the world, which was also man's sole calling. Hence 'disenchantment' has a positive meaning, too: 'that one can, in principle, *master* all things *by calculation*.'[58]

To 'master by calculation' implies science. Hence the practice of modern science is also the prototype of modern man's rational orientation towards his environment. The ethos of present-day society can accordingly be characterized as a progressive, ever broadening effort, affecting everyone and everything without exemption, to see the world rationally and control it technologically. The dominant value is the vocation, the respect for achievement, whereby the question of the existence of some further, ultimate meaning of man and the world is not answered by the society as such. This question is left to the discretion of the individual or of the small group.[59] Today's dominant value stems from the power position of the triumphant middle class, and its definition of reality is adopted by other groups, especially by the workers. Via the process of externalization it has been objectified in present-day capitalistic society and has such an overwhelming influence that, ideal-typically speaking, one can call it without qualification modern man's definition of reality.

Insofar as the relation between modern rationality and religion is concerned, it can be said that Weber never explicitly inquired whether religion or any other value in particular fulfills a (final) integrative function for society. It is rather the case that he revealed the meaninglessness of such a question in principle. That is, Weber notes the empirical fact that our society knows many different and mutually contradictory value systems and their respective institutionalizations. This is not only an empirical fact but likewise a possibility in principle, in every conceivable form of society, since meaning-giving or valuation is by definition and in principle the individual actor's prerogative. One and the same empirical reality can in principle be valued in an infinite number of ways. Weber expresses this paradoxically by saying that 'something can be 'sacred' not only in spite of its not being beautiful, but rather because and insofar as it is not beautiful'; something can be 'beautiful' although not 'good' and even 'in that very aspect' in which it is not good or not sacred. Valuations are therefore in principle strictly individual ascriptions of meaning that depend upon personal choice. 'According to our ultimate standpoint, the one is the devil and the other is the God, and the individual has to decide which is God for him and which is the devil. And so it goes throughout all the or-

180

ders of life.'[60] One can correctly assert that Weber proclaims here a philosophical epistemology that implies a subjective, individualistic doctrine of values. Certainly Weber had every right to do so in a thetical address such as the one this citation is taken from and in which he is stating the case for value-free science. What is of importance in the present context, however, is the fact that for Weber's sociology this philosophical individualism means nothing more, but also nothing less, than a 'methodical individualism,'[61] which opened his eyes to the empirically verifiable fact that social reality is a reality constructed by people, and a reality that may not be reified. Nevertheless, this construction is objectified in the social reality and leads, as it were, a supraindividual existence. This supraindividual collective definition of reality can create the appearance of unity and blind people to the 'eternal' conflict between mutually contradictory values, which actually acquire form in society at levels of both consciousness and objective structure. This was already the case during 'a thousand years' of 'allegedly or presumably exclusive orientation towards the grandiose moral fervor of Christian ethics.'[62] The history of Christianity teaches that this ethic was in fact a complex whole, and that in social and cultural reality it was driven to countless relativizations and compromises. With the increasing intellectualizing and rationalizing of life, the differences between the values became clearer, and they too were institutionalized structurally as more or less autonomous sectors of society. In the process, they lost their religious indication.[63]

> Many old gods ascend from their graves; they are disenchanted and hence take the form of impersonal forces. They strive to gain power over our lives and again they resume their eternal struggle with one another.[64]

In this pluralistic society, in which differing systems of values are locked in mutual conflict, the fundamental values that answer the question concerning the ultimate meaning of life are increasingly squeezed out of the public arena because they are meta-scientific and cannot be rebutted by these, in principle, scientifico-technological power blocs. It is true that society is not of such a nature that religious (and other basic) values necessarily must disappear, but structurally they are pressed back to the periphery of global society, to the private sector.

The fact that religion is relegated to an irrational sphere from that standpoint as the rationalization of the world picture and pattern of life deepens cannot be said to be a new, specifically modern phenomenon. Weber suggests two constitutive causes of the progressive irrationalization of religion.[65]

In the first place, every form of consistent rationalism is such that it encounters a certain point that cannot be explained rationally. Reality is never a 'calculation' that comes out even 'with nothing left over.' There is always a non-rationalizable remnant. In music, for example, 'the Pythagorean 'comma' resisted complete rationalization oriented to tonal physics.'[66] According to Weber, the systems of music of the various peoples and ages can accordingly be characterized in terms of their disposal of this irrational interval. It could be put aside, bypassed, or employed in the service of a richer tonality. Now, the same phenomenon occurs in the theoretical rationalization of the world picture and in still stronger measure in the rationalization of practical life. The 'various great ways of leading a rational and methodical life have been characterized by irrational presuppositions' that have been 'historically and socially determined.'[67] In fact, these were virtually always the social and psychological interests of the strata that left their particular mark on a given religion. Thus ascetic Protestantism was a typically bourgeois religion.

In the second place, as the world has been progressively rationalized into a cosmos running according to impersonal laws, the irrational elements of a religion have become the privileged *'loci* to which the irrepressible quest of intellectualism for the possession of supernatural values has been compelled to retreat.'[68] The unbroken primitive world picture with its concrete magic accordingly also revealed a steady tendency to become bifurcated into a rationally knowable and controllable deapotheosized nature and a 'beyond' (*Jenseits*) accessible only to individual and ineffable mystical experience. The Asiatic intellectualist religions took this second path. Only in strictly personal 'mystical union' was the supreme religious value still humanly attainable.[69]

In modern times, man with his yearning for meaning has been cast more than ever upon his own individuality. Rational empirical knowledge has today molded the disenchantment of the world into its most consistent form and transformed it into a causal mechanism.[70] Here the tension with the ethical postulate, according to which the world must, in some way or another, be a meaningful cosmos, reaches its zenith, so that now (ethical) religion becomes simply *'the* irrational or anti-rational supra-personal power.'[71]

Weber calls science the supremely 'irreligious'[72] power. The religious person is required more than ever to bring the 'sacrifice of the intellect' and to appear upon a terrain that requires vindication as totally heterogeneous and disparate to all that intellect or intuition can achieve.

This terrain is disclosed to man only through a charismatic inner enlightenment or an unconditional surrender of faith, in terms of which all interpretive reasoning seems but empty abstraction.[73] From a sociological standpoint religion thereby becomes a marginal phenomenon. The deeper explanation for this is thus that the rationality of teleological conduct, which strives to realize a modern as well as a religious value, reveals both values more sharply in their typical natures and hence is able to bring the two to a pitch.

The individualization of the person comes to correspond to the pluralizing and differentiation in modern society. Man is compelled more than ever before to free himself of the received social orders and to make a choice.[74] Because the modern industrial bureaucratic system of labor can function optimally without religious motivation or legitimation, this choice is often not made.

The above is not intended to mean that 'genuine' religion is no longer possible, but religion does become religion made private, which means it is no longer supported by a public sense of values and norms. Yet Weber sees genuine religiosity as being present in certain 'youth groups,' among other places:

> It is, however, no humbug but rather something very sincere and genuine if some of the youth groups who during recent years have quietly grown together give their human community the interpretation of a religious, cosmic, or mystical relation, although occasionally such interpretation rests on misunderstanding of self.[75]

Even less does Weber want to assert that it would in principle be impossible for a collective religious prophecy (*zingeving*) still to arise that would press the dominant value of the technocratic system in a different direction:

> No one knows who will live in this cage [of the technocratic system – ML] in the future, or whether at the end of this tremendous development entirely new prophets will arise, or there will be a great rebirth of old ideas and ideals...[76]

ABBREVIATIONS

GAR

Gesammelte Aufsätze zur Religionssoziologie.

PE

Die Protestantische Ethik. II Bd. Kritiken und Antikritiken.

Verhandlungen (1911)

Verhandlungen des Ersten Deutschen Soziologentages von 19.-22. Oktober 1910 in Frankfurt a. M.

WG

Wirtschaftsgeschichte. Abriss der universalen Sozial- und Wirtschaftsgeschichte.

WL

Gesammelte Aufsätze zur Wissenschaftslehre.

WP

Werk und Person. Dokumente ausgewühlt und kommentiert von Eduard Baumgarten.

WuG

Wirtschaft und Gesellschaft. Grundriss der verstehenden Soziologie

NOTES

Notes to Chapter 1

1. GAR I 1-16 [ET (1): 'Author's Introduction' in The Protestant Ethic and the Spirit of Capitalism]. [Material in brackets in the text, notes, and bibliography has been supplied by the translator. – HDM]
2. Thus Winckelmann, in SWP 539.
3. Archiv 20 (1904) 1-54; and 21 (1905) 1-110. In a footnote Weber refers broadly to the Archiv; the exact reference is provided by Eduard Baumgarten, who presents a chronology of Weber's life (including relevant domestic and foreign events) and works, with an extensive bibliography of his publications; see Baumgarten (1964) 679-720. My references to Weber's publications are based on this chronology [I have also used Martin Riesebrodt's more recent complete bibliography of Weber's known publications, pp. 16-32 in the publisher's Prospectus for the Max Weber Gesamtausgabe, Tübingen: J. C. B. Mohr (Paul Siebeck), May 1981 – HDM]. A somewhat less extensive bibliography of Weber's writings was included by Winckelmann in SWP 490-505.
4. GAR I 17-18n. [ET (2) 35, 186-88].
5. A summary of some of this criticism and of Weber's rejoinder appears in PE 11-345.
6. GAR I 161 [ET (2) 35, 182-83].
7. WuG 382-85 [ET 635-40]. Here Weber presents a never completed chapter explicitly about the market.
8. GAR I 83 [ET (2) 90].
9. See ch. 5, n. 1, below.
10. See, e.g., GAR I 38 [ET (2) 55-56].
11. GAR I 83 [ET (2) 90-91; italics added].
12. GAR I 83 [ET (2) 91].
13. Christliche Welt 20 (1906) 558-62; 577-83. Incorporated in SWP 382-97. [A revised version of part 1 appears in GAR I 207-36; ET (3): 'The Protestant Sects and the Spirit of Capitalism.']
14. Frankfurter Zeitung nos. 13 and 15, April 1906.
15. Troeltsch confirms this in his Die Soziallehren der christlichen Kirchen und Gruppen (Tübingen: J. C. B. Mohr (Paul Siebeck) 1912; 2d ed. 1961) 364n. [ET: O. Wyon, translator, The Social Teachings of the Christian Churches and Sects (London: Allen & Unwin, 1931)].
16. GAR I 207, n. 1 [ET (3) 302 and 450, n. 1; see GAR I ET (2) 145, 152, 254].
17. Archiv 41 (1916) 1-30 [cf. GAR I 237-75, ET (4): The Social Psychology of the World Religions].

18. [Cf. GAR I, ET (4) 267: ' – practical impulses for [economic] action which are founded in the psychological and pragmatic contexts of religions.']
19. GAR I 265 [ET (4) 293].
20. Archiv 41 (1916) 31-87; 335-86 [cf. GAR I, ET (5): The Religion of China: Confucianism and Taoism].
21. Weber says this explicitly in a footnote in the 'Einleitung' without, however, indicating what these 'internal reasons' are. See GAR I 267 [ET (4) 294, n. 10]. Thus the reasons I advance are of my own conception.
22. In his discussion of Indian philosophy of nature and religion, which reached its acme after the seventh century B.C., Weber observes in a footnote that that practically coincides with the first flowering of Chinese philosophy and with Israelitic prophecy. It is not conceivable that there was any borrowing. He firmly rejects a cosmic-biological explanation of this temporal coincidence. GAR II 155 [ET 153, 354-55, n. 25].
23. Archiv 41 (1916) 387-421 [cf. GAR I, ET (6): 'Religious Rejections of the World and their Directions']. Baumgarten does not provide the original pagination of these three subdivisions in his chronology, but Winckelmann does, in SWP 555 and 558.
24. Archiv 41 (1916) 613-744; 42 (1916-17) 345-61, 697-814 [cf. GAR II, ET: The Religion of India].
25. Weber's wife, Marianne, relates this in her foreword to the third volume. GAR III, v.
26. Von Glasenapp alludes to Jainism and recognizes that it was temporarily of great importance in India. He does not treat it separately, however, because in spite of its independence in many particular teachings, it was by nature and in the problems it addressed intimately linked to Buddhism. Von Glasenapp, Het Brahmanisme, 35.
27. Archiv 44 (1917-18) 52-138, 349-443, 601-26; 46 (1918-19) 40-113, 311-66, 541-604 [cf. GAR III, ET: Ancient Judaism].
28. [The latter passage corresponds to GAR III, ET 265-382: 'Part IV – The Establishment of the Jewish Pariah People.']
29. [See GAR III, ET 383-424: 'Part V – Supplement: the Pharisees.']
30. [On the origins of Wirtschaft und Gesellschaft, English readers may also consult the important 'Introduction' by Guenther Roth in Economy and Society (1978), xxxiii-cx; on the relation of WuG to Grundriss see especially Roth's section 9, 'The Planning of Economy and Society.' Sadly, Roth's study did not survive the manufacturing process unscathed : (1) the list of abbreviations he refers to (xxxvi) as 'following' his introduction precedes it; (2) Roth's 'Part Two: The Earlier Part' (lxvii) has wrongly become 'Part Two: The Older Part' in the page headers (lxvii-ci); (3) the sheets numbered lxxix-lxxx and lxxxi-lxxxii are incorrectly numbered and bound in the wrong sequence!) See further Ephraim Fischoff, 'The Background and Fate of Weber's 'Wirtschaft und Gesellschaft,' ' appendix 2 (280-86) in The Sociology of Religion, by Max Weber (Boston: Beacon Press, 1963, 1967.]
31. See WuG xi-xxiv. I have relied on this [German] foreword by Johannes Winckelmann and likewise on Marianne Weber's [German] foreword to the first edition (WuG xxxii) for the chronology of the separate volumes of WuG.
32. [Cf. WuG, ET 1-307: 'Part One: Conceptual Exposition.']
33. [Cf. WuG, ET 309-1372: 'Part Two: The Economy and the Arena of Normative and De Facto Powers.']
34. WuG 245-381. [The material referred to in this paragraph is presented as 'Chap-

ter VI: Religious Groups (The Sociology of Religion)' in ET 399-634; but see ET lxxxviii, n. 91; lxxxiiif., nn. 87 and 88; and ciif. An earlier English version of the same material appeared as Ephraim Fischoff, trans., The Sociology of Religion, by Max Weber (Boston: Beacon Press, 1963, 3d printing, 1967). Fischoff helped with the revision of his translation for its incorporation into ET, but the editors assumed responsibility for its final form. See n. 38, below.]

35. GAR I 15 [ET (1) 30: 'I hope to contribute something – in a systematic study of the Sociology of Religion'].
36. GAR I 237n. [ET (2) 267].
37. WuG 245-381 [ET 399-634; cf. n. 34, above].
38. See ch. 5, n. 3b, below. [ET now presents the material alluded to here and in the following discussion in fifteen sections (rather than twelve), as follows: (i) the origins of religion; (ii) magic and religion; (iii) the prophet; (iv) the congregation between prophet and priest; (v) the religious propensities of peasantry, nobility, and bourgeoisie; (vi) the religion of nonprivileged strata; (vii) intellectualism, intellectuals, and salvation religion; (viii) theodicy, salvation, and rebirth; (ix) salvation through the believer's efforts; (x) asceticism, mysticism, and salvation; (xi) soteriology or salvation from the outside; (xii) religious ethics and the world: economics; (xiii) religious ethics and the world: politics; (xiv) religious ethics and the world: sexuality and art; (xv) the great religions and the world.]
39. [See notes 34 and 38, above.]
40. [On Weber's Sociology of Domination and the translation of 'Herrschaft' in Economy and Society, see Guenther Roth's authoritative discussions at WuG, ET lxxxiii, n. 84; lxxxviii-c; 61-62, n. 31. Cf. also E. Fischoff, Translator's Preface to The Sociology of Religion, by Max Weber (Boston: Beacon Press, 1963, 1967), xv-xvi.]
41. WuG 245-381 [ET 1158-1211: 'Chapter XV: Political and Hierocratic Domination'].
42. Verhandlungen (1911).
43. Verhandlungen (1911) 39-62.
44. Verhandlungen (1911) 56-59.
45. Verhandlungen (1911) 198-99.
46. WG 300-315.

Notes to Chapter 2

1. This chapter is based mainly on the following essays:
   a. 'Die 'Objektivität' sozialwissenschaftlicher und sozialpolitischer Erkenntnis' of 1904. SWP 186-262, or WL 146-214 [ET (1): ''Objectivity' in Social Science and Social Policy']. This work appeared one year prior to 'Die Protestantische Ethik.'
   b. 'Ueber einige Kategorien der verstehenden Soziologie' of 1913. SWP 97-150, or WL 427-74. This essay belongs to about the same period as the second part of Wirtschaft und Gesellschaft, which contains Weber's systematic sociology of religion.
   c. 'Der Sinn der 'Wertfreiheit' der soziologischen und ökonomischen Wissenschaften' of 1918. SWP 263-310, or WL 489-540 [ET (3): 'The Meaning of 'Ethical Neutrality' in Sociology and Economics']. This essay appeared during the period of his publications on ancient Judaism. It is a further elabo-

ration and theoretical deepening of an address he had delivered in 1914 to a commission of the Verein für Sozialpolitik. Cf. Johannes Winckelmann in SWP 532.

d. 'Soziologische Grundbegriffe.' These were published posthumously as chapter 1 in the first part of Wirtschaft und Gesellschaft, which was written between 1918 and 1920. This chapter is at the same time a simplification and expansion of 'Kategorien der verstehenden Soziologie,' which appeared in 1913. WuG, ch. 1, pp. 1-30 [ET, ch. 1, 'Basic Sociological Terms,' pp. 3-62]. Of the seventeen sections in this chapter, only the first seven appear in Gesammelte Aufsätze zur Wissenschaftslehre (WL 541-81).

e. 'Wissenschaft als Beruf,' an address delivered in 1919. SWP 311-39, or WL 582-613 [ET (5): 'Science as a Vocation'].

Although these essays thus belong to rather widely separated periods, they do not seem to me to contain any fundamental contradictions. In this chapter I therefore make use of them without being concerned about any development that may have taken place in Weber's thought.

2. J. Winckelmann, Foreword to WL, p. ix. Tenbruck (1959) deals with the genesis of Weber's methodology in an illuminating, philosophically oriented article. Rex (1971) does the same in a less theoretical and more sociological-reflexive way.

3. WL 126-27.

4. The freedom of the will is not an obstacle but precisely the condition for such nomological knowledge. WL 132-33.

5. I am concerned here with the rationality of objective correctness (Richtigkeitsrationalität) in the empirical sciences. In mathematics or logic the correctness of the conclusions is immediately comprehensible. In such cases, according to Weber, the rationality of objective correctness and subjective understanding coincide. This can be inferred from what he says in WL 437 and 532 [cf. ET (3) 39-41].

6. [See Guenther Roth's discussion of the German term 'Evidenz' in WuG, ET and 58, n. 6.]

7. Like Weber I use the terms 'human sciences,' 'cultural sciences,' and 'social sciences' interchangeably and without distinction.

8. [See Roth's discussion of 'Verstehen', 'Deuten', 'Sinn', 'Handeln', and 'Verhalten' in WuG, ET 59, n. 2, 3.]

9. [See Roth's discussion of the relation between sinnhafte Adäquanz and causal adequacy in WuG, ET 59, n. 12.]

10. That the same approach, logically speaking, is also employed in principle in the cultural sciences, namely, working with hypotheses and their factual verification, is a matter I shall deal with in the final section of this chapter, which is devoted to sociological techniques.

11. WL 592-93 [ET (5) 137-38: 'Scientific work is chained to the course of progress – '].

12. Weber states that many and even leading representatives of the historical school, of which he is also an heir, believe in this old view of science. WL 208 [ET (1) 106].

13. WL 184, ET (1) 84.

14. This Copernican revolution in epistemology does not mean the scientist can 'rationally arrange' in an arbitrary way. It will be clear from what has already been said that (scientific) knowledge is for Weber objective in this sense, that it investigates 'aspects of the given reality' (italics added: the German phrase is Be-

standteile der gegebenen Wirklichkeit, WL 113). In doing actual research it is thus irrelevant what epistemology a scientist adheres to. One can even say with Weber that empirical disciplines necessarily adopt a 'naive realism' in doing actual research (WL 437). (This is in contrast to reflection upon the logical presuppositions of an empirical science.)

15. The above is derived mainly from the essay listed in note 1, subhead a of this chapter, namely, 'Die 'Objektivität', etc.' I have also used 'Die Kategorie der Deuting' (WL 67ff.) and 'Objektive Möglichkeit und adäquate Verursachung in der Kausalbetrachtung' (WL 266-90 [cf. ET (2) 164-88]).

16. The following section of this chapter is derived mainly from the essays listed at note 1, subheads c and e, above, namely, 'Der Sinn der 'Wirtfreiheit', etc.' and 'Wissenschaft als Beruf.' Notice should be taken of the fact that Weber places the term 'Wertfreiheit' in quotation marks. [In his introduction to Economy and Society Guenther Roth states that 'Weber uses a profusion of quotation marks as an alienating device to indicate that he employs familiar terms with reservations, with a new meaning, or in an ironic sense' (WuG, ET cvii).]

17. [WL, ET (5) 143.]

18. Weber calls attention to how the enormous progress in the natural sciences, technology, and so forth has led to the ostensible disappearance of value perspectives from the natural sciences while the values these sciences serve have been obvious at every turn. WL 185-86 [ET 85-86].

19. WL 527-30 [ET (3) 35-38].

20. WL 529-30 and passim [ET (3) 37-38].

21. [Cf. WuG, ET 38-40.]

22. WuG 23.

23. Vaskovics (1970) 1-18.

24. No cultural science would be possible in the absence of man as the meaning-giving and position-taking subject vis-à-vis the world: 'Transzendentale Voraussetzung jeder Kulturwissenschaft ist nicht etwa, dass wir eine bestimmte oder überhaupt irgend eine 'Kultur' wertvoll finden, sondern dass wir Kulturménschen sind, begabt mit der Fähigkeit und der Willen, bewusst zur Welt Stellung zu nehmen, und ihr einen Sinn zu verleihen' (Weber's italics). WL 180-81 [ET (2) 81]. The italicization of words or phrases in all the citations that follow, whether in text or notes, is Weber's own, unless otherwise indicated.

25. B. C. van Houten (1970) 265-84.

26. Cf. Van Houten's presentation: (1970) 277-78.

27. For some historical particulars on the question of 'value-free: then and now' see Tellegen (1970) 33-48. His views corroborate my conclusions concerning the verifiability in principle of Weber's sociology. Cf. also König (1971) 38-68.

   Mitzman advances a cultural-historical and psychoanalytic explanation for Weber's sociological (and political) spheres of interest. Specifically, Weber's stubborn advocacy of value-free science would be explained in terms of the traumatic experiences of his youth in combination with the suffocating, over-organized atmosphere of late bourgeois, fin-de-siècle Germany.

   Here I want to say only that even if Weber's advocacy of a value-free science was largely a defense mechanism against the all too heavy demands of society, that fact would in itself still say nothing about the ideological or nonideological character of the sociological research actually generated by it. The question concerning the psychological reasons why someone asserts something is a different one from that concerning the value of whatever it is someone asserts.

28. Sections II and III of this chapter are based mainly on the essays listed in note

1, subheads b and d, above – namely, 'Kategorien der verstehenden Soziologie' and 'Sociologische Grundbegriffe.'

29. WL 166 [ET (1) 66-68].
30. Thus Tellegen (1968) 96 and Van Houten (1970) 65.
31. Weber, as I stated, often uses the terms 'cultural sciences' and 'social sciences' in the same context without making any distinction between them. This is a consequence of the fact that his concern is the (cultural) meaning of life in society, together with its typical structural aspect.
32. 'Soziologie (im hier verstandenen Sinn dieses sehr vieldeutig gebrauchten Wortes) soll heissen: eine Wissenschaft, welche soziales Handeln deutend verstehen und dadurch in seinem Ablauf und seine Wirkungen ursächlich erklären will.' WuG 1 [ET 4].
33. Specifically, attention must be paid here not only to the interpretive (verstehende) method as over against the natural-scientific, external observational (beobachtende) one but also to the historical character of Weber's sociology. To be precise, in the first chapter of WuG Weber advances nominal definitions not only of sociology as science ('Soziologie soll heissen, etc.' – italics added) but likewise of all such basic sociological concepts as 'social selection' (Soziale Beziehung) [ET 38]; 'legitimate order' (legitime Ordnung) [ET 33]; 'conflict' (Kampf) [ET 38], etc., etc. From this as well as from explicit remarks made repeatedly in his writings on sociology of religion concerning the provisional character of his study, it is apparent just how conscious Weber was that not only the results but also the perspectives and the process of concept formation in sociology must be the permanent objects of critical research and reflection.
34. [WuG, ET 18.]
35. [Cf. WuG, ET 4.]
36. [Cf. WuG, ET 22.]
37. [Cf. WuG, ET 4.]
38. WuG 11 [ET 23; cf. 1377].
39. It is not improbable that the term 'definition of the situation' with which W. I. Thomas broke through the positivist character of American behaviorism derives from F. Znaniecki (1883-1958) who, with Thomas, published 'The Polish Peasant in Europe and America' (1927). In his methodology Znaniecki was probably influenced by Weber's emphasis on subjective meaning (der subjektiv gemeinte Sinn). See Zijderveld (1973) 86-87.
40. [Cf. WuG, ET 14.]
41. For these examples, see WL 210-12 [ET (1) 108-10].
42. [The passage at WuG, ET 9 reads: '– the subjective meaning of the action – will be called the intended meaning.' In a note to the translation, Guenther Roth explains that the pertinent German term here is gemeinter Sinn, which Weber broadens to include even cases in which the actor lacks 'a clear self-conscious awareness of such meaning' (WuG, ET 58, n. 9).]
43. Weber speaks of 'durchschnittlich und annäherend in einer gegebenen Masse von Fällen von den Handelnden – subjektiv gemeints Sinn' (WuG 1 [ET 4]). Speaking of conceptually pure types of action that are not necessarily social action, Weber says: 'Der Weg der 'Objektivation' führt nicht notwendig, freilich der Regel nach schnell zum Gemeinschaftshandeln ['communal' or 'social' action; see importantly WuG, ET lxxxiii-14, n. 88] und, wenn auch nicht notwendig immer, so in aller Regel speziell zum Einverständnishandeln ['consensual action'] (WL 462). For the term Einverständnis see WL 452-64 [cf. WuG, ET 1378] and my further discussion.

190

44. [WuG, ET 1378-79.]
45. WL 452-53.
46. [Cf. WuG, ET 18: 'Even a socialistic economy would have to be understood sociologically in – 'individualistic' terms. – The real empirical sociological investigation begins with the question: What motives determine and lead the individual members and participants?']
47. WuG 7, 8 [ET 14, 17].
48. WuG 6-9 [ET 12-18].
49. Thus Zijderveld (1966) 100, 205-6.
50. 'Organization' (Verband) is a technical term in Weber distinct from both 'communal social relationship' (Vergemeinschaftung) and 'associative social relationship' (Vergesellschaftung) (in about the same sense as in Tönnies, WuG 21-22 [cf. ET 41, 1373-80]). 'Organization' (Verband) applies from the moment a leadership function exists in a communal group or associative group that is closed to the outside. The specific element in 'organization' (Verband) is the presence of a leadership function that can act coercively (head of family, association chairman, prince, president, etc.). One does not speak of 'organization' (Verband) in connection with an erotic liaison or sib relationship. WuG 26 [ET 48-49, cf. lxxxiii-iv, n. 88, and 60, n. 24].
51. WL 466.
52. Zijderveld has incorrectly concluded from Weber's individualistic method that he had an individualistic view of reality. See note 49 to this chapter, above. Zijderveld does not draw this conclusion where Weber's actual sociological analyses are concerned. As an example of the 'dialectical' character of reality he advances the 'institutionalization of charisma.' He has borrowed this example from Weber explicitly. See Zijderveld (1966) 191-92. It is worth noting that I am not alone in my interpretation of Weber on the point of the irreducibility of social structures to individual action. Tellegen (1968), whose study, unlike Zijderveld's, is devoted exclusively to Weber, reacts against this generally accepted misconception of Weber, which he finds in Bouman, Goddijn, Martindale, and others. He rejects this mistaken 'nominalistic' interpretation of Weber. The cause of the misconception, according to Tellegen, is to be found in the fact that Weber employs nominalistic definitions in his conceptual apparatus (namely, they often include the formulation: soll heissen). Given these nominalistic definitions 'that are justified at a certain stage of the inquiry,' people incorrectly go on to conclude that Weber espoused a nominalistic view of reality. See Tellegen (1968) 186-88.
53. Deutung can also mean 'value-oriented interpretation,' the basis of every cultural science. See, e.g., WL 122. Various meanings of verstehen will be discussed in the text that follows. [Commenting on Weber's presentation of basic sociological terms in WuG, Guenther Roth says, ' 'Deuten has generally been translated as 'interpret'. As used by Weber in this context it refers to the interpretation of subjective states of mind and the meanings which can be imputed as intended by an actor. Any other meaning of the word 'interpretation' is irrelevant to Weber's discussion' (WuG, ET 57, n. 3).]
54. WUG 4 [ET 9-10].
55. WUG 9 [cf. ET 14-15, 19].
56. WL 432-36.
57. Salman (1963) 536-39 characterizes Die protestantsche Ethik as a psychological study in view of its psychological terminology and the absence of intervening variables in the form of social structures. He overlooks the fact that the attitu-

des scrutinized in it are in fact institutionalized motivations.

58. [Cf. WuG, ET 8 and 58, n. 7.]
59. WUG 3-4 [ET 8-9; cf. 58, n. 7].
60. On these two directions, see especially WuG 12-13 [ET 24-26].
61. [WUG, ET 25-26.]
62. [WUG, ET 25.]
63. [WUG, ET 26.]
64. WUG 13 [ET 26].
65. Landshut emphasizes that the dual concepts of rational versus irrational social action in Weber's methodology are to be explained in terms of the central theme of his research, namely, modern capitalism and the way of life of economically self-emancipating middle classes. See Landshut (1929), especially 54-61.
66. See, e.g., GAR III 302-3 [ET 267ff.].
67. Weber speaks of 'begrifflich reine Typen, denen sich das reale Handeln mehr oder minder annähert oder aus denen es – noch häufiger – gemischt is' (WuG 13) ['– this classification of the modes of orientation of action is – meant – only to formulate in conceptually pure form certain sociologically important types to which actual action is more or less closely approximated or, in much the more common case, which constitute its elements' (ET 26)]. An objection raised by Tellegen against this typology, namely, that 'the traditional and emotional element in goal and value-oriented behavior is misjudged' because in practice the matter is one not of 'mixed' types but of various 'aspects' of behavior is in that case also unjustified, in my opinion. See Tellegen (1968) 149.
68. WuG 9-10, 14 [cf. ET 9-11, 19-20, 29].
69. That in Weber's opinion sociology also endeavors to include future developments will be apparent from what has already been said about his views of cultural sciences in general. See above, pp. 30-34, and WL 175 [ET (3) 76].
70. GAR I 30-31 [cf. ET 47-48 (I have restored Weber's original italics to the English translation, which is by Talcott Parsons, since Professor Lemmen retained them in his Dutch translation of Weber's text. – HDM)].
71. I cite just one passage in which Weber says this explicitly: 'The following study may thus perhaps in a modest way form a contribution to the understanding of the manner in which ideas become effective forces in history.' GAR I 82 [ET 90].
72. GAR I 205-6 and n. 3 [ET 183 and 283-84, n. 118].
73. For a detailed empirical analysis (one that presents examples without aiming at completeness) of the method employed by Weber in his sociology of religion, see Prades (1966). For his analysis of Die protestantische Ethik, Prades relies largely on Weber's later interpolations, as he himself reports. See Prades, (1966) 230, n. 1. He also cited the allusions to historical materialism as one of the marks of the sociological character of this essay. See Prades (1966) 226.
74. GAR I [ET (1) 13].
75. Following a brief disquisition on his rational ideal-typical method, Weber says, 'Above all, such an essay in the sociology of religion aims at contributing to the typology and sociology of rationalism.' GAR I 537 [ET (6) 324].
76. GAR I 237-75 [ET (4): 'The Social Psychology of the World Religions'].
77. GAR I 536-73 [ET (6): 'Religious Rejections of the World and Their Directions'].
78. WuG 245-381 [ET 399-634: 'Chapter VI: Religious Groups (The Sociology of Religion'].
79. See, for instance, Lauwers (1974) 95-107.

80. GAR I 17-18 [ET 187].
81. Of the many places where he says this explicitly, see, for example, GAR I 18n. [ET 187-88]; GAR I 82 [ET 90-91]; WuG 245 [ET 399].
82. 'In order to understand the connection between the fundamental religious ideas of ascetic Protestantism and its maxims for everyday economic conduct, it is necessary to examine with special care such writings as have evidently been derived from ministerial practice.' GAR I 163 [ET 155].
83. WuG 285-314 [ET 80-137: ch. 6, 'Castes, Estates, Classes, and Religion'; ch. 7, 'Religion of Non-Privileged Classes'; ch. 8, 'Intellectuals, Intellectualism, and the History of Religion'].
84. No matter how strongly Weber emphasizes situational factors too here as conditioning religiosity, he repeatedly and explicitly maintains that the matter is not one of deterministic causality. Indeed, entirely consistently with his general sociological perspective, he also attributes to the religious position as such an originality of its own. How in spite of that Stark can assert that Weber's sociology of religion would be a form of sociologism because Weber would exaggerate the social factor in his approach and argumentation concerning the relation between social classes and religion is a great puzzle. That is all the more so since Stark himself must acknowledge that Weber sometimes insists that religious movements are not just class movements. See Stark (1964) 46. Stark's incomprehension goes so far that he even charges Weber with making a judgment as to which social strata would be bearers of authentic religiosity (especially artisans and proletarian intellectuals) and which would not (farmers, aristocrats, and bureaucrats). Furthermore, in his subconscious self Weber would espouse a particular ideal of religiosity whereby he would label Catholics as 'bad' and Calvinists as 'good.' See Stark (1964) 48.
   The explanation for all this, besides a superficial reading of Weber and a certain preoccupation with real religiosity on the part of Stark himself (namely, openness to the mystery of existence, which one can come into contact with through thought but especially through prayer), is perhaps to be found partly in the fact that until 1963 the section on 'estates, classes, and religion' was the only part of Weber's systematic sociology of religion available in English. Talcott Parsons mentions this fact in his introduction: Parsons (1966) xxxviiin.
85. WuG 245 [ET 399].
86. Peter L. Berger assumes that while avoiding an explicit definition of religion Weber in fact works with an implicit (concrete) one. See Berger (1967) 175-76, or Berger (1969) 194. Berger does not see the possibility of proceeding on the basis of a vague description of what 'people' understand by religion (which is what Weber does) and of identifying ever more precisely, while doing so, the theme which is thereby disclosed to view (which Weber also accomplishes). Weber's alternative has been to translate 'people' directly into 'purposeful actors,' so that it is no longer the conception of the observer ('people') but that of the actor which determines what religion is.
   According to Steeman, religion in Weber's view is the formulation of man's basic understanding, at every moment of history, of both man himself and the world in which he lives. It plays an irreplaceable role in man's relation with nature and with himself because it is the way life, as a task, is defined. Religion assumes different forms in different concrete situations. One could define it in Weber's spirit as follows: 'Religion is man's continuous effort to deal rationally with the irrationalities of life.' This, according to Steeman, is essentially a functional definition of religion. See Steeman (1964) 56-57.

193

This interpretation too must be rejected, I think, because according to Weber religion can vanish from society: 'But victorious capitalism, since it rests on mechanical foundations, needs its support [namely, that of ascetic Protestantism] no more.' GAR I 204 [ET 181-82].

Lennert, who raises the question of what Weber means by religiosity and of what its core would be on Weber's view, makes no distinction between the religiosity Weber describes and Weber's own conception of religiosity as this would be implicit in his sociology of religion. His conclusion – namely, that according to Weber the core of religiosity resides in man's quest for a meaning in his life independent of his own existence and in relation to which he experiences salvation (see Lennert (1935) 37-41) – also strikes me as arguable, at least in the sense that it cannot be inferred from Weber's sociology of religion in the absence of proof that he was unfaithful to his own method.

87. WuG 5-6 [ET 12].
88. WuG 5-6 [ET 12, cf. 15]; WL 436-37. To Weber statistics are not an ultimately indispensable element of interpretive (verstehende) sociology. The validity of causal connections between phenomena can be shown just as adequately in a qualitative way, as is proven by Weber's own cross-cultural studies in support of his Protestantism thesis.
89. WuG 10 [ET 20].
90. WL 191 [ET (1) 90].
91. Parsons criticizes Weber for typological rigidity and the reification of ideal types. Thus in the field of sociology of religion Weber would hypostatize religious motives by isolating them from other motives in the system of personality and from other processes in the systems of society and culture. See Parsons (1966) lxiv-lxv.
    It is not my intention to pass judgment here on Weber's use of ideal types. See, however, my comments at p. ??? below. In so far as method is concerned, Parson's reproach is entirely unwarranted. Isolation of the religious factor is pointedly necessary, in order to facilitate locating the typically religious influence on society. That Weber further restricts the influence of the religious factor to just a few processes in society is entirely consistent with the conscious selection of his field of inquiry. In 'Die Wirtschaftsethik' Weber says so expressly, and he implicitly refutes both of Parsons' objections. GAR I 238-39 [ET (4) 267-68].
92. Weber's most extensive discussion of ideal types is found in 'Die 'Objektivität' sozialwissenschaftlicher und sozialpolitischer Erkenntnis.' WL 146-214 [ET (1)], especially 185-212 [ET (1) 85ff.]. What I have said above is derived mainly from this discussion. What follows is based mainly on WL 533-36 [ET (3) 39-44] and WuG 2-3, 10 [ET 5-7; 19-22].
93. [On the translation of the German term 'Evidenz,' see WuG, ET 58n.6.]
94. [WuG, ET 21.]
95. Among others, Wach (1931) 78-79 charges that, given his method, Weber tends to regard even religiously motivated action as going on in accordance with the goal-oriented category of instrumental rationality. He speaks in this connection of the 'rationalism of this great scientist.' It should be clear, I think, that this by no means has to follow from Weber's methodology. In fact, Weber even explicitly acknowledges the irrational character of religious experience as something self-evident: 'The religious experience as such is of course irrational, like every experience. In its highest, mystical form it is even experience kat exochein, and, as James has well shown, is distinguished by its absolute incommunicability.'

GAR I 112 [ET 233n.]. ['The actor is more likely to 'be aware' of it in a vague sense than he is to 'know' what he is doing or be explicitly self-conscious about it.'

96. [WuG, ET 21.]

97. Because an ideal type often is composed of many characteristics neither the interdependence nor the alikeness in direction and degree of covariance of which are established a priori, it will be impossible using the ideal typical method to design a typology that is at once empirically valid and in possession of a high degree of generalization. The polar opposition between certain ideal types in Weber is not for that reason to be construed as entailing the extremes of a continuum the fluid transitions of which are precisely identifiable. Nevertheless, the distinction between ideal types and modern empirical typologies should not be exaggerated. After all, ideal types are designed, according to Weber, to become superfluous as they are brought into ever closer proximity to empirical reality. The results of research are likewise reported by means of ideal types.

Lazarsfeld and Oberschall (1965) survey Weber's contribution to five sociological and socio-psychological research projects (concerning the situation of agricultural and industrial workers and the attitudes of factory workers) and conclude: 'His thinking on the construction of empirical typologies was very modern– ' (191). They go on to add that the 'controversial' ideal types are totally different from the empirical ones. Their assessment of the ideal types is based, however, on a complete misunderstanding of Weber's methodological views, whereby they attribute to him a logical-deductive scheme of approach devoid of any testing (198).

Baumgarten finds a close affinity between Weber's ideal type and the modern scientific concept of the 'model,' since both aim at theoretically consistent knowledge of empirical reality. He shrinks from identifying the two, however, since the ideal type would by definition lack the flexibility needed to combine the possible variables in the way the empirical material might require. Given its extreme, one-sided selective character, he considers the ideal type suitable only for the initial approach to reality. He regards discrepancy with reality as determinative for the ideal type. See Baumgarten (1964) 595-97.

In contrast, Warner does identify the ideal type with the concept of the model. He places Weber's sharp emphasis on the one-sided selective and utopian character of the ideal type in the intellectual context of the methodological conflict between the German historical school (G. Schmoller) and the Austrian theoretical school (C. Menger), which Weber attempts to bring into synthesis. Weber's real intention, Warner thinks, can for this reason also be better inferred from Weber's actual use of his ideal types. That shows, according to Warner, that in Weber the selection and ordering criteria for the construction of ideal types are sociological in character and that they converge with the actual course of the empirical data to be ordered. See Warner (1970) 88-89.

Whatever one may think of this controversy, it seems clear that Weber's ideal types cannot all be treated in the same way. Weber's ideal type can in any case be tested in principle for reliability and validity, because irrespective of its possible origin in research-related intuition, it contains nothing but explicitly formulated unequivocal knowledge.

Notes to Chapter 3

1. On the distinction between 'rationality,' 'rationalism,' and 'rationalization' see chap. 5, n. 3a, below. Here I only want to say that in Weber the term 'rationalism' is a social or sociological category and not a philosophical concept. For all that, the concept of rationalism does sometimes occur in Weber in the philosophical sense – in the context, for example, of the prophet Isaiah's exhortation to resist the attack of the Assyrian king Sennacherib (Isaiah 36-37), which it was of course simply impossible to do in terms of the political probabilities of the day. However, the facts of the matter later proved Isaiah right. Now it is suggested, according to Weber, that Isaiah would have received information – 'even before the king!' – about the circumstances that eventually forced Sennacherib to withdraw. 'To seriously maintain that,' Weber states, '– is rationalism, indeed, equivalent to those attempts to explain the miracle at the wedding of Cana by means of liqueur which allegedly Jesus secretly brought with him' (italics added). GAR III 289 [ET 275].
   In his role as a sociologist, Weber makes no pronouncements about the miraculous or nonmiraculous character of the historical facts of Jewish or Christian history. Rather, he speaks of these facts as believers experienced them. He maintains that every philosophical rational explanation does an injustice to the fact that religious people obviously experience certain events as being charged with mystery.
2. Weber says, for example, 'The rationalization of conduct with which we have to deal here can assume unusually varied forms' (italics added). GAR I 266 [ET (4) 293).
3. The ideal type functions here (in Weber) not in the first place as a heuristic device but as the indispensable means to the (admittedly provisional) presentation of the results of research.
4. GAR I [ET (1) 13].
5. See, for example, GAR I 202-3 [ET (2) 180-81].
6. For Weber's description of the 'spirit' of capitalism, see GAR I 30-62 [ET (2) 47-48].
7. Because the rational organization of (formally) free labor as business enterprise was lacking everywhere outside the modern Orient, it was likewise impossible for a rational socialism with a 'proletariat' as a class to exist anywhere outside the modern Occident. For this description of capitalism as a socio-economic structure, see GAR I 4-9 [ET (1) 21-24). (The italics in my paraphrase [although they do not appear in the ET] are Weber's.)
8. Franklin, as quoted in GAR I (2), ET 48-49. The italics are Franklin's. The exclamation mark [which has not been carried over into the ET] is Weber's. With it Weber means to call attention to the fact that on Franklin's view anyone who is careless with money is also ethically guilty.
9. GAR I 31-32 [ET (2) 49-50].
10. [GAR I, ET (2) 51.]
11. [GAR I, ET (2) 54, 55, 57.]
12. GAR I 35 [ET (2) 53].
13. [GAR I, ET (2) 54.]
14. [GAR I, ET (2) 70.]
15. [GAR I, ET (2) 76.]
16. [GAR I, ET (2) 60.]
17. [GAR I, ET (2) 58-59.]

18. [GAR I, ET (2) 64.]
19. [GAR I, ET (2) 58, 73-74.]
20. For Weber's discussion of Protestant rationalism, see GAR I 84-206 [ET (2) 93-183].
21. [GAR I, ET (2) 157.]
22. [GAR I, ET (2) 157-58.]
23. [GAR I, ET (2) 158.]
24. [GAR I, ET (2) 158.]
25. [GAR I, ET (2) 159.]
26. [GAR I, ET (2) 159.]
27. [GAR I, ET (2) 159.]
28. [GAR I, ET (2) 124.]
29. [Cf. GAR I, ET (2) 163.]
30. [GAR I, ET (2) 220, n. 7.]
31. [GAR I, ET (2) 97.]
32. [GAR I, ET (2) 98.]
33. [Westminster Confession of Faith (1647), Chapter X, 'Of Effectual Calling,' no. 1, as quoted in GAR I, ET (2) 100.]
34. [GAR I, ET (2) 104.]
35. [GAR I, ET (2) 105.]
36. [GAR I, ET (2) 109.]
37. [GAR I, ET (2) 110.]
38. [GAR I, ET (2) 115; cf. GAR I, ET (2) 232, n. 60, where Weber cites the Helvetic Confession.]
39. [GAR I, ET (2) 116.]
40. [GAR I, ET (2) 80, 120-21.]
41. [GAR I, ET (2) 124.]
42. GAR I 117 [ET (2) 119].
43. [GAR I, ET (2) 115.]
44. GAR I 163 [ET (2) 154].
45. [GAR I, ET (2) 144.]
46. [GAR I, ET (2) 144-45.]
47. [GAR I, ET (2) 144.]
48. For the description of this class see especially GAR I 395-430 [ET (5) 107-41].
49. [GAR I, ET (5) 115.]
50. Because there is here just one distinguishing criterion and because it is present to a greater or lesser degree in every educational situation, it is possible to speak of a continuum. Usually, Weber's ideal types are too complex for that. See n. 78 in the preceding chapter.
51. For a description of the Confucian approach to life, see especially GAR I 430-58 [ET (5) 142-70].
52. GAR I 457 [ET (5) 169].
53. Weber deals with this aspect of Confucianism in the context of a comparison with Taoism, as one of the points to show that the Confucian ethic was unsuitable for the masses. See GAR I 491-93 [ET (5) 206-8].
54. For Weber's discussion of Taoism, see especially GAR I 458-512 [ET (5) 173-225].
55. For the caste system, see especially GAR II 31-109 [ET 29-110].
56. For that matter, India too had craft guilds and merchants guilds, during the period when the cities were developing. In India these guilds did not lead, however, to the emergence of an autonomous urban burgher class, as they did in the

West. The caste system prevented this. GAR II 35-36 [ET 33-34].

57. For these aspects of Brahman rationalism, see especially GAR II 116-22, 132-33, 141-47 [ET 117-23, 131-33, 143-49].

58. GAR II 120 [ET 121].

59. [GAR II, ET 121-22.]

60. GAR II 142 [ET 144].

61. As a result, rationality in the Western sense did not exist in India. What Weber has to say about administrative technique is typical: 'The rationalism of administrative technique could not offer any refinements. This was in itself not yet rational.' GAR II 167n. [ET 358].

62. See for this subject GAR II 133-40 and 148-202 [ET 137-91, where Weber distinguishes knowledge, asceticism, and mysticism].

63. This matter of possessing as if not possessing is dealt with expressly in the Bhagavad Gita, in a philosophical dialogue in which waging war is vindicated ethically in the sense that it can also lead to authentic salvation. This dialogue, part of a heroic poem, has been translated into almost every language. See GAR II 189-202 [ET 180-91. Here Weber states: 'The early Christian had his goods and women 'as if he had them not'. In the Bhagavad Gita – the man of knowledge proves himself in action – while inwardly remaining completely detached. That is, he acts as if he acted not– ' (184)].

64. GAR II 207-17 [ET 192-204].

65. [GAR II, ET 201.]

66. [GAR II, ET 198-99.]

67. [GAR II, ET 200.]

68. GAR II 217-50 [ET 204-56].

69. [GAR II, ET 220-21.]

70. [GAR II, ET 211.]

71. ['Salvation is an absolutely personal performance of the self-reliant individual.' GAR II, ET 213.]

72. ['The task is to destroy the will if one wishes to escape karma.' GAR II, ET 211.]

73. ['Whoever achieves that illumination enjoys – bliss here and now – is karma-free – has inwardly escaped the endless wheel of rebirths.– ' GAR II, ET 212.]

74. ['Will alone produces out of the bundle of psychosomatic events, which, empirically, is the 'soul', an 'ego'.– The will exerts influence beyond death and the grave. Thus the individual who dies can rise again – but not through the 'transmigration of souls', for there is no soul substance. However, when an ego is decomposing in death, 'thirst' at once joins together a new ego burdened with the curse of karma causality, which demands an ethical compensation for each ethically relevant event. Thirst alone handicaps the appearance of redemptory illumination leading to divine tranquility.' GAR II, ET 211.]

75. [GAR II, ET 206.]

76. For the self-understanding of the Jewish people, see GAR III, especially 81-173 [ET 59-138].

77. [Cf. Exodus 23:15, Deuteronomy 16:16-17.]

78. See especially GAR III 181-280 [ET 147-263].

79. [GAR III, ET 191.]

80. GAR III 281-350 [ET 265-382].

81. [GAR III, ET 289, 299.]

82. [GAR III, ET 291.]

83. On Jewish diaspora rationalism, see WuG 367-74, [ET 615-23]; on Pharisees and rabbis, see GAR III 401-22 [ET 385-404]. On the emergence of Judaism

as a purely confessional entity and its typical ethic, see GAR III 351-400 [ET 336-82].

84. Weber reports that 'today' – thus prior to the First World War – German rabbis still endeavor to press this prescription even upon the Zionistic Jews colonizing Palestine. WuG 371 [ET 618].

Notes to Chapter 4

1. GAR I 62 [ET (2) 77-78].
2. This 'dialectical' character of the social process, with the externalization, objectification, and internalization of values as the main moments, is described at length by Berger (1967) 3-28 or (1969) 13-39. Berger himself relies largely on Weber but also on more recent writers, including Arnold Gehlen, Alfred Schutz, and George Herbert Mead. Obviously this implies that Berger's view cannot be attributed integrally to Weber, although the main elements of it are certainly present in Weber, as we shall see. Yet I want to point out at this juncture that Berger does Weber an injustice by presenting this dialectic as a combination of Weber's subjectivizing view and Durkheim's objectifying view (Berger (1967) 189 n. 2). Weber regards society's material and intellectual culture not just as a product of human intentionality but also expressly as 'something' that takes a position quasi-independently of the members of society. The concept (not the term) internalization is also clearly present in Weber, as I hope to show.
3. Cf. above, pp. 49-51.
4. The element 'conscious' is a constitutive moment of rationalization. Weber often uses the terms 'rationalization' and 'sublimation' together or interchanges the one term for the other; see GAR I 541-42, 544 [ET (6) 327-28, 330]. In Weber 'sublimation' means that something – e.g., a feeling or habit – becomes 'conscious.' It is precisely by virtue of their 'conscious' character that rational actions stand in contrast to emotional or traditional actions.
5. Weber mentions the terms 'systematization' and 'rationalization' in a single breath so often that to supply references here would seem extravagant. Sometimes he explicitly uses the term 'systematic' or a synonym of it to clarify the concept of 'rationalization,' e.g., at GAR I 512 [ET (5) 226]; cf. also n. 44 to the present chapter, below.
6. SWP 293, or WL 526 [ET (3) 34-35].
7. Weber states this expressly in connection with economic actions: 'To be sure the capitalistic form of an enterprise and the spirit in which it is run generally stand in some sort of adequate relationship to each other, but not in one of necessary interdependence.' Italics added; GAR I 49 [ET (2) 64].
8. In his methodological essays Weber says this about meaningful actions in general: 'We desire something concretely either 'for its own sake' or as a means of achieving something else which is more highly desired.' Italics added; WL 149 [ET (1) 52].
9. Weber makes this generalization when observing that life-view-oriented associations become mechanisms that increasingly free themselves factually from the idea originally underlying them. See Weber's 'Geschäftsbericht' in Verhandlungen (1911) 57. Weber calls his study of Protestantism, in which it appears that the results of the Reformation were neither foreseen nor desired by the Reformers and in fact were often the opposite of what they intended, a contribution

to the illustration of the way in which 'ideas' become effective 'forces' in history. GAR I 82 [ET (2) 90]. See also notes 76 and 100 to the present chapter, below.
10. GAR I 37 [ET (2) 55].
11. GAR I 37-38 [ET (2) 55].
12. GAR I 37 [ET (2) 54-55].
13. For examples, see, e.g., WuG 835 [ET 1402-3; see also ET 957-58].
14. GAR I 204 [ET (2) 182].
15. WuG 835-37 [ET 1402-3].
16. GAR I 15-16 [ET (1) 30-31].
17. GAR I 46-48 [ET (2) 60-62].
18. Weber's definition puts one in mind of the very analogous distinction made by David Riesman between the 'inner-directed' character type that finds within itself the impulse towards a particular selectivity and the 'tradition-oriented' character whose behaviors are controlled by the culture inherited from the days of yore. In Riesman, both the first type of person, who sails by his own compass, and the second type, who lives as it were by the 'book,' are products of society. Riesman (1959) 18-23.
19. GAR I 512-36 [ET (5) 226-49, especially 231-35].
20. GAR I 517 [ET (5) 230-31].
21. GAR I 80-81, 95-96, 127-28, 164, 192, etc. [ET (2) 88-90, 95-97, 105-8, 127, 137, 173].
22. GAR II 133 [ET 132-33].
23. Reinhard Bendix criticizes Weber for inconsistency in failing to distinguish between 'impulse' (Trieb) and 'incentive' (Anreiz). Weber did not use the latter term at all. According to Bendix, the distinction between the two terms is relevant to exact characterization of the process of internalization. Bendix (1962) 273n.
24. At issue here is the distinction within the 'self' between the 'me' and the 'I' that Peter L. Berger employs, following George Herbert Mead. See Berger (1967) 192 n. 19, and 201 nn. 1 and 4.
25. Weber states expressly that the most frequent form of social action stems from 'ingrained habituation.' WuG 16 [ET 25].
26. SWP 317, or WL 593-94 [ET (5) 138-39].
27. 'A usage [Brauch] will be called a 'custom' (Sitte) if the practice is based on long standing.' WuG 15 [ET 29].
    Here I wish only to emphasize the fact of internalization, without pursuing further the differences between 'usages,' 'customs,' 'conventions,' 'norms,' and so forth. For these distinctions see WuG 14ff. [ET 29-36].
28. WuG 15-16 [ET 30].
29. Maurice Weyembergh regards goal-oriented thinking as the core of Weber's concept of rationality; the acme is reached in the axiological discussion as I summarily presented it in connection with Weber's methodological conceptions (see above, pp. 37-39). This perspective is understandable given Weyembergh's philosophical position. According to him, the axiological discussion is the point of departure from which to explain the coherence of Weber's entire oeuvre (Weyembergh (1972) 182, 203, etc.). This view does not conflict with mine. Sociologically, however, our concern is not with Weber the person but with Weber's view of rationality as a socio-cultural process.
    Given my conception of rationality as a 'dialectical' process, I accordingly stand closer to Talcott Parsons, who likewise distinguished three senses of rationalization in Weber's sociology of religion, namely (1) intellectual clarification or

specification and systematization of ideas; (2) normative control or sanction; and (3) motivational attachment or 'commitment' (Parsons (1966) xxxii-xxxiii). Parsons does not, however, allude explicitly to the dialectic between these three senses.

I agree with Bendix's statement that in Weber rationalization acquires various substantive meanings depending on the sphere of life being rationalized. Certainly I agree with him that rationalization is not an inevitable or irreversible process. In addition, according to Bendix, the concept of rationality has two other senses in Weber. Namely, it is 'the manifestation of individual liberty.' This was both appropriate in a capitalist era and congenial to Weber personally, Bendix observes. I am in agreement with Weyembergh (1972, 203, n. 3) that what is at issue here is not rationality itself, however, but a precondition of it, the possibility of (rational) choice (cf. above, p. 39). The third sense of the concept of rationality Bendix distinguishes is the synonym 'clarity.' From Bendix's discussion I conclude he means by this the construction of ideal types. I would prefer not to distinguish these as a separate sense, and to view them instead as a special case of 'conscious and orderly thought,' the (logical) first moment of a possible dialectical socio-cultural process, in casu: practicing science. Bendix (1962) 278-79, n. 33.

30. The terms 'dialectic' and ''dialectical' method' occur in Weber's sociology of religion [Economy and Society ch. 6] and sociology of law [Economy and Society ch. 8] in the sense of 'method of argumentation': in connection, for example, with the typical argumentation of the petty bourgeois intellectuals of St. Paul's day, which finds expression also in his epistles (WuG 310 [ET 511]); ' 'dialectical' method' as practiced in the medieval universities (WuG 343 [ET 790]); the since vanished, typically Western dialectics of the Talmudic diaspora-Judaic Pumbeditha academy of Babylon (WuG 478 [ET 825]); and the typification of Jewish rationalism (WuG 720 [ET 1201]).

31. GAR I 203-4 [ET (2) 181-82; Weber quotes from Richard Baxter's Saint's Everlasting Rest, ch. xii].

32. See, e.g., GAR I 249-51 [cf. ET (4) 277-78, where the text reads 'a cosmic love'].

33. See, e.g., WuG 245 [ET 399-400].

34. For the psychological concept of 'rationalization,' see, e.g., A. M. J. Chorus (1953) 124ff.

35. SWP 293, or WL 526 [ET (3) 34-35].

36. Of course, I have presented Nietzsche here in terms of Weber's summarizing version. See GAR I 241-42 [ET (4) 270] and WuG 301ff. [ET 494-99].

37. WuG 301-3 [ET 494-96].

38. GAR III 421 [ET 404].

39. As the context indicates, Weber means by 'ideas' human knowledge at the theoretical level.

The concept of 'interests' (Interesse) plays an important role in Weber's sociology. For all that, he never defines the term explicitly, nor does he deal explicitly with the relation between 'interests' and 'values' (or 'worth'). It seems a correct interpretation to understand by 'interests' all the goods, whatever their nature, that an actor considers worthy of his concrete pursuit. Health, certitude, prestige, possessions, knowledge, power, the status quo in society, rebirth, etc., Weber calls 'interests.' To the extent that interests are objects of social action, they are also to be regarded as concretizations of values for the actor concerned.

40. GAR I 252 [ET (4) 280].

41. GAR I 252 [ET (4) 280].

42. GAR I 258-59 [ET (4) 286].
43. Weber explicitly states this basis for constructing ideal types. GAR I 537 [ET (6) 323-24].
44. GAR I 512 [ET (5) 226].
45. GAR I 259-60 [ET 287].
46. GAR I 260, n. 1 [ET 287 and 450, n. 5].
47. On magic and the ethic of magic, see especially WuG 245-59 and 261-68 [ET 399-424, 427-39].
48. A clear example of the fact that magical charisma must constantly prove itself in terms of the data of experience is provided by the case of the Chinese emperor and the mandarins as individual persons; see above, p. 79.
49. WuG 259 [ET 424]. This distinction between magic and religion is not in conflict with what I said earlier about Weber's refusal to define religion (see above, p. 57), for Weber has no intention of determining here what a sociologist is to understand by religion. He means only to distinguish two affinitive forms of intentionality (he often uses the terms 'magical' and 'religious' in a single breath to indicate comparable phenomena – see, e.g., WuG 245 [ET 399-400] – which because of their experiential differences can be indicated scientifically by different terms. Yinger (1968), who advances a functional definition of religion (Yinger, 9), regards it as necessary to distinguish religion and magic scientifically, even though the two very often actually go together in his view too – so much so, in fact, that he expresses agreement with Herskovits's assertion that magic is in fact an integral part of religion (Yinger, 42). For the rest, Yinger's definition of magic agrees almost completely with Weber's: magic in Yinger's view, too, is aimed in the first place at the realization of immediate objectives (weather, harvest, victory, health) through human manipulation and control of meta-empirical forces (Yinger, 41-42).
50. The fact that magical ethics are unbreakably tied to concrete worldly objectives does not mean that 'artificial' social institutions based on magical ethics cannot arise. Weber uses totemism as an illustration, since in certain cases it generates an artificial and functional organization (Zweckverband) through which the 'brotherhood' achieve a magically-religiously guaranteed fraternalism which does not coincide per se with local or political social groups but which instead is diffused right through them. Meanwhile, Weber condemns as a gross and by now generally repudiated exaggeration the belief that totemism was virtually universal and that practically all social groups and religions derived from it. WuG 264-654 [ET 434].
51. This does not detract from the fact that incidental tensions could arise between magical orgiasticism and sexuality: magicians and also priests had at times temporarily to observe cultic abstinence. The origin of this practice is to be found in the fact that from the standpoint of a strongly stereotyped group ritual, sexuality appeared to be specifically demonic. Yet this pertains to a purely cultic chastity linked to magical or desdemonic motives. GAR I 557 [ET (6) 334] and WuG 362-63 [ET 602-4]. This tension is of course in principle different in nature from that between religious ethics and sexuality, as what follows will make clear.
52. For this matter see especially GAR I 536-37 [ET (6)] and WuG 348-67 [ET 576-610].
53. [WuG, ET 578.]
54. GAR I 538-39 [ET (6) 325]. (I have added the italicization of 'asceticism' and 'mysticism.' – ML)
55. [WuG, ET 579.]

56. [WuG, ET 600.]
57. [WuG, ET 596.]
58. [WuG, ET 583ff.]
59. [WuG, ET 589.]
60. [WuG, ET 608.]
61. [WuG, ET 601.]
62. Here one must be careful not to attribute to Weber an unqualified form of religious evolutionism.

    In the first place, such an attribution would be in conflict with his views on the theory of science. In his methodological works Weber warns explicitly against the peril of exchanging an ideal-typical development model for an actual historical development process. The temptation is great to regard something that follows logically as something that must necessarily develop historically. On the point of religious development, Weber reacts in this connection against Hermann Usener, who distinguishes three phases in the rise of belief in God. See Winckelmann, in SWP 531; WuG 247 [ET 402]. In the second place, a reading of the texts I shall principally rely upon in the expositions to follow – namely, 'Die Entstehung der Religionen' (WuG 245-59 [ET 399-424, 'The Origins of Religion']) and 'Gottesbegriff. Religiöse Ethik. Tabu' (WuG 261-68 [cf. ET 432-39]) – leads to the conclusion that Weber was engaged here in an elaboration of theoretical stages of development of advancing rationalization. Of such theoretically constructed levels of rationality (theoretisch konstruierten Rationalitätsstufen) Weber states explicitly in his sociology of law what repeatedly appears to be the case in his discussion of 'the origin of religions' as well: in historical reality these phases neither occur everywhere in this sequence nor are everywhere present; the bases for the kind and degree of rationalization were totally different historically. WuG 504-5 [cf. ET 655, 753, 801, 809-10, 892].

    There is a difference between Weber's way of speaking about the development of magic and his way of speaking about the development of the great religions. He speaks of '... the stages of magic, which are rather similar the world over...' WuG 261 [ET 427]. However, of the religions he says in contrast, 'In no respect can one simply integrate various world religions into a chain of types, each of them signifying a new 'stage.' ' GAR I 264-65 [ET (4) 292].
63. [WuG, ET 402.]
64. Pantheon formation becomes possible, sociologically speaking, only when power positions have developed which call for reflection on man's relationship to the suprasensual world. This will be clear from the discussion of rationalization as a socio-cultural process that follows in section III of this chapter.
65. See for a description of salvation religiosity GAR I 242-67 [ET (4) 270-95]; GAR I 536-73 [ET (6)]; WuG 314-19 [ET 500-506].
66. GAR I 253 [ET (4) 281]. Weber calls attention to the fact that the rational name for a theodicy of suffering and death was not a powerful influence in the past alone. As recently as 1906 a poll of proletarians concerning the grounds of their disbelief indicated that only a minority related it to the conclusions of natural science. The majority referred to the 'injustice' in the world essentially 'because they believed in a revolutionary compensation in this world.' GAR I 247 [ET (4) 275-76].
67. [The translation of the following passage on Weber's presentation of theodicy is based on WuG, ET 519-26.]
68. Peter Berger has adopted Weber's concept of 'legitimation' in order to shed light on its 'world-maintenance' function, or, in other words, its function of preser-

ving the objective social order once generated by collective definition. He has worked this concept of legitimation out further than Weber did, by distinguishing a number of levels of legitimation. In doing so he remains, however, within Weber's line of thought. Specifically, the fact that legitimations effectively fulfill their stabilizing function not only by saying what 'should be' but also by saying what 'is' is entirely within Weber's line of thought, which of course also ascribed legitimating force to tradition. See Weber, WuG 16-20 [ET 31-38]; Berger (1967) 29-32, or (1969) 41-44.

69. See the discussion of the internalization of values in section I. C. of this chapter, above.

70. Cf. Berger (1967) 32 or (1969) 44.

71. WuG 16-17 [ET 32].

72. Thus formulated, the rationalization process is intensionally poor in content, relatively speaking. This is probably why Weber, given his conception of science, speaks repeatedly of the indefiniteness but never of the definiteness of the concept of rationality. He does set two criteria for determining the degree of religious rationalization. See section II B in this chapter, above. One can ask why in this connection Weber advances the absence of magic as one of these criteria without supporting his case with explicit argumentation. This could be considered indicative of an unconscious esteem for rationality that would regard Western rationality as the 'authentic,' objectively correct attribution of meaning. However, this interpretation is not correct.

In the first place, Weber recognizes that, from a subjective view, magic too can be rationalized, in at least as great a measure as modern medical science. See section I A, above. The rationalization of magical charisma from naturalism to symbolism meant an ever more thoroughgoing abstraction vis-à-vis concrete empirical reality, so that this could be explained and manipulated via the 'original' world of spirits and demons. This symbolism could be further rationalized to a 'science' based on arguments by analogy, so that even more sectors of life were rendered vulnerable to manipulation, until the world became one great enchanted garden. Thus here too rationalization entails advancing systematic insight and power over people.

Yet magical rationality differs from religious rationality in that the former does not necessitate the rationalization of human behavior; on the contrary, it augments the possibility of arbitrary human actions. The magician enhances his power not by rationalizing his actions to a consistent pattern of behavior but by enlarging his power over the spirits, which he can then arbitrarily employ for his own or another's good or evil. The 'laity' in a magical community are thereby made subject to what are for them opaque, alien powers, with the result that they are bereft of any capacity to account for their behavior from a central vantage point or to shape it consistently in the light of such a vantage point. A society dominated by magic accordingly does not lead to a rationalism in which man can achieve personal autonomy by shaping his life in conformity to a central system of meaning attribution. Such a society leads at most to a practical rationalism focussed directly on the attainment of concrete ends. Cf. chap. 3, section III B, above.

The explanation of the fact that Weber advances the absence of magic as a criterion of religious rationalization lies, in Levin's view, too, in the potential for arbitrary human intervention in the world of gods and in the behavior of non-magicians. Levin (1970) 172-73.

73. GAR I 264 [ET (4) 291].

74. GAR I 253 [ET (4) 280-81].
75. WuG 28 [ET 53, cf. 942].
76. WuG 28 [ET 53].
77. WuG 549 [ET 952].
78. WuG 544-45 [ET 946-48].
79. A summary description of these three types of domination is provided by Weber in GAR I 267-73 [ET (4) 295-300]. A short essay on the subject appeared posthumously in SWP 151-66. A more extensive theoretical exposition can be found in WuG 122-76 [ET 212-301]. Weber's sociology of domination deals with them even more extensively, but in an empirical-descriptive way. See WuG 541-868 [ET 942-1372, especially 954].
80. In presenting his basic sociological concepts, Weber contrasts the acceptance of a particular social order for reasons of legitimacy to conformity out of custom alone or for goal-rational considerations alone as follows: 'Only then will an order be called 'valid' if the orientation toward these maxims occurs, among other reasons, also because it is in some appreciable way regarded by the actor as in some way obligatory or exemplary for him.' WuG 16 [ET 31; italics added]. It seems to me not at all far-fetched to suppose that in defining legitimacy Weber had in mind as the prototypes of legitimacy the two forms of prophecy, that is, the exemplary (vorbildlich) and the ethical (verbindlich). Prophets find the basis of their legitimacy within themselves and must be regarded as incarnations of values.
81. This mechanism (the routinization of charisma) is dealt with explicitly only in a very summary way in Weber's sociology of religion. See GAR I 270-73 [ET (4) 297-99]. Implicitly, however, one encounters it there time and again. Weber deals with it at the theoretical level in WuG 142-48 [ET 246-54] and more extensively and descriptively in the fifth section of his sociology of domination: WuG 654-87 [ET 1111-56]. My discussion is based largely on the last of these passages.
82. WuG 654 [ET 1111-12].
83. WuG 661 [ET 1121].
84. [WuG, ET 1119.]
85. It is Rudolf Sohm's contribution, Weber says, that he thought through consistently and described sociologically this kind of domination (Kategorie der Gewaltstruktur), be it in but one historical case, that of the rise of the ecclesiastical authority of the early Christian church. WuG 654-55 [ET 1112].
86. Nor does this distinction lie, furthermore, Weber observes, in intuition's being an inward and rationalization's being an outward something: '(Parenthetically, in the value sphere, which does not concern us here, all these kinds of ideas – including artistic intuition – have in common that to objectivate themselves, to prove their reality, they must signify a grasp on demands of the 'work' or, if you prefer, a being seized by them; they are not merely a subjective feeling or experience.)' WuG 658, n. 1 [ET 1116]; italics added.
87. WuG 658 [ET 1116].
88. See section I C in this chapter, above.
89. For Weber the distinction between 'intuition' and 'understanding' [rendered 'reason' in WuG, ET 1116] was sociologically irrelevant. This is not, however, true for the terms 'ratio' and 'intellect.'
In Weber the terms 'Intellekt' and 'Ratio,' 'Intellektualismus' and 'Rationalisierung' occur very frequently and are repeatedly used in combination with each other and even interchangeably. Yet they are not identical. 'Intellectualism' and

'intellectualizing' pertain exclusively to subjectively conscious rationality, not to its objectified forms. Hence the term 'rationality' has a greater extension than the term 'intellectuality': 'The likewise revolutionary force of 'reason' [in contrast to 'charisma'] works from without: by altering the situations of life and hence its problems, finally in this way changing men's attitudes toward them; or it intellectualizes (italics added – ML) the individual. Charisma, on the other hand, may effect a subjective or internal reorientation...' WuG 142 [ET 245].

90. WuG 661 [ET 1121].
91. [Cf. WuG, ET 1118.]
92. [Cf. WuG, ET 1122.]
93. [WuG, ET 1123.]
94. Weber deals with the various ways in which the problem of the succession of the charismatic leader can be resolved at two places in WuG. At the first, WuG 143-48 [ET 246-49], he distinguishes six ways, and at the second, WuG 671-75 [ET 1135-41], he distinguishes three. As the criterion of the threefold distinction Weber employs the routinization of charisma. The sixfold distinction is more a summary of actual cases, only the last of which involves mention of the routinization of charisma. The threefold distinction, however, embraces all the cases presented in the sixfold survey. Given the relevance to my discussion of 'routinization,' I have based my remarks mainly on WuG 671-75 [ET 1135-41].

The threefold distinction is an organic part of the empirically descriptive argument of the sociology of domination; the sixfold analysis is found in the more conceptual and theoretical section of WuG.

In addition to providing references, this note is meant to serve as an illustration of the difference – a frequent source of confusion – between the conceptual-abstract, 'staccato' first part of WuG and the empirical-sociological, more leisurely flowing second part. See chap. 1, section IV, above.
95. The term 'personally acquired' in contrast to 'by virtue of birth' suggests that there should be some mention here of the current dichotomy of 'achievement' versus 'ascription.' The latter terminology is related, however, to (voluntary or involuntary) entry into a group and not to the assignment of a position by third parties, which is Weber's concern in this case.
96. [WuG, ET 247-49.]
97. [WuG, ET 1140.]
98. [WuG, ET 1143, 249.]
99. WuG 155-56 [ET 266-67].
100. [WuG, ET 1140.]
101. WuG 675 [ET 1141].
102. [WuG, ET 1121.]
103. [WuG, ET 267.]
104. [WuG 155, ET 266.]
105. For Weber this need for legitimation is not a speculative or philosophical matter but an empirically established fact. Every 'power,' indeed every advantage in life (health, wealth, happiness), however obvious the 'accidentalness' of its acquisition, bears with it for its privileged possessor, according to Weber, 'the never ceasing need to look upon his position as in some way 'legitimate', upon his advantage as 'deserved', and the other's disadvantage as being brought about by the latter's 'fault.' ' In times of social stability, when power relations are no 'problem,' even the less privileged accept this 'myth.' In times of social instability, however, when the class situation becomes clearly visible as a power fac-

tor decisively influencing life's advantages and disadvantages, this 'myth' of legitimacy becomes the object of bitter struggle. This was so not only earlier but also in the modern class struggle, where this need for self-justification clearly occupies a place in the foreground. WuG 549 [ET 953].

106. WuG 156 [ET 266-68; cf. 1113, 1141].
107. [Cf. WuG, ET 1150.]
108. WuG 686 [ET 1156].
109. Der Begriff der 'Diziplin' schliesst die 'Eingeübtheit' des kritik- und widerstandslosen Massengehorsams ein. WuG 29 [ET 53].
110. WuG 682 [ET 1150].
111. WuG 680 [ET 1147].
112. The term Konflikt occurs repeatedly in Weber, but is nowhere precisely defined. From the context, however, it is evident that it may be identified with Kampf. WuG 20 [ET 38].
113. WuG 20 [ET 38].
114. WuG 20 [ET 38].
115. WuG 21 [ET 39].
116. WuG 21 [ET 40].
117. [Cf. WuG, ET 248, point e, and 1135-39.]
118. WuG 673 [ET 1138].
119. [Cf. WuG, ET 248-49, points a, b, c, and d, and 1138.]
120. [Cf. WuG, ET 248-49, point f, and 1139-41.]
121. WuG 148 [ET 252].
122. Elsewhere Weber uses the term 'objectivate' [also translated 'objectify'] for this phenomenon. See note 86 to this chap., above.
123. GAR I 524 [ET (5) 238].
124. WuG 21 [ET 39].
125. Zijderveld (1966) criticizes both Weber and Durkheim for taking a dualistic view of social reality in which the individual aspects and the structural aspect of the process of institutionalization remain juxtaposed in the theory without, however, any explanation being offered for their mutual interdependence. In Weber's case, this would follow from his 'nominalistic' and 'anascopic' method, which takes as its starting point the meaning-oriented actions of individuals. The deposit of social structures found in the theory would in this case amount to little in reality. Durkheim would proceed in exactly the opposite direction, following a 'realistic' and 'katascopic' method based on the whole as the analytical starting point. Durkheim's approach would terminate in the reification of social 'structures' and neglect of the 'individual' component. Zijderveld would solve the problem by incorporating Durkheim's method into Weber's. Thus he advocates a 'katascopic-anascopic' method or, to put it in other terms, a dialectical model of thought in which the process of institutionalization is disclosed as a dialectical social process. He closes his study with the 'value judgment' that 'the true dialectic is a matter for the future,' since 'our time – is still too dominated by instances of one-sidedness.' Zijderveld (1966) 208.
I would conclude, given my own study, that the 'true dialectic' belongs to sociology's most recent past. Although Weber does not employ a dialectical model of thought, he may be interpreted dualistically neither with respect to his methodological analyses (see above, chap. 2, section II A) nor, certainly, with respect to his factual analyses. Where factual analyses are concerned, Zijderveld, who is making primarily a methodological study, suggests it would be worthwhile to investigate whether Weber applied his method consistently. Zijderveld (1966)

207

103, n. 49. He is probably prompted to ask this question in part because of an immediately preceding quotation (102) from Weber in which Weber says that charismatic domination will 'turn into an 'institution' ' (ins 'Institutionelle' transponiert) (see chap. 4 at n. 90, above, for the context of this remark). Zijderveld italicizes this phrase and calls attention to its dialectical character.

That Weber's actual sociological analyses must be viewed as dialectical is also the view of Jean Seguy (1976), 76 and n. 30. By that he means only to say, however, that Weber can properly be viewed neither as a 'materialist' nor as an 'idealist' and that in Weber the religious factor is neither only a function of structures nor the only factor to influence the structures in question. In Weber no single explanatory factor can be qualified as the 'final' one.

Richard C. Levin, too, speaks of 'the dialectic of charisma and routinisation,' without, however, going into the matter any further. Levin (1970) 197.

126. For this subject see especially WuG 245-49 [ET 399-407].
127. [WuG, ET 401-2.]
128. 'Continuous rational activity of a specified kind will be called an enterprise; an association with a continuously and rationally operating staff will be called a formal organization.' WuG 28 [ET 52].
129. The notion that peasants would be outstandingly religious and pious people is according to Weber a very recent phenomenon. The view is entertained especially in Lutheranism and in modern Slavophile Russian religiosity. Both cases involve ecclesiastical organizations having strong ties to royal and aristocratic interests and antipathy towards modern urban rationalism (in the philosophical and social senses of the term). Historically, both in East Asia and the West, peasants were often regarded as the religiously inferior ones while the cities were considered the places of 'authentic' religiosity. WuG 287 [ET 470-71].
130. For this subject see especially WuG 268-85 [ET 439-67].
131. 'It is more correct for our purpose,' says Weber, 'in order to do justice to the divine and mixed manifestations of this phenomenon, to set up as the crucial manifestation of the priesthood the specialization of a particular group of persons in the continuous operation of a cultic enterprise, permanently associated with particular norms, places and times, and related to specific social groups.' WuG 260 [ET 426].
132. The concept of a 'congregation' (Gemeinde) indicates an already institutionalized communal 'organization' (Verband) and is defined by Weber as distinct from both a 'parish' and an 'intermittent community' (e.g., an orgy). The term can apply to a religious community and also to a secular local community: 'We want to use the term [congregational religion] only when the laity has been organized permanently in such a manner that they can actively participate. A mere administrative unit which delimits the jurisdiction of priests is a parish, but not yet a congregational community.'
133. [WuG, ET 464.]
134. [WuG, ET 465.]
135. [WuG, ET 487.]
136. WuG 285-314 [ET 468-99].
137. [WuG, ET 472-73.]
138. [WuG, ET 477.]
139. [WuG, ET 477.]
140. [WuG, ET 483.]
141. [WuG, ET 483.]
142. [WuG, ET 490-91.]

143. [WuG, ET 507.]
144. Pierre Bourdieu advances an interesting and, I believe, largely justified interpretation of Weber's sociological analyses of religion by reformulating them with
the help of a conceptual scheme that combines elements of symbolic interac-
tionism and sociology of conflict. He analyzes the direct (defining) interactions
between the various religious actors in terms of competing interests and power
of the position holders in an objective social structure. The pertinent positions
are prophets, priests, sorcerers (in a mutual and reciprocal structure of competition) and lay persons, who are subdivided into ruling and ruled strata. Bourdieu (1971) 3-21.

Notes to Chapter 5

1. Reinhard Bendix, among others, asserts that Weber's only objective in his Protestantisch Ethik was to show an inward affinity between the Protestant ethic
and the spirit of capitalism. Showing a causal coherence between the two would
not have been part of that objective: 'Weber himself stated explicitly that his
purpose had not (italics added by Bendix) been to explain the origin or expansion of capitalism.' Bendix (1962 50, n. 2). 'The protestant ethic does not contain a direct approach to the problem of causal imputation; it deals only (italics
added – ML) with the affinity between religious precepts and the self-discipline
of mundane conduct.' Bendix (1962) 280; Dutch trans. in Dobbelaere and Laeyendecker (1974) 67. By that Bendix means that Weber proceeded on the assumption of the actual existence of a correlation between Protestantism and
economic expansion and that Weber's intention was to render comprehensible
a connection that, in his time, was already established. Even an established connection still always needs an 'interpretive explanation.' It was this alone that
Weber meant to furnish, through an ideal-typical comparison of the two variables. Bendix (1972, 2d ed.) 388-90.
Opposed to this position are Weber's own express statements: 'One of the fundamental elements of the spirit of modern capitalism, and not only of that but
of all modern culture: rational conduct on the basis of the idea of calling, was
born – that is what this discussion has sought to demonstrate (italics added) –
from the spirit of Christian asceticism.' GAR I 202 [ET (2) 180]. Weber characterizes his Protestantische Ethik as follows: 'Here we have only attempted
to trace the fact (Tatsache) (italics added) and direction (Art) of [ascetic Protestantism's] influence to their motives in one, though a very important point
[of modern culture].' GAR I 205 [ET (2) 183]. From this and other statements
it is clear that ideal-typical 'interpretive explanation' was, indeed, Weber's foremost aim. He emphasizes 'direction' (Art) in contrast to 'fact' (Tatsache), but
this does not exclude the possibility that Weber also meant to pose the problem of causal attribution directly, if perhaps only tentatively. He observes that
his investigation requires to be carried forward by hypothetically differentiating
the causal influence of Protestantism by country, etc., but especially by the differences within Protestantism. The influence of Calvinist, Baptist, and pietist
ethics on the respective ways of life needs to be examined. Yet it is very clear
that in this essay Weber already wishes to show that at least in some particular places (England, America) and at sometime (the seventeenth century), ascetic Protestantism had a causal influence. Weber's selection of source material

provides additional methodical evidence of this. Popular pamphlets, tracts, sermons, testimonies from the literature of the period, etc., can be used in a 'supplementary' way, but the only authentic sources are books on the care of souls, obviously 'drawn from life' and answering 'life's concrete, practical questions.' See, e.g., GAR I 163-65 [ET (2) 155] and PE 316-25.

An entirely different question is that of whether Weber, in leaving countless intervening variables out of the picture, made the causal attribution in his Protestantisch Ethik in a valid way. For the literature on this 'endless discussion,' see Sprondel (1972), in PE 395-405. Here I wish to point out only that the criticism often overlooks Weber's actual intentions. A fairly recent example is provided by Kurt Samuelson (1964, 2d ed.). He suggests that Weber views ascetic Protestantism as the only decisive factor, while Weber in fact does not mean to indicate even its relative importance. Moreover, Samuelson uses the concept of capitalism in a much broader sense than Weber does. Among others, Parsons (1965) 235 writes very negatively about Samuelson's view.

2. See chap. 1, above.

3. *a.* Swidler (1973) 35-42 also distinguishes between the concepts 'rationality,' 'rationalism,' and 'rationalization.' He writes that while Weber never carried the distinction through fully himself ('as Weber never fully did,' 35), it is nonetheless present in his sociology of religion. This distinction, according to Swidler, is eminently suited to making the relation between ideas and actions intelligible. By the same token, it sheds light on the theoretical relevance of the concept of rationality to our time.

'Rationalism' is the pragmatic, efficient modulating of means to immediate ends without regard to ideas in a broader context of meaning. Rationalism is the simplest and least precise term for rationality. Rationalism bears mention in the case of magical actions, for example, or in the case of farmers who pursue immediate material interests in everyday life.

'Rationalization' is the process of systematization in which ideas are ordered, integrated in terms of abstract principles, and applied ever more widely. It is the development of ideas according to an internal logical dynamic. One encounters it in priests and prophets.

'Rationality,' finally, establishes a direct connection between rationalization so conceived and the concrete conduct of life. It is methodical, deliberate action whereby one permits his whole life to be led consistently by ideas. Rationality differs from rationalism in that here goal-oriented action is consciously related to a broader system of meanings and values. It appears in its full scope in the pattern of life of the ascetic Protestant and bourgeois capitalist. According to Swidler, Weber's genius is revealed in the assertion that irrationality is always at the basis of rationality, as its motor: for example, the desire for certainty of salvation is the driving force for the ascetic Protestant, and vocation as 'duty' drives the young capitalist.

Herein lies the actual relevance of Weber's concept of rationality for understanding a concrete culture or social situation. In contrast to the pragmatic attitude that is aimed directly at the attainment of goals (rationalism), 'unnatural' rationality is the product of strong cultural forces. Here, commitment to ultimate values creates rationality. For example, modern social movements – from 'encounter' groups to movements for altering the family structure – can be viewed as attempts made in terms of some 'commitment to values' to bring new areas of life or experience under the conscious control of ideas. Ascetic Protestantism's concept of 'vocation' as 'calling' gives way by this time to 'authenticity' or 'self-actualization,' which goes on to dominate the whole of life as the focal point of 'inner-worldly asceticism.' 'Rationality' goes further than 'rationalism' and is not a cold or routine matter but an emotionally charged commitment to values brought consciously under the control of a system of knowledge.

Swidler advances what is to my mind a substantially correct analysis of the various forms of rationality in Weber, but his threefold terminological distinction finds too little support in Weber himself. Weber often uses the term 'rationalism' to indicate precisely the system of ideas as such. For example, he calls the theoretically meaningful cosmos 'the core of genuinely religious rationalism.' GAR I 253 [ET (4) 281; italics added). By 'rationalization' Weber also means the technical subjugation of nature, which revolutionizes man from without and which, I would emphasize, is not internalized. WuG 658 [ET 1116-17]; see also chap. 4, section A 1, above.

Weber is done more justice terminologically when, in keeping with present-day usage, 'rationality' is taken to be the concept with the greatest extension: it is action which goes on 'consciously and in accordance with one criterion or another' (cf. chap. 4, section I A, and chap. 4, n. 4, above). In that case 'rationalism' means rationality 'as a situation,' and 'rationalization' means rationality 'as process.' Rationalization in Swidler's sense is the cultural aspect of that process.

b. From all I have now discussed it is clear that the problem of rationality also runs like a scarlet thread through the systematic sociology of religion in WuG. At first glance this systematic presentation may seem to contain a disparate complex of topics (cf. chap. 1, part IV, above). Even after a first reading this thread may not be clearly apparent, because of the enormous erudition Weber displays here and because of his countless associative excursions. It should accordingly not be at all surprising that the commentators organize this systematic sociology in a variety of ways.

Nelson (1965) 595 advances a fourfold division: a religious phenomenological part, §1-§3; an essentially religious-sociological part, §4-§7; the terrain of value commitments and life styles, §8-§10; and the relation of the cultural religions of the world, §11-§12. Nelson does not perceive that the problem of rationality is the central unifying problem.

Parsons, in his introduction to Fischoff's translation of Weber's Sociology of Religion (19643), xxvii-lx, distinguishes the following problem areas: religion and the problem of social evolution; the main elements of a social system; the problem of rationalization; prophecy, charisma, and the process of breakthrough; radical salvation and the orientation of action; types of religious ethics and their relation to the world. Parsons does perceive, in contrast to Nelson, that progressive rationalization is the central problem. However, he criticizes Weber for failing, as a result of 'typological rigidity,' to be adequately aware of gradual and cumulative processes of change and for overemphasizing the 'prophetic breakthrough.' Parsons sees this as a theoretical 'bias' in Weber (lxiv-lxv).

That there might be a theoretical 'bias' here is a matter I shall leave to Parsons to resolve. But Weber did, most certainly, have an eye for gradual processes of change. Even leaving aside the fact that a priesthood could develop gradually, without the intrusion of prophecy, from the sorcerer's enterprise, priestly rationalism is a supremely gradual and cumulative process of change. My own view agrees with that of Bendix, expressed in his study of Weber's political sociology: '. . . [Weber] did not subscribe to a theory of history that sees history's dynamic element in the charismatic 'break-throughs' of great men and its stable element

211

in the 'decline of charisma' through routinization.' Here Bendix is challenging Gerth's and Mill's interpretation of Weber. Bendix (1962) 328.

Personally, I would present the line of rationality in Weber's sociology of religion briefly as follows: 'The Origins of Religion' (§1) pictures advancing rationalization from naturalism to monotheism. The 'magicians and priests' (§2) are the driving forces behind magical rationalization and religious rationalization, respectively. The latter presupposes an ethical 'concept of God' and a religious ethic as against a magical taboo (§3). The breakthrough to it generally involves the 'prophet' (§4), who influences the priestly 'congregation' (§5) in such a way that 'sacred' (magical, esoteric) knowledge makes way for (rational) 'preaching and pastoral care' (§6). The lay congregation displays a varying selective affinity for rationality depending on 'rank, classes, and religion' (§7). The rationalization of religion creates the 'problem of theodicy' (§8), the question concerning a theoretically meaningful cosmos which tints the quest for 'salvation and rebirth' (§9) and leads to various ways of salvation (asceticism and mysticism) and their (more or less systematizing) influence on the pattern of life (§10). The rationalized religious ethic and the world come into conflict with each other (§11). Presented lastly are the great cultural religions (and their respective rationalities) and the world (§12).

4. Cf. the opening discussion in chap. 4, section II B, above.

5. See the opening paragraphs of chap. 4, section II B 2, above.

6. The suggestion for this graphic representation comes from Parsons, who speaks of 'cross-tabulating' distinctions between asceticism and mysticism on the one hand and inner-worldly and other-worldly tendencies on the other hand. Parsons (1966) li. Weyembergh provides an articulated scheme, which I have adapted and added to for our present purposes. Weyembergh (1972) 308.

7. The ideal-typical element is over-accented here. For example, the Brahmans who lived in the world were highly comparable to the Chinese gentleman insofar as their everyday ethics were concerned. They took pride in their training and bore themselves diplomatically. GAR I 152 [ET 139, 149].

8. The scheme of four main types of value-orientation (which can also be regarded as alternatives for personal behavior) presented by Parsons (1967, 5th ed.) 102 reveals a remarkable measure of agreement with Weber's typology. Type A, the 'universalistic-achievement pattern,' and type B, the 'particularistic-achievement pattern,' Parsons illustrates with the American and Confucian patterns of culture respectively. For type C, the 'universalistic-ascription pattern,' Parsons uses philosophical 'idealism' and the German cultural ideal as an example. Weber's Brahmanism could, as I see it, provide a second example, because here too the focus of behavioral orientation is on an ideal state of affairs that can be regarded as permanently valid (the ascription element), while general rules of conduct are required because the reality does not meet the demands of the ideal (the universalistic element). For type D, the 'particularistic-ascriptive pattern,' Parsons uses Latin American culture as an example. Weber's magic could also serve as an example here, as I see it, because here the social order is regarded as something given (the ascriptive element) to which one can orient oneself concretely (the particularistic element). Parsons (1967, 5th ed.) 101-11.

9. GAR I 395-401, 426-430, 498-511, and passim [ET (5) 107-13, 138-41, 213-24].

10. The allusion is to the Chinese doctrine of predestination (cf. the closing passage of chap. 3, part III A, above.

11. GAR I 504-9 [ET (5) 219-24].

12. GAR I 440 [ET (5) 152].

212

13. GAR I 131 [ET (5) 131]. For the process aspect of the Indian social system, see GAR II 8-22, 51-57, 122-32, 134-48, 316-27, and passim [ET 9-25, 49-54, 123-33, 137-54, 290-328].

14. For the dialectical 'process of routinization' see, for India proper, GAR II 241-79 [ET 233-56]; for Ceylon, Burma, China, Korea, Japan, and Inner Asia, see GAR II 279-316 [ET 257-90].

15. Weber's discussion of Judaism emphasizes the change of status groups and power groups more than do his discussions of Hinduism and Confucianism, where the stability of the social stratification is central. The explanation for this is probably to be found both in the character of the pertinent societies and in Weber's knowledge of their cultures. The latter is not only borne out by the greater scope of the study of Judaism; Weber says as much himself, speaking of 'the definitely provisional character of these studies, and especially of the parts dealing with Asia' and adding explicitly that 'they are destined to be superseded in a much more important sense than this can be said, as it can be, of all scientific work.' GAR I 13-14 [ET (2) 28].

16. [GAR III, ET 380.]

17. GAR III 220-21 [ET 206-7].

18. See WuG 273-74 [ET 454-55] in combination with GAR III 219-21 [ET 205-7].

19. GAR III 224-25 [ET 210].

20. GAR III 221 [ET 207].

21. On the Chinese city, see GAR I 276-78, 290-98, 380 [ET (5) 3, 13-20, 90-91]. For India, see GAR II 86-89 [ET 84-88]. For Palestine, see GAR III 16-27, 108-9 [ET 13-23, 98-100].
    For a brief survey of the differences between the ancient Hellenic, Hellenistic, and Roman city on the one hand and the typical medieval city on the other hand, see Weber's essays, 'Die sozialen Gründe des Untergangs der antiken Kultur' (1896) (SWP 1-26 [ET (1)]) and 'Wirtschaft und Gesellschaft im Rom der Kaiserzeit' (1909) (SWP 27-58). My discussion is based on these sources. An extensive sociology of the city is found in WuG 727-814 [ET 1212-1372]. It was first published in 1920 -21. Abramowski (1966) 83-117 provides a summary of it and notes that there is still no extensive appraisal available of Weber's urban sociological investigations (p. 85, n. 8).

22. See chap. 1, part I, above.

23. WuG 287-88 [ET 472].

24. [WuG 334, ET 472.]

25. WuG 334-37 [ET 551-56].

26. The Roman law had its origin, according to Weber, in religio, that is, the commitment to precisely defined cultic formulas and to an extraordinary number of highly specialized numina that the Roman had to take into account in his everyday life. Not just every activity but even its components fell under the jurisdiction of special gods. In important dealings it was necessary to invoke not just the gods whose jurisdiction embraced a certain activity (dii certi) but even those whose jurisdiction in the matter was ambiguous (dii incerti). In certain agricultural activities, for example, it was necessary to invoke up to twelve dii certi. In this way Roman ritual practice became a rational juridical casuistry derived in large measure from the analysis of various activities. WuG 250-51 [ET 408-9].
    Roman law also contributed in a direct way, in interaction with economic expansion, to the rise of Western capitalism. See, e.g., GAR I 11 [ET (1) 25]. Yet it was not a necessary condition for it. In England, for example, 'the Renais-

sance of Roman law was overcome by the power of the great legal corporations.'
GAR I 62 [ET (2) 77]. As a result of 'the autonomy of the economically powerful stratum' guaranteed by laws created by these guilds of jurists, England still
provided fertile soil for capitalism. GAR I 438 [ET (5) 149-50].

27. For this process, by which ascetic Protestantism developed into modern capitalism, see especially GAR I 37-62, 183-204 [ET 55-78, 161-81].

28. GAR I 192 [ET (2) 172].

29. From the statistics pertaining to religious affiliation and 'the social distribution of the population' with which Weber opens his study of Protestantism, it
is clear that the socialization process in question requires to be differentiated
along confessional lines and that the bourgeois work ethic was still by no means universally accepted in his day, although it has to be regarded as the modern lifestyle from an ideal-typical standpoint. GAR I 17-30 [ET (2) 35-48].

30. For a typifying citation concerning the sociological genesis of Western rationalism, see p. 113, above.

31. Among others, Wilson (1969, 2d ed.), Berger (1967), Fenn (1969), Jacobs (1971).

32. SWP 389-90 [cf. GAR I,ET (3) 305-6].

33. See chap. 5, section I C 1, above.

34. GAR I 235 [ET (3) 321].

35. Actually, the term 'sect membership' should be used here, but Weber himself
repeatedly uses terms related to 'church' (Kirche, Kirchlichkeit) in the sense of
(affiliation with) a religious group, regardless of whether it should be characterized as a 'church' or a 'sect.' See, e.g., GAR I 209 [ET (3) 304].

36. SWP 397 [cf. GAR I 214, ET (3) 308-9: '. . . where I listened. . . the sermons
were delivered with obvious inner conviction; the preacher was often moved.'].

37. GAR I 212 [ET (3) 307].

38. Nijk (1968) asserts correctly that Weber is aware of the original meaning of the
word secularization ('transfer of ecclesiastical sovereignty rights and property
rights to the state or any other worldly institution' (Nijk (1968) 20), as is clear
from the fact that Weber puts the term in quotation marks whenever he uses it
in precisely that sense (Nijk (1968) 61-62).

Nijk's assertion that Weber made no valuable preparatory contribution to con-
verting this term into a scientific category because he never defined its meaning
precisely enough (Nijk (1968) 29-30) is patently arguable. For the argumentation, see note 65 to this chapter, below.

39. [Cf. GAR I, ET (3) 309.]

40. [GAR I, ET (3) 310.]

41. GAR I 217 [cf. ET (3) 311].

42. [GAR I, ET (3) 311-12.]

43. SWP 395.

44. See, e.g., GAR I 214, with n. 1 [ET (3) 308].

45. Weber uses the term 'denomination' (Denomination) repeatedly, but not as a
terminus technicus to distinguish ecclesiastical or sectarian structures. He uses
it like the term 'confession' (Konfession) in the very general sense of religion,
without respect to structure. See, for example, SWP 390 [GAR I, ET (3) 307,
314, 321].

Weber sometimes also uses the term 'free church' (Freikirche) (e.g., SWP 396
and WuG 314 [cf. ET 516]). However, he does not define this term, nor does he
state its characteristic origins or consequences. From the context it is clear he
distinguishes these 'free churches' from both 'churches' and 'sects'; they neither
'could nor would' be 'sects' and are a 'fairly recent' phenomenon. It is legiti-

214

mate to surmise that Weber borrowed this term from his friend Ernst Troeltsch. Laeyendecker (1967) 48-49 presents the characteristic features of the 'free churches' according to Troeltsch.

46. See GAR I 211, n. 1 [cf. ET (3) 305] and SWP 387-88. I have chosen this example of Weber's expressly, in order to show that the social structural 'pluralism' and the 'market situation' of the religious groups spoken of by Berger were already noted implicitly by Weber. First, Berger seems to suggest that 'cartel forming' is a phenomenon typical of secularization, while Weber shows that it can arise from typically religious considerations. In the second place, Berger cites cartel forming as a sign of secularization at the social structural level. In Weber, in contrast, this structure, which had existed since olden times, now serves to some extent the advancing process of secularization at the level of consciousness. See especially in this connection Berger (1967) 126-53 or Berger (1969) 143-71; for the term 'cartel' in this connection see Berger (1967) 142 or Berger (1969) 159.

47. GAR I 199 [ET (2) 177].

48. See pp. 171-72, above.

49. GAR I 199 [ET (2) 177]. See pp. 145-47, above.

50. This secularization mechanism or, to use Weber's terminology, this 'line of development which we have again and again observed,' is described by Berger as the phenomenon whereby 'religion might appear as a formative force in one situation and as a dependent formation in the situation following historically.' Berger speaks of 'a 'reversal' in the 'direction' of causal efficacy as between religion and its respective infrastructures' and of the 'irony in the relation between religion and secularization, an irony that can be graphically put by saying that, historically speaking, Christianity has been its own gravedigger.' Apparently there is an irony between human intentions and their historical consequences. Berger (1967) 127-28 or Berger (1969) 1144-45.

What is of interest here is that in a note Berger correctly refers in this connection to Weber's theory about charisma and the 'routinization' of charisma, which according to Berger 'provides a model for this kind of differentiated analysis.' Berger (1967) 209, n. 3 or Berger (1969) 234, n. 3.

Yet it is striking, I think, that Weber's 'routinization' mechanism, which 'affords a very nice opportunity to show in concreto' (Berger) – i.e., in an empirically observable way – the dialectical connection between religion and society, is not perceived by Berger to be a concretization of what I take to be a general dialectical perspective of Weber's concerning the relation between idea and reality, between ' 'idealist' and 'materialist' interpretations' (Berger). The dialectical relation between religion and society as a general theoretical insight Berger defends as if it were a new and personal theory of his own, integrating at the theoretical level Weber's one-sidedly idealist conception and Marx's equally one-sided materialist conception. Berger (1967) 126-27 and 208-9, n. 2; or Berger (1969) 143-44 or 234, n. 2.

51. See p. 66, above.

52. The absence of any reference to religious motivation in these citations afforded Weber a technical research advantage as well: he could set about demonstrating the affinity between Protestant rationality and capitalist rationality and, since the relation of dependence was not explicit in the citations themselves, assert that his investigation was therefore 'free of preconceptions' (voraussetzungslos). GAR I 31 [ET (2) 48].

53. GAR I 54 [cf. ET (2) 70].

54. GAR I 204 [ET (2) 181-82].

Jacobs (1971) 1-9 sees in the current increase in criminality in America not so much an increase in 'immorality' as a growing tendency towards 'amorality,' which has developed from Protestantism into an ethic of 'rational capitalism.' He bases his historical analyses largely on Weber.

The link between the increase in criminality and the disappearance of religious values from society is assumed by other sociologists, too. See, for example, Wilson (1969, 2d ed.) 262.

Weber speaks time and again of 'genuine' religiosity in contrast to the 'humbug or self-deception' of many present-day intellectuals. See, e.g., WuG 314 [cf. ET 500-517]; GAR I 251-52 [ET 280-81]; SWP 337 [WL, ET (5) 154-55]. This must not be interpreted as if Weber were making a value judgment here about religiosity as such. He remains within the framework of his sociology, which judges religious motivation solely in relation to its actually influencing individual or social life. The denigrating tone in which Weber describes this ineffectual, snobbish religiosity of the intellectuals betrays, I should rather say, the passion with which he practices 'value-free' science. To him, science as such is a 'passionate' enterprise. WL 589 [ET (5) 135].

55. See, e.g., SWP 397; SWP 338-39 [ET (2)], or WL 612-13 [ET (5) 154-56].

56. In addition to his writings in sociology of religion, I have relied in dealing with this question on Weber's essay 'Wissenschaft als Beruf' [Science as a vocation]. It contains a number of situation sketches from modern society, which I made some use of in the preceding discussion.

57. See WL 582-613 [ET (5) 129-56]. The most important part also appears in SWP 311-41 [ET (2)].

58. SWP 317, or WL 594 [cf. ET (5) 139].

59. It is justifiable to assert that according to Weber the masses caught up in the modern system of labor regard the actual system of vocations as a given and play their roles without pursuing the question of its legitimacy any further. It is highly disputable, however, to assert, as Fenn does, that Weber would characterize as typically secular behavior this approach whereby people motivate and legitimate their activity solely through the work itself and through the demands of life as they arise from day to day. According to Fenn, Weber regards as typically secular every system of beliefs or values which deems the question of transcendent, ultimate meaning to be irrelevant. The typically religious orientation of behavior arises, on Fenn's view, from the perception that human existence as such has an ultimate meaning, and it arises, furthermore, when people take a definitive decision consistent with that perception and become totally engaged and strive to show through their behavior what is humanly worth-while. (On the religious approach, 'human nature is fulfilled only in vocation, choice, wholeness and authenticity.')

Given his view of the typically religious together with his interpretation of Weber's view of what is typically secular, Fenn finds himself compelled to ascribe to Weber an ambivalence: Weber would be at once religious to the core and a showcase exhibit of the typical features of the secular person. Fenn bases his conclusions (the substance of the typically secular, and Weber's ambivalence) exclusively on a close analysis, he says, of a single essay of Weber's, that is, the one on science as a vocation. Here Weber asserts, among other things, that 'yearning and tarrying' (for a divine message of salvation) as the Jewish people have yearned and tarried for more than two millennia will no longer do; people will have to 'set to work' and, both as people and in their vocations, they will

216

have to do justice to the 'demands of the day' [WL, ET (5) 156]. According to Fenn, Weber's secular orientation can be discerned here in that for him, the time of 'yearning and tarrying' for a God who never comes is gone for good. Meanwhile, Weber says that the need to meet the 'demands of the day' is 'plain and simple, if each finds and obeys the demon who holds the fibers of his very life' (Weber's italics). This statement would testify to Weber's typically religious orientation of conduct: here one finds 'an ultimate commitment to penultimate concerns.' Fenn (1969) 159-69.

Fenn advances his personal view of what is typically religious and typically secular here in a way that would make it seem he is presenting Weber's view of what is particularly secular. Certainly, Weber would without reservation have called himself secular despite his clear orientation to final (individually chosen) values, which to him were precisely what makes existence humanly worthwhile. Cf. p. 39, above.

60. SWP 329-30, or WL 604 [ET (5) 147-48].
61. See chap. 2, section II A, above.
62. [WL, ET (5) 149.]
63. See p. 123-26, above.
64. SWP 330, or WL 605 [ET (5) 149].
65. On the two reasons behind the progressive irrationalization of religion, see GAR I 253-54 [ET (4) 281-82].
66. [GAR I, ET (4) 281.]
67. [GAR I, ET (4) 281.]
68. [GAR I, ET (4) 281-82.]
69. [GAR I, ET (4) 282.]
70. [GAR I, ET (6) 350.]
71. [GAR I, ET (6) 351.]
72. [WL, ET (5) 142.]
73. GAR I 564-67 [ET (6) 350-52].
74. In recent literature as well, individualization and the compelling necessity to make a choice are discussed as typical of modern society in contrast to agricultural-artisan society. Kooij (1967) 183-204.
75. SWP 337, or WL 611-12 [ET (5) 155].
76. GAR I 204 [ET (2) 182]. Cf. chap. 4, n. 14, above.

In contrast to Lauwers, who ascribes an ideological character to Weber's secularization or rationalization theory, I believe such an interpretation should be rejected. See Lauwers (1974) 73-83; 91-93. I take the same position towards Marcuse, who likewise regards Weber's concept of rationality as ideologically charged. See Marcuse (1970, 8th ed.) 107-29. For my critique of this position, see Lemmen (1975) 155-74.

Baum fills in concretely the possibility left open by Weber of a rebirth of religion. Joining the analysis of modern society with rationality in Weber's sense as the key concept, Baum determines that now, precisely as a consequence of this modern rationality, a reinterpretation of the Christian religion is taking place that is unquestionably pertinent to public life. This redefining of Christianity is in fact a 'rationalization' (in Weber's sense and hence also in that intended by Baum) of Christianity whereby the content of the Christian message today is brought to greater clarity and more intense consciousness. Baum finds this fresh Christian self-understanding in the present trend in theology, he finds it amongst many Christians, and he finds it in a somewhat superficial form in some sub-varieties of the youthful counter-culture. From a sociological standpoint, this 'rationalization' of Christianity means a 'functionalization of the sacred.' In the process, the sharp traditional distinction between sacred and profane, between believers and unbelievers is abolished, and Christianity comes to see itself – precisely, moreover, through its interpretation of reality in terms of the divine mystery that acquired form in Christ – as the source of inspiration for universal solidarity in the cooperative construction of a new society. Christianity can fulfill this function because the development of the technocratic system has led to a new historical self-understanding of man amongst non-Christians, too. Technology has compelled (Western) man to reflect more fully, and in a broader circle, on the question of what it means to be human. The need to humanize the world is ever more pressing. That need finds expression, for instance, in virtually all sub-varieties of contemporary counter-culture. The recent development in the field of technology (e.g., the computer) has enhanced the flexibility of organizational structures, thereby affording a better possibility than existed in Weber's day to employ these structures in the service of new values. The reinterpretation of Christianity and the new historical self-understanding of the non-Christian man do not exclude but rather are cast upon or consigned to each other. Herein lies the opportunity for a fresh, socially relevant form of religiosity, which Weber regarded as being at once possible in principle but improbable in practice. Baum (1970) 153-202.

Weber views secularization as a phenomenon whereby earlier religious definitions of reality yield to secular ones, but he does not take the measure of secularization in terms of already religiously defined norms or functions. In other words, he sees secularization in terms of the actor and not in terms of particular criteria of the observer. In doing so, Weber also remained true to his value-free method, by virtue of which he also declined to advance a definition of religion; cf. pp. 56-57, above. In this way he avoids having the secular become a residual category of the religious, or vice versa. 'Religiosity' and 'secularity' alike thereby acquire a logical status independent of each other and can in principle be studied as sociologically independent of each other.

According to Rendtorff (1965) 241-45 the pertinence of Weber's secularization thesis to present-day sociology of religion is to be found in the fact that it analyzes processes of change in societies holistically considered without ascribing to such processes an irrevocable and definitive character. That is in contrast, he believes, to currently prevalent secularization theories, which accordingly attempt broadly either to assent to or else to reject the secular society. In contrast, according to Rendtorff, Weber's sociology of religion aimed to study the development of society scientifically, free from every (evolutionistic) dogmatism, and to leave the future open to perennially renewed empirical study.

BIBLIOGRAPHY

a. Writings by Max Weber

[Listed here are the German editions cited by professor Lemmen in the original Dutch version of his book, together with the English translations (ET) adopted for citation in the present English version. - HDM]

Gesammelte Aufsätze zur Religionssoziologie. Vol. I. Tübingen: J. C. B. Mohr (Paul Siebeck), 1920; 5th ed. 1963. Abbreviation: *GAR I.*

GAR I contains the following:

(1) pp. 1-16: 'Vorbemerkung' (ET: 'Author's Introduction.' In *The Protestant Ethic and the Spirit of Capitalism,* pp. 13-31, 185-86. New York: Charles Scribner's Sons, 1958);

(2) pp. 17-206: 'Die protestantische Ethik und der Geist des Kapitalismus' (ET: *The Protestant Ethic and the Spirit of Capitalism,* pp. 35-183, 186-284. Translated by Talcott Parsons. New York: Charles Scribner's Sons, 1958);

(3) pp. 207-36: 'Die protestantischen Sekten und der Geist des Kapitalismus' (ET: 'The Protestant Sects and the Spirit of Capitalism.' In *From Max Weber: Essays in Sociology,* pp. 302-22. Translated by H. H. Gerth and C. Wright Mills. New York: Oxford University Press, 1946; reprint. ed. 1967);

(4) pp. 237-75: 'Die Wirtschaftsethik der Weltreligionen. Vergleichende religionssoziologische Versuche. Einleitung' (ET: 'The Social Psychology of the World Religions.' In *From Max Weber: Essays in Sociology,* pp. 267-301. Translated by H. H. Gerth and C. Wright Mills. New York: Oxford University Press, 1946; reprint. ed. 1967);

(5) pp. 276-536: 'Die Wirtschaftsethik der Weltreligionen. Vergleichende religionssoziologische Versuche. [Part] I. Konfuzianismus und Taoismus' (ET: *The Religion of China: Confucianism and Taoism.* Translated and edited by Hans H. Gerth. Glencoe, Illinois: The Free Press; 2d printing 1959);

(6) pp. 536-73: 'Zwischenbetrachtung. Theorie der Stufen und Richtungen religiöser Weltablehnung' (ET: 'Religious Rejections of the World and Their Directions.' In *From Max Weber: Essays in Sociology,* pp. 323-59. Translated by H. H. Gerth and C. Wright Mills. New York: Oxford University Press, 1946; reprint. ed. 1967).

Gesammelte Aufsätze zur Religionssoziologie. Vol. II. 'Die Wirtschaftsethik der Weltreligionen. Vergleichende religionssoziologische Versuche. [Part] II. Hinduismus und Buddhismus.' Tübingen: J. C. B. Mohr (Paul Siebeck), 1921; 4th ed. 1964. Abbreviation: *GAR II.*

ET: *The Religion of India: The Sociology of Hinduism and Buddhism.* Translated and edited by Hans H. Gerth and Don Martindale. Glencoe, Ill.: The Free Press, 1958.

Gesammelte Aufsätze zur Religionssoziologie. Vol. III. 'Die Wirtschaftsethik der Weltreligionen. Vergleichende religionssoziologische Versuche. [Part] III. Das antike Judentum.' Tübingen: J. C. B. Mohr (Paul Siebeck), 1921; 5th ed. 1971. Abbreviation: *GAR III.*
ET: *Ancient Judaism.* Translated and edited by Hans H. Gerth and Don Martindale. Glencoe, Ill.: The Free Press, 1952.

Gesammelte Aufsätze zur Wissenschaftslehre. Tübingen: J. C. B. Mohr (Paul Siebeck), 1922; 2d ed., revised and expanded by Johannes Winckelmann, 1951; 3d ed. 1968. Abbreviation: *WL.*
Parts of *WL* – i.e., of the 3d ed. unless otherwise indicated – are available in English translation as follows:
  (1) 2d ed., pp. 146-214: 'Die 'Objektivität' sozialwissenschaftlicher und sozialpolitischer Erkenntnis' (1904) (ET: "Objectivity' in Social Science and Social Policy.' In *The Methodology of the Social Sciences,* pp. 49-112. Translated and edited by Edward A. Shils and Henry A. Finch. Glencoe, Ill.: The Free Press, 1949; 4th printing 1968);
  (2) 2d ed., pp. 215-90: 'Kritische Studien auf dem Gebiet der kulturwissenschaftlichen Logik' (1905) (ET: 'Critical Studies in the Logic of the Cultural Sciences: I. A Critique of Eduard Meyer's Methodological Views; II. Objective Possibility and Adequate Causation in Historical Explanation.' In *The Methodology of the Social Sciences,* pp. 113-63; 164-88. Translated and edited by Edward A. Shils and Henry A. Finch. Glencoe, Ill.: The Free Press, 1949; 4th printing 1968);
  (3) pp. 489-540: 'Über den Sinn der 'Wertfreiheit' der soziologischen und ökonomischen Wissenschaften' (1917-18) (ET: 'The Meaning of 'Ethical Neutrality' in Sociology and Economics.' In *The Methodology of the Social Sciences,* pp. 1-47. Translated and edited by Edward A Shils and Henry A. Finch. Glencoe, Ill.: The Free Press, 1949; 4th printing 1968);
  (4) pp. 541-81: 'Soziologische Grundbegriffe' (ET: 'Basic Sociological Terms,' sections 1-7. In *Economy and Society: An Outline of Interpretive Sociology,* pp. 4-38. Edited by Guenther Roth and Claus Wittich. Berkeley, Los Angeles, and London: University of California Press, 1978. Cf. *WuG.*);
  (5) pp. 582-613: 'Wissenschaft als Beruf' (ET, based on 1st ed., pp. 524-55: 'Science as a Vocation.' In *From Max Weber: Essays in Sociology,* pp. 129-56. Translated by H. H. Gerth and C. Wright Mills. New York: Oxford University Press, 1946; reprint. ed. 1967).

Die Protestantische Ethik. II Bd. Kritiken und Antikritiken. Edited by Johannes Winckelmann. Hamburg: Siebenstern Taschenbuch Verlag, 1968; 2d rev. ed., 1972. Abbreviation: *PE.*

Soziologie, Weltgeschichtlichen Analysen, Politik. Edited and annotated by Johannes Winckelmann, with an introduction by Eduard Baumgarten. Kröners Taschenausgaben, no. 229. Stuttgart: Kröners Taschenausgeben, 1956. 2d ed. 1959.
This pocket anthology of texts selected from Weber's major works includes, among others, the following:
  (1) pp. 1-26: 'Die sozialen Gründe des Untergangs der antiken Kultur' (1896)

(ET: 'The Social Causes of the Decay of Ancient Civilization.' Translated by Christian Mackauer. Pp. 254-75 in *Max Weber: The Interpretation of Social Reality*. Edited with an introduction by J. E. T. Eldridge. London: Michael Joseph, 1971).
(2) pp. 311-41: 'Wissenschaft als Beruf' (ET: see *WL* (5), above).

Werk und Person. Dokumente ausgewähhlt und kommentiert von Eduard Baumgarten. Mit Zeittafel und Bildtafeln [Work and person: Documents selected and annotated by Eduard Baumgarten, with a chronology and illustrations]. Tübingen: J. C. B. Mohr (Paul Siebeck), 1911. Abbreviation: *WP*.

Verhandlungen des Ersten Deutschen Soziologentages von 19.-22. Oktober 1910 in Frankfurt a. M. Tübingen: J. C. B. Mohr (Paul Siebeck), 1911. Abbreviation: *Verhandlungen* (1911).

Wirtschaftsgeschichte. Abriss der universalen Sozial- und Wirtschaftsgeschichte. Edited by Siegmund Hellmann and Melchior Palyi. Munich and Leipzig: Duncker & Humblot, 1923. [Other German editions are: 2d ed. 1924; 3d ed. revised by Johannes Winckelmann, 1958.] Abbreviation: *WG*.
ET: *General Economic History.* Translated by Frank H. Knight. London and New York: Allen & Unwin, 1927; paperback ed. New York: Collier Books, 1961.

Wirtschaft und Gesellschaft. Grundriss der verstehenden Soziologie (1921-22). 5th ed. Studienausgabe, revised and edited by Johannes Winckelmann. Tübingen: J. C. B. Mohr (Paul Siebeck), 1972. Abbreviation: *WuG*.
ET: *Economy and Society: An Outline of Interpretive Sociology.* Edited by Guenther Roth and Claus Wittich and translated by Ephraim Fischoff, Hans Gerth, A. M. Henderson, Ferdinand Kolegar, C. Wright Mills, Talcott Parsons, Max Rheinstein, Guenther Roth, Edward Shills, and Claus Wittich. 1968; 2d printing Berkeley, Los Angeles, and London: University of California Press, 1978. 2 vols., cx, 1469, lxiv pages.
While this translation of *WuG* is based on the 4th German edition (1956), the editors had access to Professor Winckelmann's text revisions for the 5th edition, then in preparation – see ET xxxi-xxxii and cviii. It incorporates and/or supersedes various earlier English versions of parts of *WuG* as follows:
(1) Ephraim Fischoff, trans., *The Sociology of Religion* (Boston: Beacon Press, 1963), pp. 1-274;
(2) H. H. Gerth and C. Wright Mills, trans. and eds., *From Max Weber: Essays in Sociology* (New York: Oxford University Press, 1946), pp. 159-244, 253-62;
(3) Ferdinand Kolegar, trans., 'The Household Community' and 'Ethnic Groups,' in Talcott Parsons, et. al., eds., *Theories of Society* (New York: The Free Press of Glencoe, 1961), vol. 1, pp. 296-98, 302-9;
(4) Talcott Parsons, ed.; and A. M. Henderson and Talcott Parsons, trans., *The Theory of Social and Economic Organization* (1947; 2d ed. New York: The Free Press of Glencoe, 1964), pp. 87-423;
(5) Max Rheinstein, ed.; and Edward Shils and Max Rheinstein, trans., *Max Weber on Law in Economy and Society* (Cambridge, Harvard University Press, 1954), pp. 11-348.

b. Secondary literature

Abramowski, Günther. *Das Geschichtsbild Max Webers. Universalgeschichte am Leitfaden des okzidentalen Rationalisierungsprozesses.* Stuttgart: Ernst Klett Verlag, 1966.

Aron, Raymond. *La philosophie critique de l'histoire. Essai sur une théorie allemande de l'histoire.* Paris: Librairie philosophique J. Vrin, 1969.

Ashcraft, Richard. 'Marx and Weber on Liberalism as Bourgeois Ideology.' *Comparative Studies in Society and History* 14 (1972): 130-68.

Baum, Gregory. 'Does the World Remain Disenchanted?' *Social Research* 37 (1970): 153-202.

Baumgarten, Eduard. 'Einleitung' to *Max Weber: Soziologie, Weltgeschichtliche Analysen, Politik.* Edited by Johannes Winckelmann. Krüners Taschenausgaben, no. 229. Stuttgart: Krüners Taschenausgaben, 1956. 2d ed. 1959. Pp. xi-xxxvi.

Baumgarten, Eduard, ed. *Max Weber: Werk und Person. Dokumente ausgewählt und kommentiert von Eduard Baumgarten. Mit Zeittafel und Bildtafeln* [Work and person: Documents selected and annotated by Eduard Baumgarten, with a chronology and illustrations]. Tübingen: J. C. B. Mohr (Paul Siebeck), 1911.

Beerling, R. F. 'Max Weber 1864-1920.' In *Wijsgerig-socologische verkenningen,* vol. 2, pp. 188-212. Arnhem: Van Loghum Slaterus, 1965.

Bellah, Robert N. *Tokugawa Religion.* New York: The Free Press, 1957; 2d ed. 1969.

Bendix, Reinhard. *Max Weber: An Intellectual Portrait.* New York: Doubleday & Company, Inc., 1960; 2d ed. 1962.

Bendix, Reinhard. 'Die *Protestantische Ethik* im Rückblick.' In *Max Weber, Die Protestantische Ethik. II Bd. Kritiken und Antikritiken,* pp. 380-94. Edited by Johannes Winckelmann. Hamburg: Siebenstern Taschenbuch Verlag, 1968; 2d rev. ed., 1972.

Berger, Peter. L. 'Charisma and Religious Innovation: The Social Location of Israelite Prophecy.' *American Sociological Review* 28 (1963): 940-50.

Berger, Peter. L. *Het hemels baldakijn. Bijdrage tot een theoretische godsdienstsociologie.* Translated from the English by W. Veugelers and H. de Hingh. Utrecht: Ambo, 1969.

Berger, Peter. L. *The Sacred Canopy: Elements of a Sociological Theory of Religion.* New York: Doubleday & Company, Inc., 1967.

Bonus, Arthur. 'Studien zur Religionssoziologie von Max Weber.' *Christliche Welt* 36 (1922): 656.

Bourdieu, Pierre. 'Une interprétation de la théorie de la religion selon Max Weber.' *Archives européennes de sociologie* 12 (1971): 3-21.

Braam, A. van. 'Inleiding: Max Weber over gezag en bureaucratie.' In *Max Weber. Gezag en bureaucratie,* pp. 1-18. Edited by A. van Braam. Rotterdam: Universitaire Pers, 1972.

Breuer, Stefan. 'Die Evolution der Disziplin. Zum Verhältnis von Rationalität und Herrschaft in Max Webers Theorie der vorrationalen Welt.' *Kölner Zeitschrift für Soziologie und Sozialpsychologie* 30 (1978): 409-37.

Buchigani, Norman I. 'The Weberian Thesis in India.' *Archives de sciences sociales des religions* 42 (1976): 17-33.

Burger, Thomas. *Max Weber's Theory of Concept Formation: History, Laws, and Ideal Types.* Durham, North Carolina: Duke University Press, 1976.

Butts, Stewart. 'Parsons' Interpretation of Weber: A Methodological Analysis.' *Sociological Analysis and Theory* 7 (1977): 227-40.

Butts, Stewart. 'Parsons, Weber, and the Subjective Point of View.' *Sociological Analysis and Theory* 5 (1975): 185-217.

Chorus, A. M. J. *Grondslagen der sociale psychologie.* Leiden: Kroese, 1953.

Cohen, Jere; Hazelrigg, Laurence E.; and Pope, Whitney. 'De-Parsonizing Weber: A Critique of Parsons' Interpretation of Weber's Sociology.' *American Sociological Review* 40 (1975): 229-41.

Davis, Wallace M. 'Anticritical Last Word on *The Spirit of Capitalism* by Max Weber.' *American Journal of Sociology* 83 (1978): 1105-31.

Dieckmann, Johann. *Max Webers Begriff des 'modernen okzidentalen Rationalizmus.'* Dusseldorf, 1961. Dissertation, Cologne.

Dobbelaere, Karel, and Layendecker, Leo, eds. *Godsdienst, kerk en samenleving. Godsdienstsociologische opstellen.* Rotterdam: Universitaire Pers, 1974.

Dow, Thomas E. 'Analysis of Weber's Work on Charisma.' *British Journal of Sociology* 29 (1978): 83-93.

Drehsen, Volker. 'Religion und die Rationalisierung der modernen Welt: Max Weber.' In *Das Jenseits der Gesellschaft,* pp. 89-154. Edited by K. W. Dahm. Munich: Claudius Verlag, 1975.

Dux, Günther. 'Religion, Geschichte und sozialer Wandel in Max Webers Religionssoziologie.' *Internationales Jahrbuch für Religionssoziologie* 7 (1971): 60-94.

Eisen, Arnold. 'Called to Order: The Role of the Puritan *Berufsmensch* in Weberian Sociology.' *Sociology* 13 (1979): 203-18.

223

Eisen, Arnold. 'The Meanings and Confusions of Weberian 'Rationality'.' *British Journal of Sociology* 29 (1978): 57-93.

Eisenstadt, S. N., ed. *The Protestant Ethic and Modernization: A Comparative View.* New York and London: Basic Books, 1968. This work contains an extensive bibliography.

Eisenstadt, S. N. 'Some Reflections on the Significance of Max Weber's Sociology of Religions for the Analysis of Non-European Modernity.' *Archives de sociologie des religions* 32 (1971): 29-52.

Eister, Allan W. 'Comment on 'Max Weber on Church, Sect and Mysticism.'' *Sociological Analysis* 36 (1975): 227-28.

Eliaeson, Sven. 'Some Recent Interpretations of Max Weber's Methodology.' *Sociological Analysis and Theory* 7 (1977): 21-71.

Farganis, James. 'An Exposition of Weber's Approach to *Verstehende Soziologie*.' *Sociological Focus* 7 (1974): 66-87.

Faul, Erwin. 'Die Religionssoziologie M. Webers.' In *Einführung in die Soziologie,* pp. 392-99. Edited by A. Weber. Munich: R. Piper & Co., Verlag, 1955.

Fenn, Richard K. 'Max Weber on the Secular: A Typology.' *Review of Religious Research* 10 (1969): 159-69.

Forbes, Richard P. 'The Problem of 'Laissez-faire' Bias in Weber's Concept of Formal Rationality.' *Sociological Analysis and Theory* 5 (1975): 219-36.

Freund, Julien. 'Le charisme selon Max Weber.' *Social Compass* 23 (1976): 383-95.

Freund, Julien. 'L'éthique économique et les religions mondiales selon Max Weber.' *Archives de sociologie des religions* 26 (1968): 3-25.

Freund, Julien. 'La hiérocratie selon Max Weber.' *Revue européene des sciences sociales* 34 (1975): 65-79.

Freund, Julien. *Sociologie de Max Weber.* Paris: Presses universitaires de France, 1966; 2d ed., 1968.

Freund, Julien. *The Sociology of Max Weber.* Translation M. Ilford. New York, 1965.

Gabel, Joseph. 'Une lecture marxiste de la sociologie religieuse de Max Weber.' *Cahiers internationaux de sociologie* 46 (1969): 51-66.

Gerth, Hans H. and Gerth, Hedwig Ida. 'Bibliography on Max Weber.' *Social Research* 16 (1949): 70-89.

Gerth, Hans H. and Mills, C. Wright. *From Max Weber: Essays in Sociology.* Translated, edited and with an introduction by Hans H. Gerth and C. Wright Mills. New

York: Oxford University Press, 1946. [Reprint editions appeared in 1958 and 1967.]

Giddens, Anthony. 'Marx and Weber: A Reply to Mr. Walton.' *Sociology: The Journal of the British Association* 5 (1971): 395-97.

Girndt, H. *Das soziale Handeln als Grundkategorie erfahrungswissenschaftlicher Soziologie.* Foreword by Johannes Winckelmann. Bibliography by Walter M. Sprondel. Tübingen: J. C. B. Mohr (Paul Siebeck), 1967.

Glasenapp, Helmuth von. *Het Boeddhisme.* Translated from the German by A. A. Bouwmeester and J. Bouwmeester-Fortuin. The Hague: Kruseman's Uitgeversmaatschappij, 1971.

Glasenapp, Helmuth von. *Het Brahmanisme.* Translated from the German by A. A. Bouwmeester and J. Bouwmeester-Fortuin. The Hague: Kruseman's Uitgeversmaatschappij, 1971.

Glasenapp, Helmuth von. *Het Chinese universalisme.* Translated from the German by A. A. Bouwmeester and J. Bouwmeester-Fortuin. The Hague: Kruseman's Uitgeversmaatschappij, 1971.

Glasenapp, Helmuth von. *De Islam.* Translated from the German by A. A. Bouwmeester and J. Bouwmeester-Fortuin. The Hague: Kruseman's Uitgeversmaatschappij, 1971.

Goddijn, Hans P. M., ed. *Max Weber. Zijn leven, werk en betekenis. Een inleiding.* Baarn: Ambo, 1980.

Goddijn, Hans P. M. et. al. *Geschiedenis van de sociologie. Achtergronden, hoofdpersonen en richtingen.* Meppel: J. A. Boom & Zn, 1971.

Goodman, Mark Joseph. 'Type Methodology and Type Myth: Some Antecedents of Max Weber's Approach.' *Sociological Inquiry* 45 (1975): 45-58.

Goodridge, R. Martin. 'The Secular Practice and the Spirit of Religion.' *Social Compass* 20 (1973): 19-30.

Grab, Hermann J. *Der Begriff des Rationalen in der Soziologie Max Webers. Ein Beitrag zu den Problemen der philosophischen Grundlegung der Sozialwissenschaft.* Karlsruhe: G. Braun, 1927.

Graf zu Sohms, M. Ernst. 'Vorwort, Einleitung.' In *Max Weber. Aus den Schriften zur Religionssoziologie,* pp. 5-37. Frankfurt am Main: Schauer, 1948.

Greeley, Andrew M. 'The Protestant Ethic: Time for a Moratorium.' *Sociological Analysis* 25 (1964): 20-33.

Greeley, Andrew M. *Religion and Career.* New York: National Opinion Research Center, 1963.

Grimm, Klaus. 'Niklas Luhmann's 'soziologische Aufklärung' oder das Elend der aprioristischen Soziologie. Ein Beitrag zur Pathologie der Systemtheorie im Licht der Wissenschaftslehre Max Webers.' *Kölner Zeitschrift für Soziologie und Sozialpsychologie* 26 (1974): 850-54.

Habermas, Jürgen. 'Technik und Wissenschaft als 'Ideologie'. Für Herbert Marcuse zum 70. Geburtstag am 19. VII 1968.' In *Technik und Wissenschaft als 'Ideologie,'* pp. 48-103. Frankfurt am Main: Suhrkamp Verlag, 1968; 5th ed. 1971.

Hasenfuss, Joseph. 'Die Beziehungen zwischen Religion und Gemeinschaft bei Max Weber.' *Philosophisches Jahrbuch* 55 (1942): 20-44.

Hassan, Riaz. 'Belief Systems and Job Satisfaction: An Empiricist Test of the Weberian Hypothesis.' *Sociologus* 20 (1970): 57-71.

Helmer, Hans Joseph. *Religion und Wirtschaft. Die neuere Kritik der Weberthese.* Cologne: Sülz, 1970.

Herberg, Will. *Protestant, Catholic, Jew: An Essay in American Religious Sociology.* New York: Doubleday & Company, Inc., 1955; 2d rev. ed. 1960.

Hilhorst, Hendricus W. A. *Religie in verandering. Een kritische analyse en evaluatie van de sociologische optiek van Peter L. Berger en Thomas Luckmann.* Utrecht: Elinkwijk, 1976. Doctoral dissertation, University of Utrecht. With a summary in English.

Hintze, Harry. *Kritische sociologie. Inleiding tot het sociologische denken der 'Frankfurter Schule.'* Alphen aan den Rijn: Samson Uitgeverij, 1973.

Houtart, François, and Lemercier, G. 'Weberian Theory and Ideological Function of Religion.' *Social Compass* 23 (1976): 345-54.

Houten, B. C. van. *Tussen aanpassing en kritiek. De derde methodenstrijd in de Duitse sociologie.* Deventer: Van Loghum Slaterus, 1970.

Howe, Richard H. 'Max Weber's Elective Affinities: Sociology Within the Bounds of Pure Reason.' *American Journal of Sociology* 84 (1978): 366-85.

Hunt, Larry L., and Hunt, Janet G. 'Black Catholicism and the Spirit of Weber.' *Sociological Quarterly* 17 (1976): 368-77.

Israel, Joachim. *Der Begriff Entfremdung. Makrosoziologische Untersuchungen von Marx bis zur Soziologie der Gegenwart.* Translated from the English by M. Kreckel. Hamburg: Rowohlt, 1972.

Jacobs, Jerry. 'From Sacred to Secular: The Rationalisation of Christian Theology.' *Journal for the Scientific Study of Religion* 10 (1971): 1-9.

Jaspers, Karl. *Max Weber. Rede bei der von der Heidelberger Studentenschaft am 17. Juli 1920 veranstalteten Trauerfeier.* Tübingen: J. C. B. Mohr (Paul Siebeck), 1926.

Johnson, Benton. 'Church and Sect Revisited.' *Journal for the Scientific Study of Religion* 10 (1971): 124-37.

Jonas, Friedrich. *Geschichte der Soziologie.* Vol. 4: *Deutsche und amerikanische Soziologie. Mit Quellentexten.* Reinbek bei Hamburg: Rowohlt Taschenbuch Verlag, 1965; 2d ed. 1972.

Jones, Bryn. 'Max Weber and the Concept of Social Class.' *Sociological Review* 23 (1975): 729-57.

Käsler, Dirk, ed. *Max Weber. Sein Werk und seine Wirkung.* Munich: Nymphenburger Verlagsbuchhandlung, 1972.

Käsler, Dirk, and Fogt, Helmut. 'Max-Weber-Bibliographie.' *Kölner Zeitschrift für Soziologie und Sozialpsychologie* 27 (1975): 703-30.

Kalberg, S. 'The Search for Thematic Orientations in a Fragmented Oeuvre: The Discussion of Max Weber in Recent German Sociological Literature.' *Sociology* 13 (1979): 127-39.

Kolegar, Ferdinand. 'The Concept of 'Rationalization' and Cultural Pessimism in Max Weber's Sociology.' *The Sociological Quarterly* 5 (1964): 355-73.

König, René. 'Einige Überlegungen zur Frage der Werturteilsfreiheit bei Max Weber.' In *Studien zur Soziologie. Theme mit Variationen,* pp. 38-68. Frankfurt am Main: Fischer Bücherei, 1971.

König, René, and Winckelmann, Johannes, eds. *Max Weber zum Gedächtnis. Materialen und Dokumente zur Bewertung von Werk und Persönlichkeit.* Kölner Zeitschrift für Soziologie und Sozialwissenschaft, Sonderheft 7. Cologne and Opladen: Westdeutscher Verlag, 1963.

Kooij, G. A. *Het modern westers gezin. Een inleidende gezinssociologische beschouwing.* Hilversum: Paul Brand, 1967.

Kreis, Friedrich. 'Max Webers Religionssoziologie.' *Logos* 10 (1921): 244-47.

Küenzlen, Gottfried. *Die Religionssoziologie Max Webers. Eine Darstellung ihrer Entwicklung.* Berlin: Duncker & Humblot, 1980.

Küenzlen, Gottfried. 'Unbekannte Quellen der Religionssoziologie Max Webers.' *Zeitschrift für Soziologie* 7 (1978): 215-27.

Laeyendecker, Leo. *Religie en conflict. De zogenaamde sekten in sociologisch perspectief.* Meppel: J. A. Boom & Zn., 1967.

Landshut, Siegfried. *Kritik der Soziologie. Freiheit und Gleichheit als Ursprungsproblem der Soziologie.* Munich and Leipzig: Duncker & Humblot, 1929.

Lauwers, Jan. *Secularisatietheorieën. Een studie over de toekomstkansen van de godsdienstsociologie.* Leuven: Universitaire Pers, 1974.

Lazarsfeld, Paul F., and Oberschall, Anthony R. 'Max Weber and Empirical Social Research.' *American Sociological Review* 30 (1965): 185-99.

Lefèvre, Wolfgang. *Zum historischen Character und zur historischen Funktion der Methode bürgerlicher Soziologie. Untersuchungen am Werk Max Webers.* Frankfurt am Main: Suhrkamp Verlag, 1971.

Lemmen, Mathieu Martin Willem. 'Doden priesters de profeten? Een sociologische analyse van de godsdienst van Israël.' In *Schrift in veelvoud*, pp. 97-114. Edited by Ernst Henau et al. Boxtel: Katholieke Bijbelstichting, 1980.

Lemmen, Mathieu Martin Willem. 'De godsdienstsociologie van Max Weber.' In *Max Weber. Zijn leven, werk en betekenis. Een inleiding*, pp. 134-55. Edited by Hans P. M. Goddijn. Baarn: Ambo, 1980.

Lemmen, Mathieu Martin Willem. 'De kritiek van H. Marcuse op het rationaliteitsbegrip van Max Weber.' *Politica* 25 (1975): 155-74.

Lemmen, Mathieu Martin Willem. 'Rationaliteit en seculariteit bij Max Weber.' *Politica* 27 (1977): 41-51.

Lennert, Rudolf. *Die Religionstheorie Max Webers*. Stuttgart: Kohlhammer, 1935.

Lenski, Gerhard. *The Religious Factor: A Sociological Study of Religion's Impact on Politics, Economics, and Family Life*. New York: Doubleday & Company, Inc., 1961; 2d ed. 1963.

Levin, Richard C. 'Max Weber's Concept of Rationality.' B. Litt. thesis, Oxford University, 1970. Copy in Bodleian Library.

Löwith, Karl. 'Max Weber und Karl Marx.' *Archiv für Sozialwissenschaft und Sozialpolitik* 67 (1932): 53-99; 175-214.

Luckmann, Thomas. *Das Problem der Religion in der modernen Gesellschaft. Institution, Person und Weltanschauung*. Freiburg im Bresgau: Verlag Rombach & Co., 1963.

Manasse, E. M. 'Max Weber on Race.' *Social Research* 14 (1947): 191-221.

Marcuse, Herbert. 'Industrialisierung und Kapitalismus im Werk Max Webers.' *In Kultur und Gesellschaft* vol. 2, pp. 107-29. Frankfurt am Main: Suhrkamp Verlag, 1965; 8th ed. 1970.

Meijers, Daniel. 'Singular and Plural Ethical Systems: A Critical Analysis of the Weber Thesis.' Translated by G. Kilburn. In *Religion, Nationalism and Economic Action: Critical Questions on Durkheim and Weber*, pp. 53-94. Assen: Van Gorcum, 1978.

Meurer, Bärbel. *Mensch und Kapitalismus bei Max Weber. Zum Verhältnis von Soziologie und Wirklichkeit*. Berlin: Duncker & Humblot, 1974.

Mitzman, Arthur. *The Iron Cage: An Historical Interpretation of Max Weber*. New York: Alfred A. Knopf, 1970.

Mommsen, Wolfgang J. 'Neue Max-Weber-Literatur.' *Historische Zeitschrift* 211 (1970): 616-30.

228

Mühlmann, Wilhelm E. *Max Weber und die rationale Soziologie.* Tübingen: J. C. B. Mohr (Paul Siebeck), 1966.

Münch, Richard. 'Max Webers Anatomie des okzidentalen Rationalismus: eine systemtheoretische Lektüre.' *Soziale Welt* 29 (1978): 217-46.

Munch, Peter A. ' 'Sense' and 'Intuition' in Max Weber's Theory of Social Action.' *Sociological Inquiry* 45 (1975): 59-65. With a short commentary by M. L. Wax, p. 67.

Nelson, Benjamin. 'Max Weber's 'Author's Introduction (1920): A Master Clue to His Main Aims.' *Sociological Inquiry* 44 (1974): 269-78.

Nelson, Benjamin. 'Max Weber's Sociology of Religion.' *American Sociological Review* 30 (1965): 595-99.

Nijk, A. J. *Secularisatie. Over het gebruik van een woord.* 2d ed. Rotterdam: Lemniscaat, 1968.

Nowak, Leszek. 'Social Action Versus Individual Action.' *Polish Sociological Bulletin* (1971): 84-93.

Parsons, Talcott. Introduction to Ephraim Fischoff, trans., *The Sociology of Religion,* by Max Weber. Pp. xix -lxvii. Boston: Beacon Press, 1963; paperback ed., 3d printing, 1967.

Parsons, Talcott. 'Neuere angelsächsische Literatur zu Max Webers Religionssoziologie.' In *Max Weber und die Soziologie heute,* pp. 234-41. Edited by Otto Stammer. Tübingen: J. C. B. Mohr (Paul Siebeck), 1965.

Parsons, Talcott. 'Preface to New Edition' of *The Protestant Ethic and the Spirit of Capitalism,* by Max Weber. Pp. xiii-xvii. New York: Charles Scribner's Sons, 1958.

Parsons, Talcott. *The Social System.* London: Routledge & Kegan Paul, 1951; 5th ed. 1967.

Petersen, David M. 'Max Weber and the Sociological Study of Ancient Israel.' *Sociological Inquiry* 49 (1979): 117-49.

Prades, J. A. *La sociologie de la religion chez Max Weber. Essai d'analyse et de critique de la méthode.* Louvain and Paris: Editions Nauwelaerts, 1966.

Raphaël, Freddy. 'Les Juifs en tant que peuple paria dans l'oeuvre de Max Weber.' *Social Compass* 23 (1976): 397-426.

Raphaël, Freddy. 'Max Weber et la judaïsme antique.' *Archives européennes de sociologie* 11 (1970): 297-336.

Rendtorff, Trutz. 'Die Säkularisierungsthese bei Max Weber und ihrer Bedeutung für die gegenwärtige Religionssoziologie.' In *Max Weber und die Soziologie heute,* pp. 241-45. Edited by Otto Stammer. Tübingen: J. C. B. Mohr (Paul Siebeck), 1965.

Rex, J. 'Typology and Objectivity: A Comment on Weber's Four Sociological Methods.' In *Max Weber and Modern Sociology,* pp. 17-36. Edited by Arun Sahay. London: Routledge & Kegan Paul, 1971.

Riesman, David. *De eenzame massa. Over cultuur en karakter in de moderne samenleving.* Translated from the English by E. J. Zwaan. Assen: Van Gorcum, 1959.

Riesman, David. *The Lonely Crowd: A Study of the Changing American Character.* With Nathan Glazer and Reuel Denney. New York: Doubleday & Company, Inc., 1950; 2d ed. 1953.

Ritzer, George. 'Professionalization, Bureaucratization and Rationalization: The Views of Max Weber.' *Social Forces* 53 (1975): 627-34.

Rotenberg, Mordechai. 'The Protestant Ethic Against the Spirit of Psychiatry: The Other Side of Weber's Thesis.' *British Journal of Sociology* 26 (1975): 52-65.

Roth, Guenther. 'Abscheid oder Wiedersehen? Zur fünften Auflage von Max Webers *Wirtschaft und Gesellschaft.' Kölner Zeitschrift für Soziologie und Sozialpsychologie* 31 (1979): 318-27.

Roth, Guenther. 'History and Sociology in the Work of Max Weber.' *British Journal of Sociology* 27 (1976): 306-18.

Roth, Guenther. 'Max Weber: A Bibliographical Essay.' *Zeitschrift für Soziologie* 6 (1977): 91-118.

Roth, Guenther. 'Religion and Revolutionary Beliefs: Sociological and Historical Dimensions in Max Weber's Work. In Memory of Ivan Vallier.' *Social Forces* 55 (1976): 257-72.

Sahay, Arun, ed. *Max Weber and Modern Sociology.* London: Routledge & Kegan Paul, 1971.

Salman, D. H. 'Psychology and Sociology in Max Weber's Theories.' *Social Compass* 10 (1963): 536-39.

Samuelson, Kurt. *Religion and Economic Action: A Critique of Max Weber.* Translated from the Swedish by E. Geoffrey French. New York and Evanston: Harper, 1961; 2d ed. 1964. The original Swedish version was published in 1957.

Savramis, Demosthenes. *Religionssoziologie. Eine Einführung.* Munich: Nymphenburger Verlagsbuchhandlung, 1968.

Schluchter, Wolfgang. *Die Entwicklung des okzidentalen Rationalismus. Eine Analyse von Max Webers Gesellschaftsgeschichte.* Tübingen: J. C. B. Mohr (Paul Siebeck), 1979.

Schluchter, Wolfgang. 'Die Paradoxie der Rationalisierung. Zum Verhältnis von 'Ethik' und 'Welt' bei Max Weber.' *Zeitschrift für Soziologie* 5 (1976): 256-84.

Schluchter, Wolfgang. *Rationalismus der Weltbeherrschung. Studien zu Max Weber.* Frankfurt am Main: Suhrkamp Verlag, 1980.

Schmidt, Gert. 'Max Weber and Modern Industrial Sociology: A Comment on Some Recent Anglo-Saxon Interpretations.' *Sociological Analysis and Theory* 6 (1976): 47-73.

Schoffeleers, Matthew, and Meijers, Daniel, eds. *Religion, Nationalism and Economic Action: Critical Questions on Durkheim and Weber.* Assen: Van Gorcum, 1978.

Schreuder, Osmund. *Gedaanteverandering van de kerk.* Nijmegen and Utrecht: Dekker & v. d. Vegt, 1969. Translation of *Gestaltwandel der Kirche.* Olten, Switzerland: Walter Verlag, 1967.

Seguy, Jean. 'Max Weber et la sociologie historique.' *Archives de la sociologie des religions* 33 (1972): 71-103.

Seyfarth, Constans. 'The West German Discussion of Max Weber's Sociology of Religion Since the 1960s.' *Social Compass* 27 (1980): 9-25.

Seyfarth, Constans, and Schmidt, Gert. *Max Weber Bibliografie. Eine Dokumentation der Sekundärliteratur.* Stuttgart: Euke, 1977.

Sharon, Allan N. 'Max Weber and the Origins of the Idea of Value-free Social Science.' *Archives européennes de la sociologie* 15 (1974): 337-53.

Siefer, Gregor. 'De ecclesiologische implicaties van Max Webers ideaaltypische distinctie tussen gemeente en gemeenschap.' *Concilium* 10 (1974): 88-100.

Sprondel, Walter M. 'Sekundärliteratur zu Max Webers Protestantismusstudien.' In Max Weber, *Die Protestantische Ethik. II Bd. Kritiken und Antikritiken,* pp. 395-405. Edited by Johannes Winckelmann. Hamburg: Siebenstern Taschenbuch Verlag,1968; 2d rev. ed., 1972.

Sprondel, Walter M., and Seyfarth, Constans, eds. *Max Weber und die Rationalisierung sozialen Handelns.* Stuttgart: Ferdinand Enke Verlag, 1981.

Stammer, Otto, ed. *Max Weber und die Soziologie heute. Verhandlungen des 15. Deutschen Soziologentages.* Tübingen: J. C. B. Mohr (Paul Siebeck), 1965.

Stark, Werner. 'Max Weber's Sociology of Religious Belief.' *Sociological Analysis* 25 (1964): 41-49.

Stark, Werner. 'The Place of Roman Catholicism in Max Weber's Sociology of Religion.' *Sociological Analysis* 29 (1968): 202-10.

Steemann, Theodore M. 'Max Webers [sic] Sociology of Religion.' *Sociological Analysis* 25 (1964): 50-58.

231

Stob, Henry John. 'Eine Untersuchung zu Max Webers Religionssoziologie.' Dissertation, Göttingen, 1938.

Stokes, Randall G. 'Afrikaner Calvinism and Economic Action: The Weberian Thesis in South Africa.' *American Journal of Sociology* 81 (1975): 62-81.

Swidler, Ann. 'The Concept of Rationality in the Work of Max Weber.' *Sociological Inquiry* 43 (1973): 35-42.

Tellegen, E. *De sociologie in het werk van Max Weber.* Meppel: J. A. Boom & Zn., 1968.

Tellegen, E. 'Waardevrijheid: toen en nu.' In *Max Weber: Wetenschap als beroep en roeping, met een nawoord van E. Tellegen,* pp. 33-51. Alphen aan den Rijn: Samson, 1970.

Tenbruck, Friedrich H. 'Die Genesis der Methodologie Max Webers.' *Kölner Zeitschrift für Soziologie und Sozialpsychologie* 11 (1959): 573-630.

Tenbruck, Friedrich H. 'Das Werk Max Webers.' *Kölner Zeitschrift für Soziologie und Sozialpsychologie* 27 (1975): 665-702.

Troeltsch, Ernst. *Gesammelte Schriften.* Vol. I: *Die Soziallehren der christlichen Kirchen und Gruppen.* Tübingen: J. C. B. Mohr (Paul Siebeck), 1912; 3d ed. Aalen: Scientia Verlag, 1977.

Turner, Bryan S. 'The Structuralist Critique of Weber's Sociology.' *British Journal of Sociology* 28 (1977): 1-16.

Turner, Bryan S. *Weber and Islam: A Critical Study.* London and Boston: Routledge & Kegan Paul, 1974.

Valk, Jakobus J. M. de. 'Webers karakteristiek van de moderne samenleving.' In *Max Weber: Zijn leven, werk en betekenis,* pp. 211-28. Edited by H. P. M. Goddijn. Baarn: Ambo, 1980.

Vaskovics, Laszlo A. 'Methodologische Konzeptionen der Soziologie. Ein Ueberblick.' In *Oesterreichisches Jahrbuch für Soziologie,* pp. 1-18. Edited by E. Bodzenta. Vienna: Springer Verlag, 1970.

Verhandlungen des 15. Deutschen Soziologentages vom 28. bis 30. April 1964 in Heidelberg. Max Weber und die Soziologie heute. Edited by Otto Stammer. Tübingen: J. C. B. Mohr (Paul Siebeck), 1965.

Vidich, Arthur J., ed. 'Charisma, Legitimacy, Ideology, and Other Weberian Themes.' *Social Research* 42 (1975): 567-811.

Voeglin, Erich. 'Ueber Max Weber.' *Deutsche Vierteljahrsschrift für Literaturwissenschaft und Geistesgeschichte* 3 (1925): 177-93.

Vogel, Ulrike. 'Einige Uberlegungen zum Begriff der Rationalität bei Max Weber.' *Kölner Zeitschrift für Soziologie und Sozialpsychologie* 25 (1973): 532-50.

Vogel, Ulrike. 'Das Werk Max Webers im Spiegel aktueller soziologischer Forschung.' *Kölner Zeitschrift für Soziologie und Sozialpsychologie* 29 (1977): 343-54.

Wach, Joachim. 'Max Weber als Religionssoziologe.' In *Einführung in die Religionssociologie,* pp. 65-98. Tübingen: J. C. B. Mohr (Paul Siebeck), 1931.

Wach, Joachim. *Sociology of Religion.* Chicago and London: The University of Chicago Press, 1944; 10th ed. 1964.

Wagner, Helmut. 'The Protestant Ethic: A Mid-Twentieth Century View.' *Sociological Analyses* 25 (1964): 34-40.

Walton, Paul. 'Critical Notes: Ideology and the Middle Class in Marx and Weber.' *Sociology: The Journal of the British Sociological Association* 5 (1971): 389-94.

Warner, R. Stephen. 'The Role of Religious Ideas and the Use of Models in Max Weber's Comparative Studies of Non-Capitalist Societies.' *The Journal of Economic History* 30 (1970): 74-99.

Weisz, Johannes. *Max Webers Grundlegung der Soziologie. Eine Einführung.* Munich: Verlag Dokumentation Saue, 1975.

Weyembergh, Maurice. *Le voluntarisme rationnel de Max Weber.* Brussels: Palais des Académies, 1972.

Wheeler, Wayne, ed. 'Max Weber, 1864-1964: A Symposion.' *The Sociological Quarterly* 5 (1964): 311-99.

Wilson, Bryan R. *Religion in Secular Society.* London and Baltimore, 1966; 2d ed. 1969.

Wilson, Bryan R., ed. *Rationality.* Oxford: Basil Blackwell & Mott, 1970.

Wilson, H. T. 'Reading Max Weber: The Limits of Sociology.' *Sociology* 10 (1976): 297-315.

Winckelmann, Johannes. 'Anmerkungen und Erläuterungen.' In *Max Weber: Soziologie, Weltgeschichtlichen Analysen, Politik,* pp. 509-62. Edited and annotated by Johannes Winckelmann, with an introduction by Eduard Baumgarten. Kröners Taschenausgeben, no. 229. Stuttgart: Kröners Taschenausgeben, 1956. 2d ed. 1959.

Winckelmann, Johannes. Foreword to *Die Protestantische Ethik. II Bd. Kritiken und Antikritiken.* Pp. 7-10. Edited by Johannes Winckelmann. Hamburg: Siebenstern Taschenbuch Verlag,1968; 2d rev. ed., 1972.

Winckelmann, Johannes. Foreword to *Wirtschaft und Gesellschaft. Grundriss der verstehenden Soziologie,* by Max Weber. 5th ed., pp. xi-xxiv and xv-xxxi. Studien-

ausgabe, revised and edited by Johannes Winckelmann. Tübingen: J. C. B. Mohr (Paul Siebeck), 1972.
See also Winckelmann's foreword to 4th edition.

Yinger, J. Milton. *Religion, Society, and the Individual: An Introduction to the Sociology of Religion.* New York: MacMillan, 1957; 11th ed. 1968.

Zijderveld, Anton C. *Institutionaliserung. Een studie over het methodologisch dilemma der sociale wetenschappen.* Hilversum: Paul Brand, 1966.

Zijderveld, Anton C. *De theorie van het symbolisch interactionisme.* Meppel: Boom, 1973.

INDEX OF NAMES AND SUBJECTS

2x, 102, 113 2x, 117, 120-121, 122-123, 123-124, 125, 126 2x, 132, 154, 157-160, 163, 170, 171, 173, 174, 178, 187, noot 38, 198, noot 62, 202, noot 54, 209, noot 1, 210v, noot 3, 212, noot 6; see also Protestantism; Rationalism

Association, 42, 84 2x, 94, 148, 174 2x, 176, 191, noot 50, 199, noot 9; compulsory, 47; voluntary, 47 2x, 173, 176 2x; *see also* *Verbände; Verein*

Astrology, 82

Astronomy, 15, 82

Atheism, 87, 90

B

Baptist movement, 17, 74, 75; *see also* Ethics, Baptist

BAUDELAIRE, Charles, 123

BAUM, Gregory, 217-218, noot 76

BAUMGARTEN, Eduard, 185, noot 3, 186, noot 23, 195, noot 97

BAXTER, Richard, 69, 70, 113, 201, noot 31

Bedarfdeckungswirtschaft, 68

Begreifen, 32 2x

BENDIX, Reinhard, 200, noot 23, 200-201, noot 29, 209-212, de noten 1 en 3

BERGER, Peter L., 11, 12, 193-4, noot 86 4x, 199, noot 2 5x, 200, noot 24 2x, 203-4, noot 68 2x, 204, noot 70, 214, noot 31, 214-5, noot 46 7x, noot 50 14x

Bureaucracy, 108 2x, 134, 136, 140 2x, 162, 168, 170, 176

Bhagavad Gita, 198, noot 63

Biology, 15, 32, 37, 43

Bodhisattvas, 153

BOUMAN, J., 191, noot 52

BOURDIEU, Pierre, 208-9, noot 144

Brahma, 88

Brahman, the divine World-Spirit, 88

Brahmanism: asceticism of, 163; and the caste system, 22, 83-84, 88, 109; genteel pattern of life of, 88, 163, 212, noot 7; and magic, 162; and the masses, 23, 109, 164; mysticism of, 163; 'organismic' social ethic of, 86; religious techniques of, 89; and world rejection, 121, 160; *see also* Hinduism; Jainism; Rationalism, Brahman

Brahmans: bearers of Hindu rationalism, 83, 88, 163; charisma of, 163; communities and schools of, 89; as gurus, 91-2, 152; as hermits, 88; and Musselmen, 164; as priests, 88, 159, 162; as *purohitas,* 152; and rulers, 87, 162, 164, 168; and vocational *dharma,* 86, 87

Brauch, 200, noot 27

BRENTANO, Lujo, 16
Brüderlichkeitsethik, 121
BUDDHA, 22, 135, 152
Buddhism, Buddhists, 19, 21, 22-24, 55, 63, 83, 91-2, 106, 114, 121, 153, 157-8, 160, 161, 163, 164, 186, noot 26
Buddhist ethic, 91
Business enterprise, 26, 196, noot 7

C
CAESAR, 37
Caesaropapistic church-state, 161
Calculability, 30, 31, 32
Calligraphy, 77
Calvinism, Calvinists, 17, 71-5, 107, 111, 116, 193, noot 84, 209-210, noot 1
Capitalism, 15, 16, 17, 20, 21, 64, 65-69, 71, 91, 100, 102, 106, 107, 108, 109, 113 2x, 160, 168-9, 170-1, 172-4, 178, 192, noot 65, 193-4, noot 86, 196, noot 7, 209-210, noot 1, 197, noot 26, 27, 54; spirit of, 16, 18, 28, 53, 65, 68, 68-9, 170, 185, noot 1 en 13, 196, noot 6, 209-210, noot 1
Cartel, 214-5, noot 46
Castes, caste system, 22, 27, 55, 83-85, 85-87, 89, 107, 108, 115, 163-4, 165, 193, noot 83, 197, noot 55, 56
Casuistry, 98; and priests, 150; rational juridical, 213, noot 26; of sins, 96; and the systematization of truths, 152
Catholicism, Catholics, 73, 74, 75, 78, 116, 119, 121, 141, 152, 153, 157-8, 193, noot 84
Causality, causation, 32 7x, 35, 36, 44, 60, 193, noot 84, 198, noot 74
Certitudo salutis, 72, 74, 114
Charisma, 82, 119, 122, 152, 161, 162, 163, 164, 169, 173, 183, 205-6, noot 89, 207-8, noot 125, 210-2, noot 3; in education, 77; heroic, 161; institutionalization of, 137-145, 191, noot 52, 207-8, noot 125; Laotse on, 82-3; magical, 119, 126, 147, 154, 163, 202, noot 48, 204, noot 72; prophetic, 152; routinization of, 135-147, 163, 205, noot 81, 206, noot 94, 210-2, noot 3; *see also* Domination, charismatic
Chemistry, 15, 32, 43
CHEN Ki Tong, 79
CHORUS, A. M. J., 201, noot 34
CHRIST, 100; and cult of Christ the Lord, 24; *see also* JESUS
Christian apologetics, 169

Christian calendar, 162

Christianity, 19, 20, 24 2x, 84, 97; expansion of, and rise of an autonomous urban bourgeoisie, 167, 169-172; history of, 181; and modern Western rationality, 169-171; and Roman law, 170

Christians, 69, 72-4, 126, 173, 198, noot 63

Chronomancy, 82

Church(es), 11, 18-9, 27, 47 2x, 60, 72, 73, 74-6, 134 2x, 139, 141 2x, 143, 145, 161, 165, 170, 173 2x, 175 2x, 176 2x, 178, 179, 185, noot 15, 205, noot 85, 214, noot 35 en 45; future of, 179; *see also* Sects; Religion, future of

Clan, 163

Classes, 21, 27, 44, 57, 65, 69, 71, 76, 77 3x, 79, 80 3x, 81, 83, 84, 85 3x, 86, 87 2x, 88, 91, 95, 140, 154 2x, 155, 161, 169, 171 2x, 175 2x, 180, 192, noot 65, 193, noot 83 en 84, 196, noot 7, 197, noot 48 en 56, 206, noot 105, 210-2, noot 3; *see also* Ethic, class

Class struggle, 206, noot 105

Clubs, 18, 76, 176

Commandments, 72, 73, 90, 94, 95, 96 2x, 99, 101 2x, 102, 126, 128 2x, 152

Commensality, 84 2x, 139

Compensation, 85, 89, 154, 198, noot 74, 203, noot 66; *see also* Karma

Computers, 217-8, noot 76

Conflict, 143, 190, noot 33

Confucianism, 19, 20-21, 55, 63, 76-81, 82, 83 2x, 159 2x, 162; and cities, 167; norms of, 106; and Taoist pantheon, 153, 186, noot 20, 212, noot 8; *see also* Rationalism, Confucian

Confucian personality, 110

CONFUCIUS, 21, 82

Congregation, 26, 149, 150 4x, 151, 152-3, 161, 169, 170, 173 2x, 175, 176, 187, noot 38, 208, noot 132, 210-2, noot 3

Connubium, 85, 101

Conviviality, 85

Corporations, 44 3x, 173, 213, noot 26

Counter-culture, 217-8, noot 76

Crime, criminality, 57, 215-6, noot 54

Custom, 112 3x, 133, 189, noot 27, 193, noot 80

D

Dance, dancers, 117, 120, 148

'Definition of the situation,' 113, 190, noot 39; as object of Weber's sociology, 44; *see also* Reality, definitions of

DE LA COURT, Pieter, 177
Demagogues, 134, 137, 152
Denomination, 214, noot 45
Deuten, 32, 37, 48, 188, noot 8, 190, noot 32, 191, noot 53; *see also* Understanding, interpretive; *Verstehen*
Deutsche Gesellschaft für Soziologie, 42
Dharma, 86-7
Disenchantment of the world, 148-9, 179, 180, 182
DOBBELAERE, Karel, 209-10, noot 1
Domination, 141, 142, 160, 205, noot 79; charismatic type, 133-5, 136, 138, 139, 205, noot 85, 207-8, noot 125; hierocratic, 27, 187, noot 41; legal type, 133-4, 139, 142; political, 27, 187, noot 41; traditional type, 134 2x, 139 2x; Weber's definition of, 133; *see also* Sociology of domination
DURKHEIM, Emile, 11, 199, noot 2, 207-8, noot 125 4x

E
Economics, 25, 31, 36, 37, 42, 123, 187, noot 38, 187-8, noot 1
Education, 80, 82, 83, 87, 96, 102, 110, 141, 144, 153, 155; Chinese mandarin system of, 76-8; types of, 76-7, 197, noot 50
Einmaligkeit, 33
Einverständnishandeln, 45, 47, 190, noot 43; *see also* Action, consensual
Einzigartigkeit, 33
Election: divine, 72, 73, 74, 114, 158; by the majority, 144, 145; *see also* Predestination
Enlightenment: charismatic, 183; eighteenth-century, 35, 178; mystical, 155
Enterprise, 26, 64, 65 2x, 68 2x, 102, 124, 134 2x, 148, 149, 150 2x, 151-2, 169, 171, 174, 196, noot 7, 199, noot 7, 208, noot 128 en 131, 210-2, noot 3, 216, noot 55
Epistemology, 181, 188-9, noot 14
Erkenntnisinteresse, 36; *see also Interesse*
Erwerbswirtschaft, 68
Ethic(s), ethical ideas: 16-7, 35, 36, 39, 51, 62, 67, 68, 69, 71, 77, 78 2x, 173, 174, 187-8, noot 1, 196, noot 8; of adaptation, 78, 80; ascetic, 17, 123-4, 125-6, 132; Baptist, 209-10, noot 1; bourgeois, 171, 174, 214, noot 29; Buddhist, 91-2; Calvinist, 209-10, noot 1; capitalistic, 15, 17, 54, 106, 171, 215-6, noot 54; caritative inward, 121-3; Catholic, 72-3, 77-8; Christian, 181; class, 22; of compensation, 154; and competition, 174; Confucian, 77-81, 197, noot 53; of deliverance, 87; economic, 19, 20 2x; fraternal, 121-5; Hindu and

Brahman, 85-9, 198, noot 63, 212, noot 7; inner-worldly utilitarian, 79; of intramundane actions, 96, 99; of inwardness, 98, 117-8, 120-6, 128-9, 131, 157; Jewish business, 102-3; of Judaism, 93, 94, 95-6, 97, 98-9, 102-3, 198, noot 83; legitimation of, 114; of magic, 117-20, 126, 147-8, 149, 202, noot 47 en 50; mystical, 132; pietist, 209-10, noot 1; Protestant, 16, 156, 167, 170, 172, 173, 209-10, noot 1; Puritan, 174 2x; rational, 96-7, 153; religious, 20, 27 2x, 55, 96, 98, 99, 115, 122, 126, 128, 153, 187, noot 38, 202, noot 51, 210-2, noot 3; and sexuality, 202, noot 51; social, 67, 77-8, 86, 94; tradi-tional(istic), 98, 103; and universal love, 121; and war, 122; worldly heroic, 123; see also Rationalism, ethical; Rationalization of ethics
Everyday life, 15, 16, 19, 38, 45, 55, 56, 63, 64 2x, 69, 81, 91, 94, 96, 98, 100, 101, 102, 112, 113, 118, 120, 128 2x, 129, 137, 138 2x, 139, 142, 145, 147, 149, 152 2x, 193, noot 82, 210-2, noot 3, 212, noot 7, 213, noot 26
Evidenz, 31, 61, 188, noot 6, 194, noot 93

F
Fachmenschentum, 64, 71
Facts, 26, 30, 31 2x, 33, 35 2x, 37, 39, 42, 43 2x, 98, 116, 196, noot 1
Family, 26, 44, 45, 139, 141, 169, 191, noot 50, 210-2, noot 3
Fate, 80, 81, 109, 113, 146, 153
FENN, Richard K., 216-7, noot 59
FISCHOFF, Ephraim, 26-7, 186, noot 30, 187, noot 34 en 40, 210-2, noot 3
FRANKLIN, Benjamin, 66 5x, 67, 69 2x, 107, 178, 196, noot 8
Freikirche, 214, noot 45

G
GAUTAMA, 22; *see also* SIDDHARTHA
Gedankenbild, 59
GEHLEN, Arnold, 199, noot 2
Gemeinde, 26, 150, 208, noot 132; *see also* Congregation
Gemeinschaftshandeln, 190, noot 43
Geography, 21; science of, 43, 48
Geomancy, 82 2x
Geometry, 15
GERTH, Hans H., 27, 210-2, noot 3
Gesellschaften, 176; *see also* Clubs
Gesinnungsethik, 96, 98, 117, 120, 128; *see also* Ethic of inward-ness

GLASENAPP, Helmuth von, 186, noot 1
Gnosis, 88-9, 99, 159
GODDIJN, Hans P. M., 191, noot 52
Gottesdienst, 119; see also Religion
Gotteszwang, 119; see also Magic
Grace, 72, 73, 92, 141 2x, 142, 173, 174
GROOT, A. B. de, 82
Guilds, 76, 84-5, 163, 167-8, 174 3x, 197, noot 56, 213, noot 26
Gurus, 91-2, 152, 153

H
HABERMAS, Jürgen, 41 2x
Handelen, 43; see also Action, social; *Handeln*
Handeln, 188, noot 8, 190, noot 32 en 43, 192, noot 67; see also
Action, social
Hellenistic world, 24, 168, 213, noot 21
Helvetic Confession, 197, noot 38
Henotheism, 94
Hermits, 88
Heroes, heroism, 77, 81, 134, 135, 137, 138, 139, 163
Herrschaft, 27 2x, 133, 187, noot 40; see also Domination
HERSKOVITS, M. J., 202, noot 49
Hinduism, Hindus, 13, 19, 22-3, 55, 83-90, 101, 115, 152, 153; *see
also* Brahmanism
History, 15, 28, 31, 37, 42, 65, 86, 93, 94, 95, 97, 99, 108, 111, 113,
117, 144, 193-4, noot 83 en 86, 196, noot 1; ideas in, 192, noot 71,
199, noot 9; and sociology, 42-3, 53-6, 110; theory of, 210-2, noot
3; universal, 55; *see also* Research, historical
Homo politicus, 122
HOUTEN, B. C. van, 41, 189, noot 25 en 26, 190, noot 30

I
Idealtypus, 58
Individualism: Anglo-American, 111; methodical, 45-6, 181; mo-
dern, 174; philosophical, 181
Institutions, 15, 45, 46, 47 7x, 75, 111, 125, 136, 138, 141, 144,
214, noot 38; *see also* Charisma, institutionalization of
Intellectuals, intellectualism, 23, 57, 79, 81 2x, 82, 87 2x, 89, 91,
100, 102, 155 2x, 159, 164, 165, 182, 187, noot 38, 193, noot 83
en 84, 201, noot 30, 205-6, noot 89, 216, noot 55
Intelligibility, 32, 58
Intentionality, intentions, 43, 44, 45 3x, 46, 48, 49, 50, 52, 66, 69,

241

71, 105 2x, 107, 109, 114, 132, 133, 143, 144, 146, 172, 199, noot 2, 202, noot 49, 215, noot 50; and structures, 109
Interesse, 201, noot 39
ISAIAH, 97, 196, noot 1
Islam, 19, 20, 22, 24 2x, 152, 153

J

JACOBS, Jerry, 215-6, noot 54
Jainism, Jains, 22-3, 63, 83, 89-91, 159-60, 163, 164, 186, noot 26
JAMES, William, 194-5, noot 95
JEREMIAH, 97
JESUS, 121; and wedding at Cana, 196, noot 1; *see also* CHRIST
Jewish history, Weber on miraculousness of facts of, 196, noot 1
Job, Book of, 24
Jurisprudence, 15
Justification, 75; by faith, 116

K

KANT, Immanuel, 34
Karma, 85 3x, 86, 90 2x, 92 4x, 130, 131, 132, 164, 198, noot 72, 73 en 74; *see also* Compensation
Kausaladäquanz, 31
Knowledge, 24, 30, 31 2x, 32 6x, 33 6x, 34, 39, 40 2x, 41 2x, 46, 77 2x, 78, 82 3x, 88, 89 2x, 90, 91, 96 2x, 101 3x, 151, 152, 160, 180, 182, 188, noot 4, 188-9, noot 14, 194, noot 92, 198, noot 62 en 63, 201, noot 39, 210-2, noot 3, 213, noot 15
KÖNIG, Renè, 189, noot 27
Kollektivbegriffe, 44
Kollektivgebilde, 46
Konfession, 214, noot 45
Konflikt, 207, noot 112; *see also* Conflict
KOOIJ, G. A., 217, noot 74

L

LAEYENDECKER, Leo, 209-10, noot 1, 214, noot 45
LANDSHUT, Siegfried, 192, noot 65
Language groups, 45
LAOTSE, 21, 82 2x
LAUWERS, Jan, 192, noot 79, 217-8, noot 76
Law(s): canon, 69; civil, 47; of consumption, 85, 88; corporate, 44; criminal, 132; empirical, of nature, 30, 32-3 36, 39, 46, 58-9, 60, 86, 127, 135, 182; God's, 96 2x, 98 2x, 100, 101-3; Roman, 170;

sacred, 120; science of, 46
LAZARSFELD, Paul F., 195, noot 97
LEMMEN, M. M. W., 192, noot 70, 217-8, noot 76
LENNERT, Rudolf, 193-4, noot 86
LEVIN, Richard C., 204, noot 72, 209-10, noot 125
Levites, 93 3x, 96, 98 2x, 158
Logic, 30, 77, 86, 113, 188, noot 5
LOYOLA, Ignatius of, 143
LUCKMANN, Thomas, 11
Lutheranism, 75, 111, 116, 208, noot 29

M
Machines, 43, 108, 113; as objectified mind, 108
Magic, magician, 23, 26, 46, 72 2x, 75 2x, 77, 79, 80 2x, 81-3, 85,
88, 97, 98, 102, 105, 117-20, 126-8, 135, 147-9, 150, 152, 153, 154,
157-60, 161, 162, 164, 179, 182
MAHAVIRA, 22
MARCUSE, Herbert, 217-8, noot 76
Markets, 17, 36, 45 3x, 47, 65 4x, 66, 74, 100, 108, 123, 131, 144,
185, noot 7, 214-5, noot 46
MARTINDALE, Don, 191, noot 52, 220 2x
MARX, Karl, 11, 18, 215, noot 50
Marxism: view of religion, 18, 54; conception of history, 37
Massen religiosität, 132; *see also* Religiosity, popular
Mathematics, mathematicians, 77, 137, 188, noot 5
MEAD, George Herbert, 199, noot 2, 200, noot 24
Mechanics, science of, 15
MENGER, C., 195, noot 97
Metaphysics, 87-8 2x, 90, 92, 116, 170
Meteorology, 82
Meteoromancy, 82
Method(s), 11 2x, 15, 29-30, 38, 39, 40, 41, 45-6, 47, 48, 49, 57 2x,
58, 61 2x, 64, 65, 69, 73, 74, 89, 91, 96, 101, 150, 170, 181, 190,
noot 33, 191, noot 52, 192, noot 73 en 75, 193-4, noot 86 en 91,
194-5, noot 95 en 97, 199, noot 8, 201, noot 30, 207-9, noot 125,
209-10, noot 1, 217-8, noot 76
Methodicalness, 69, 73, 74 2x, 75 2x, 88, 106 2x, 120, 122, 146,
158, 159, 160, 174, 182
Methodism, 17, 74 2x
Methodology, 12, 13, 17, 25, 29 2x, 30-31, 33, 34, 37, 40, 41 2x,
42v, 43, 45, 46, 48, 53, 54, 56, 57, 58, 61, 109, 188, noot 2, 190,
noot 39, 192, noot 65, 194-5, noot 95, 195, noot 97, 200-1, noot

29, 203, noot 62, 207-8, noot 125
MILLS, C. Wright, 210-2, noot 3
Miracles, miraculousness, 96, 196, noot 1
MITZMAN, Arthur, 189, noot 27
MOHAMMED, 135
Monalatry, 94
Monks, 22-3, 73, 74, 89-91, 114, 117, 121, 155, 157-8, 160, 164
Monotheism, 94, 99, 128, 150, 165-7, 210-2, noot 3
MOSES, 93, 96, 166
Music, 15, 148, 182; religiously 'musical' persons, 39, 117, 176
Mysticism, 27, 91, 120, 123-125, 157, 158, 159, 163, 169, 187, noot
38, 198, noot 62, 202, noot 54, 210-2, noot 3, 212, noot 6

N
NAHUM, 97
Narcotics, 148
Necromancers, 127
NELSON, Benjamin, 210-2, noot 3
NIETZSCHE, Friedrich, 115, 201, noot 36
NIJK, A. J., 214, noot 38
Nirvana, 88, 90, 91, 114, 153

O
OBERSCHALL, Anthony R., 195, noot 97
Oracles, 141
Organization(s), 15, 23, 42, 47, 64, 66, 71, 84, 86, 101, 108, 136,
139, 148, 161, 163, 168, 169, 170, 173, 174, 176, 191, noot 50, 196,
noot 7, 202, noot 50, 208, noot 128, 129 en 132, 217-8, noot 76;
see also Verband
Orgiasticism, orgies, 88, 96, 202, noot 51, 208, noot 132

P
Pantheon, formation of, and rational thought, 127-8, 203, noot 64;
rank of a city god in, in China, 77
Papal infallibility, 134
Pariah people, 24 2x, 97, 101, 103, 116, 154, 163, 164, 165, 176,
186, noot 28
Parish, 208, noot 132
PARSONS, Talcott, 27, 192, noot 70, 193, noot 84, 194, noot 91,
200-1, noot 29, 209-10, noot 1, 210-2, noot 3, 212, noot 6 en 8, 221
Pastor(s), 134, 152 2x
Pastoral care, 11, 27, 56, 69, 96, 151, 152, 210-2, noot 3

Paterfamilias, 134
PAUL, 70, 199, noot 3
Pharisee(ism), 24, 100, 102, 186, noot 29, 198, noot 83
Physics, 15, 32, 43, 77, 105, 182
Physiology, 48
Pietism, pietists, 74, 152; *see also* Ethics, pietist
Political science, 15, 39
PRADES, J. A., 192, noot 73
Preaching, 27, 151, 210-2, noot 3
Predestination, 72, 74 2x, 80, 212, noot 10; *see also* Election
Predictability, 31, 47, 80, 154
Priesthood, priests, 27, 72, 73, 76, 99, 134, 139, 141, 149, 150-155,
165, 169, 187, noot 38, 202, noot 51, 208, noot 131 en 132, 208-
9, noot 144, 210-2, noot 3; Brahman, 22, 83, 84, 87, 88 2x, 159,
162-3; Catholic, 78, 119, 141; and Chinese polity, 76, 77; Levitic,
24, 95; of magic, 83, 97, 162; Taoist plebeian, 81, 82, 159, 161
Printing, 15
Prophecy, prophetic message, 134, 135, 151, 152, 205, noot 80,
210-2, noot 3
Prophets, 24, 26, 52, 93 2x, 95 4x, 97, 98-101, 109, 135, 137, 138,
139, 151 3x, 152, 153 2x, 187, noot 38, 196, noot 1, 205, noot 80,
208-9, noot 144, 210-2, noot 3; emissary or ethical, 98, 135, 149,
151, 162, 165, 205, noot 80; exemplary, 135, 149, 162, 205, noot 80
Protestantism, 16-7, 18, 20 2x, 178, 194, noot 88, 199, noot 9; ascetic, 17 2x, 53 2x, 63, 69 2x, 71, 74, 106, 121, 123, 124, 157, 160,
170, 172 2x, 173, 179, 182, 193, noot 82, 193-4, noot 86, 209-10,
noot 1, 210-12, noot 3, 213-4, noot 27
Psalms, 24
Psychology, 43, 48-50, 185-6, noot 17, 192, noot 72
Pumbeditha academy of Babylon, 200-1, noot 29
Puritan(s), Puritanism, 17, 21, 23, 69, 70, 71, 73, 101, 113, 114,
126, 130 2x, 140, 146, 174 2x
Pythagorean comma, 182

R
Rationalism, 15, 19, 24, 26, 29, 63 2x, 64, 196, noot 1, 104, 128,
129, 130, 136; and administrative technique, 198, noot 61; ancient
Buddhist, 22, 23, 63, 91-2; ascetic Protestant, 63, 69-76, 111, 197,
noot 20, 215, noot 52; bourgeois, 171, 174; Brahman or Hindu, 22,
63, 83-9, 91-2, 162-165, 197-8, noot 57; bureaucratic, 154, 162; capitalistic, 64-69, 167-172, 215, noot 52; Chinese, 21, 160-2; concept
of, 13, 26, 29, 196, noot 1; Confucian, 19, 76-81, 81, 159; of the

245

force, 136, 137, 205-6, noot 89; of religion, 107, 114, 117, 126, 128-132, 135, 147, 149-156; and the religiosity of the masses, 132, 137; and religious virtuosi, 132; and salvation, 106, 121, 124, 129; scientific, 105; of sexuality, 124; of social relations, 106; as socio-cultural process, 13, 104-56, 200-1, noot 29; of spheres of value; 118, 130; and 'sublimation', 199, noot 4; and 'systematization', 199, noot 5; of values, 112; of vengefulness, 116; of work, 106; of the world picture, 129, 133, 181; and world-renunciation, 22; *see also* Rationalism; Rationality

Reality, 34, 40, 41, 58, 59, 79, 88, 181, 188-9, noot 14, 191, noot 52, 205, noot 86, 212, noot 8, 215, noot 50; definitions of, 63, 180, 181, 217-8, noot 76; empirical, 13, 30-32, 58, 60-1, 180, 195, noot 97; historical, 53, 54, 203, noot 62; and ideal types, 59, 195, noot 97; nominalistic view of, 191, noot 52; socio-cultural, 13, 33, 34, 48, 49, 51, 53, 173, 181 2x, 207-8, noot 125; *see also* 'Definition of the situation'

Reformation, 18 2x, 199, noot 9

Reification: of ideal types, 194, noot 91; of social reality, 181; of structures, 46, 47, 207-8, noot 125

Religio, 213, noot 26

Religion(s), 11, 13, 20, 26, 27, 39, 56 2x, 57, 62, 74, 79, 84, 89, 91 2x, 114, 115, 116, 117, 118, 119, 126, 131, 150, 151, 154, 155 2x, 158, 164, 172, 178, 180, 181, 182, 186, noot 18 en 22, 187, noot 38, 193, noot 83 en 84, 202, noot 49 en 50, 208, noot 132, 208-9, noot 144, 210-2, noot 3, 214, noot 45, 215, noot 50; Asian intellectualist, 182; and the believer, 56; bourgeois, 182; Catholic, 119; of China, 186, noot 20; cultural, 24, 210-2, noot 3; definition of, 57, 193-4, noot 86, 194-5, noot 95, 202, noot 49, 203, noot 62, 217-8, noot 76; ethical, 182; future of, 175; genuine, 183; history of, 117, 193, noot 83; of India, 186, noot 24; irrationalization of, 182, 217, noot 65; Jewish, 24, 115; Marxism on, 54; origins of, 26, 114, 187, noot 38, 210-2, noot 3; primitive, 114; rebirth of, 217-8, noot 76; salvation, 154, 187, noot 38; and society, 11, 54, 156, 179, 215, noot 50; sociological view of, 11; urban, 169; Western, 172; world, 19 2x, 20 2x, 22, 24 2x, 55, 185-6, noot 17, 187, noot 38, 192, noot 76, 203, noot 62; *see also* Rationality and religiosity; Rationalization of religion; Religiosity; Sociology of Religion

Religiosity, 48, 193, noot 84, 193-4, noot 86, 216, noot 55 en 56; ancient Buddhist, 23; ascetic, 114, 154; authentic or genuine, 179, 183, 193, noot 84, 208, noot 129, 216, noot 55; Calvinist, 73; in China, 20-1; congregational, 150-151, 154, 169; emotional, 23; ethical, 154; heroic, 117; Indian, 21-3; of intellectuals, 216, noot 55;

247

irrational, 154; Jewish, 21, 100, 116; and magic, 23, 129; Near Eastern, 20; popular, 23 2x, 117, 132, 173; prophetic, 154; Puritan, 114; and rationality, 179-183; salvation, 162, 203, noot 65; and a savior, 23; and secularity, 217-8, noot 76; Slavophile Russian, 208, noot 129; virtuoso, 117; Western, 20

RENDTORFF, Trutz, 217-8, noot 76

Research, 13, 17, 18, 20 2x, 36, 38, 39 2x, 54, 55, 185, noot 3, 188-9, noot 14, 190, noot 33, 192, noot 65, 195, noot 97, 215, noot 52; comparative, 54; empirical, 29, 54, 57; historical, 26; and ideal types, 62, 196, noot 3; scientific, 11, 38, 42; sociological, 13, 29 2x, 52, 189, noot 27

Researcher, 33 2x, 34, 35, 59, 60 2x

Resentment, and Hinduism, 115; and Jewish religiosity, 115; Nietzsche's theory of, and Weber 115

REX, J., 188, noot 2

RHEINSTEIN, Max, 27, 221

Richtigkeitsrationalität, 31, 32, 58, 212, noot 5; *see also* Rationality of objective correctness

Richtigkeitstypus, 62; *see also* Types, ideal

RIESEBRODT, Martin, 185, noot 3

RIESMAN, David, 200, noot 18

ROCHFAHL, F., 16

Roman Empire, province, cities, 166, 168 3x, 213, noot 21

Roman law: *see* Law, Roman

ROTH, Guenther, 221; on terms and concepts in Weber, 187, noot 40, 188, noot 6, 8, en 9, 189, noot 16, 190, noot 42, 191, noot 53; on Weber's *Economy and Society,* 186, noot 30

S

Sacrament, 72, 75, 116, 151, 153, 157-8, 165; *see also* Magic Saints, 77, 92, 113, 153, 173, 201, noot 31

SAMUELSON, Kurt, 209-10, noot 1

SALMAN, D. H., 191-2, noot 57

Salvation, 23, 27, 71-6, 81, 83, 86-9, 93, 95, 97, 99, 100, 102, 106, 114-5, 116, 120, 121, 124, 126, 129 2x, 130, 133, 135, 138, 149, 151, 152-4, 157-9, 162, 170, 171, 173, 180, 187, noot 38, 193-4, noot 86, 198, noot 63 en 71, 203, noot 65

SCHMOLLER, G., 195, noot 97

SCHÄFFLE, Albert, 45

SCHUTZ, Alfred, 199, noot 2

Science(s), 11, 15, 25, 32, 33, 34 2x, 35, 41, 42, 44, 46, 48-9, 53, 60, 61, 82, 92, 105, 109, 112, 180, 182, 190, noot 33, 200-1, noot

29, 204, noot 72, 216, noot 57, 216-7, noot 59; application of, 39, 41; cultural, 32 3x, 33 2x, 34, 36, 39, 42 2x, 58, 59, 188, noot 7 en 10, 189, noot 24, 190, noot 31, 191, noot 53, 192, noot 69; deductive, 30; definition of, 31, 188, noot 12; empirical, 30-5, 44, 188, noot 5, 189, noot 15; human, 32, 33, 188, noot 7; medical, 204, noot 72; natural, 32 5x, 33, 39, 40, 58, 189, noot 18, 203, noot 66; social, 31, 33 2x, 34 2x, 37, 40, 42 2x, 44, 58, 59, 187-8, noot 1, 188, noot 7, 190, noot 31; technical, 86; theory of, 12, 29 2x, 41, 203, noot 62; and values, 29, 35-40, 181, 189, noot 27, 216, noot 55; see also Rationality and science; Values Sects, sectarianism, 17, 18 2x, 22, 23, 24, 27 2x, 47 2x, 52, 60, 74, 75 2x, 89, 90, 100, 117, 139, 154, 161, 172-4, 175 2x, 176, 177, 179

Secularization, 172 2x, 175-9, 214, noot 38, 214-5, noot 46, 215, noot 50, 217-8, noot 76

SEGUY, Jean, 207-8, noot 125

Self-understanding: historical non-Christian, 217-8, noot 76; Jewish, 93, 198, noot 76

Sermon on the Mount, 122

SENNACHERIB, 196, noot 1

Shiva, 153

Sib, 26, 76, 120, 134, 163, 167, 169, 191, noot 50

SIDDHARTHA, 22; *see also* BUDDHA

Sinn, 43, 50, 57, 187-8, noot 1, 188, noot 8, 189, noot 16 en 24, 190, noot 32, 39, 42 en 43

Sinnadäquanz, 31

Sitte, 112, 200, noot 27; *see also* Custom

Sociology, 11, 12 2x, 29, 30, 42 2x, 43, 46 2x, 53, 63, 110, 133, 197, noot 39, 207-8, noot 125, 216, noot 55; and causal explanation, 45, 48, 58; concept formation in, 190, noot 33; definition of, 42, 49, 190, noot 32 en 33; and economics, 187-8, noot 1; emancipatory, 40; empirical-nomological, 40-1; and ethical neutrality, 187-8, noot 1; heuristic value of, 46; and history, 43, 53-6, 190, noot 33; individualistic, 42, 43-8, 181; interpretive, 42, 43 2x, 44, 46, 48 2x, 194, noot 88; methodology of, 42; and natural science, 59; object of, 43, 44, 50, 52, 62, 192, noot 69; problem-oriented, 41, 47; and psychology, 43, 48-53; rationalistic, 13, 29, 57, 61; as a social science, 42; socio-critical, 40-1; and sociology of religion, 43, 56-7; techniques of, 57-63; value-free, 41, 189, noot 27; *Verstehende,* 40-1, 43, 46, 194, noot 88

Sociology of authority, 27

Sociology of the city, 167, 213, noot 21

Sociology of conflict, 208-9, noot 144

Sociology of domination, 27, 187, noot 40, 205, noot 79 en 81, 206, noot 94

Sociology of imperative control, 27

Sociology of knowledge, 177, 178

Sociology of law, 56, 197, noot 30, 198, noot 62

Sociology of politics, 56, 210-2, noot 3

Sociology of rationalism, 55, 192, noot 75

Sociology of religion, 11-3, 14, 29, 39, 53, 65, 134-5, 192, noot 75 en 78, 193-4, noot 86, 194, noot 91, 197, noot 29 en 30, 198, noot 81, 210-2, noot 3, 217-8, noot 76; comparative, 26; method of, 42-57, 192, noot 73; object of, 63 2x, 156, 217-8, noot 76; as socio-logism, 193, noot 84; systematic, 26 2x, 56-7, 187-8, noot 1, 193, noot 84, 210-2, noot 3; Weber's writings on, 15-29, 29, 53-6, 56, 186, noot 30, 187, noot 34, 190, noot 33, 216, noot 57; *see also* Sociology

SOHM, Rudolf, 205, noot 85

SOMBART, Werner, 16, 68 2x, 100, 101

Sorcerers, sorcery, 81, 89, 119, 134, 148-9, 150, 151, 179, 208-9, noot 44, 210-2, noot 3

SPANN, Othmar, 45

Specialization of task, 64, 208, noot 131; *see also Fachmenschentum*

SPRONDEL, Walter M., 209-10, noot 1

STARK, Werner, 193, noot 84

State, 19, 37, 44 2x, 45, 47, 76, 78, 79, 109, 122, 126, 134, 139, 141, 142, 143, 144, 145, 160, 161 2x, 165, 167 2x, 168, 173 2x, 176 2x, 214, noot 38

STEEMAN, Theodore M., 193-4, noot 86

Stock exchange, 49, 61, 100

Sublimation, 52, 96, 98, 120, 129, 199, noot 4

SWIDLER, Ann, 210-2, noot 3

Symbolism, 118, 126, 127, 204, noot 72

T

T'ai P'ing Rebellion, 162

Talmud, 24, 100, 102, 116, 201, noot 30

Taoism, Taoists, 20-1, 55, 63, 76, 79, 81-3, 106 2x, 159, 161 2x, 163

Taoist pantheon, and Confucianism, 153

Technicians, 152, 176; and technocratic system, 183, 217-8, noot 76

Technique(s) or technical means, 82, 89, 141, 143, 145, 166; administrative, 37, 160, 198, noot 61; Buddhist meditation, 91; construction, 86; erotic, 86; ideal types as, 57, 58-63; investigative, 34; of law, 137; and logic, 86; magical, 141, 148; oracles as, 141; and scientific rationality, 31, 39, 40-1; sociological, 29, 57-63, 188, noot 10; statistics as, 57; yoga, 89

Technology, 25, 82, 112, 154, 189, noot 18, 217-8, noot 76; and conditions of machine production, 113; and being human, 217-8, noot 76; and ethos, 181; and power blocs, 181; and progress, 171; and social production relations, 18

TELLEGEN, E., 189, noot 27, 190, noot 30, 191, noot 52, 192, noot 67, 216, noot 57

TENBRUCK, Friedrich H., 188, noot 2

Theodicy, 27, 80, 164, 187, noot 39, 203, noot 67, 210-2, noot 3; Brahman, 85-6; inner-worldly-oriented Confucian, 81; and legitimation, 132; pure types of, 130-2; of suffering and death, 203, noot 66; rational, 149

Theologians, theological approach to religion, theology, 35, 56, 69, 71, 75, 87, 141, 217-8, noot 76

THOMAS AQUINAS, 70

THOMAS, W. I., 44, 190, noot 39

TÖNNIES, Ferdinand, 176, 191, noot 50

Torah, 95-7, 98, 99, 101

Totemism, 163, 201, noot 39

Tradition, traditionalism, 61, 66, 67, 68, 77, 80 2x, 95, 98, 101, 103, 108, 110, 112 2x, 131-2, 133-4, 136 2x, 137, 138, 139 2x, 141, 152, 153 2x, 160-1, 162, 168, 170, 171, 172, 174, 178, 192, noot 68, 200, noot 18, 203-4, noot 68, 217-8, noot 76; see also Action, traditional type

Tribe, 26, 120, 163 2x, 164

TROELTSCH, Ernst, 19, 27, 189, noot 15, 214, noot 45

Truth(s), 30, 38, 92, 105 3x, 130, 152

Truthfulness, 90

Type(s): of asceticism, 73; of association, 27; average, 58, 59; of behavior, 57; of city, 168, 213, noot 21; conceptually pure, 190, noot 43, 192, noot 67; cultural, 46; of doctrine, 23; of domination, 205, noot 79; of education, 77-8; of ethics, 210-2, noot 3; of ethos, 20; ideal, 18-9, 21, 53, 57, 58-62, 63-4, 67, 71, 104, 112, 114, 117, 133 2x, 140, 142 2x, 143, 147 2x, 157, 173 2x, 180, 192, noot 75, 194, noot 91 en 92, 195, noot 97, 196, noot 3, 197, noot 50, 200-1, noot 29, 201, noot 43, 203, noot 62, 209-10, noot 1, 212, noot 7, 214, noot 29; interpretable, 57; mixed, 192, noot 67; of people, 39, 98, 200, noot 18; of prophet, 135; of rationalism, 17, 20, 21 2x, 24, 26, 85, 93, 95, 97, 101, 130-1, 192, noot 75; of rationality, 36-7, 105-6,

251

107, 112, 118, 156, 160; of religiosity, 20; of revolution, 126; of social action, 49-53, 190, noot 43; sociological, 58; of sociology, 40; of theodicy, 130, 132, 149, 150; of value-orientation, 212, noot 8

U

Understanding, 46, 48, 57 2x, 62, 72, 78, 96, 137, 179, 192, noot 71, 193-4, noot 86, 205-6, noot 89, 210-2, noot 3, 217-8, noot 76; causal, 20; direct observational, 50; explanatory, 50; interpretive, 26, 32, 33, 42; irrational, 50; rational, 50; sociological, 43; subjective, 188, noot 5; see also Self-understanding; Verstehen
USENER, Hermann, 203, noot 62
'Universist' philosophy of Taoism, 82

V

Value(s), 22, 27, 29, 44, 46, 50-2, 55, 57, 58, 59, 61-2, 64, 65, 67-70, 71, 77, 78, 81, 93, 96, 102, 114, 118 2x, 120, 122, 124 3x, 125 2x, 129 3x, 130, 131, 134, 137, 145, 147, 150, 154, 159, 171, 178 3x, 180 3x, 181 6x, 182 2x, 183 4x, 191, noot 53, 192, noot 67, 205, noot 80 en 86, 207-8, noot 125, 210-2, noot 3, 212, noot 8, 215-6, noot 54, 216-7, noot 59, 217-8, noot 76; externalization of, 105-7, 135, 199, noot 2; and interests, 201, noot 39; internalization of, 109-113, 135, 199, noot 2, 204, noot 69; and meaning, 40; objectification of, 107-9, 135, 199, noot 2; and science, 30, 35-42, 181, 189, noot 16, 18 en 27, 202, noot 55, 216, noot 55, 217-8, noot 76; see also Science
Variable(s), 17 2x, 20, 54, 157, 191-2, noot 57, 195, noot 97, 209-10, noot 1
VASKOVICS, Laszlo A., 40, 189, noot 23
Vedas, 87, 152
Verband, 47, 176, 191, noot 50, 208, noot 132; see also Organization; Zweckverband
Verbände, 176; see also Association, voluntary
Verein, 47; see also Association, voluntary
Verein für Sozialpolitik, 42, 187-8, noot 1
Vergemeinschaftung, 191, noot 50
Vergesellschaftung, 191, noot 50
Verstehen, 26, 32 2x, 33, 37 3x, 42, 48, 50 5x, 51, 62, 188, noot 8, 190, noot 32, 191, noot 53; see also Sociology, interpretive; Sociology, verstehende
Vishnu, 153

W

WACH, Joachim, 194-5, noot 95
WARNER, R. Stephen, 195, noot 97
WEBER, Marianne, 24, 25 2x, 30, 186, noot 25 en 31
WEBER, Max, passim; in America, 175; on the application of science, 39, 41; on conducting empirical sociological research, 57-63; and definition of religion, 57, 193-4, noot 86, 202, noot 49, 217-8, noot 76; on general scientific methodology, 30-42; on 'genuine' religiosity, 179, 183, 210-2, noot 3, 216, noot 55; between history and sociology, 53-55; on the 'iron cage', 109, 113, 183; and the marxist materialist view of religion, 18, 215, noot 50; methodological essays of, 29, 187-8, noot 1; on psychology, 43, 48-53, 185-6, noot 17, 192, noot 76; on the religiously 'musical' person, 39, 117, 176; on science and religion, 182-3; on sociological methodology, 42-57; question posed by, 15, 156; writings of, on sociology of religion, 16-29
Weltanschauung, 132
Wertbezogenheit, 36
Wertfreiheit, 189, noot 16
Wertrationalität, 36, 41, 50-2, 67, 105; *see also* Rationality, value-oriented
Wertrationalisierung, 112; *see also* Rationalization of values
Westminster Confession of Faith, 197, noot 33
WEYEMBERGH, Maurice, 200-201, noot 29, 212, noot 6
WILSON, Bryan R., 216-7, noot 54
WINCKELMANN, Johannes, 25, 30, 185, noot 2 en 3, 186, noot 23 en 31, 187-8, noot 1, 188, noot 2, 203, noot 62
World renunciation, 21-2
Worldview, 162; *see also Weltanschauung*
WYON, O., 185, noot 15

Y

Yahweh, Yahwehism, 24, 93-100, 102, 115, 158
YINGER, J. Milton, 202, noot 49
Yoga, 89; *see also* Brahmanism, religious techniques of

Z

ZEPHANIAH, 97
ZIJDERVELD, Anton C., 190, noot 39, 191, noot 49 en 52 4x, 207-8, noot 125 6x
ZNANIECKI, F., 190, noot 39
ZOROASTER, 135